EDUCATION IN A COMPETITIVE AND GLOBALIZING WORLD

ELEMENTARY SCHOOL CHILDREN'S SPELLING-SPECIFIC SELF-BELIEFS

LONGITUDINAL ANALYSES OF THEIR RELATIONS TO ACADEMIC ACHIEVEMENT, SCHOOL ATTITUDES, AND SELF-ESTEEM

EDUCATION IN A COMPETITIVE AND GLOBALIZING WORLD

Additional books in this series can be found on Nova's website under the Series tab.

Additional e-books in this series can be found on Nova's website under the e-books tab.

EDUCATION IN A COMPETITIVE AND GLOBALIZING WORLD

ELEMENTARY SCHOOL CHILDREN'S SPELLING-SPECIFIC SELF-BELIEFS

LONGITUDINAL ANALYSES OF THEIR RELATIONS TO ACADEMIC ACHIEVEMENT, SCHOOL ATTITUDES, AND SELF-ESTEEM

GÜNTER FABER

New York

Copyright © 2012 by Nova Science Publishers, Inc.

All rights reserved. No part of this book may be reproduced, stored in a retrieval system or transmitted in any form or by any means: electronic, electrostatic, magnetic, tape, mechanical photocopying, recording or otherwise without the written permission of the Publisher.

For permission to use material from this book please contact us:
Telephone 631-231-7269; Fax 631-231-8175
Web Site: http://www.novapublishers.com

NOTICE TO THE READER

The Publisher has taken reasonable care in the preparation of this book, but makes no expressed or implied warranty of any kind and assumes no responsibility for any errors or omissions. No liability is assumed for incidental or consequential damages in connection with or arising out of information contained in this book. The Publisher shall not be liable for any special, consequential, or exemplary damages resulting, in whole or in part, from the readers' use of, or reliance upon, this material. Any parts of this book based on government reports are so indicated and copyright is claimed for those parts to the extent applicable to compilations of such works.

Independent verification should be sought for any data, advice or recommendations contained in this book. In addition, no responsibility is assumed by the publisher for any injury and/or damage to persons or property arising from any methods, products, instructions, ideas or otherwise contained in this publication.

This publication is designed to provide accurate and authoritative information with regard to the subject matter covered herein. It is sold with the clear understanding that the Publisher is not engaged in rendering legal or any other professional services. If legal or any other expert assistance is required, the services of a competent person should be sought. FROM A DECLARATION OF PARTICIPANTS JOINTLY ADOPTED BY A COMMITTEE OF THE AMERICAN BAR ASSOCIATION AND A COMMITTEE OF PUBLISHERS.

Additional color graphics may be available in the e-book version of this book.

Library of Congress Cataloging-in-Publication Data

Elementary school children's spelling-specific self-beliefs : longitudinal analyses of their relations to academic achievement, school attitudes, and self-esteem / editor, Günter Faber.
       p. cm.
 Includes bibliographical references and index.
 ISBN 978-1-62257-006-5 (hardcover)
 1. Spelling ability--Psychological aspects--Longitudinal studies. 2. Academic achievement--Longitudinal studies. 3. Self-esteem in children--Longitudinal studies. I. Faber, Günter, 1954-
  LB1574.E44 2012
  372.63'2--dc23
                            2012018493

Published by Nova Science Publishers, Inc. ✢ New York

Contents

Preface		vii
Introduction		ix
Chapter 1	Academic Self-Beliefs	1
Chapter 2	Empirical Analyses of Academic Self-Beliefs in the Spelling Domain	37
Chapter 3	Academic Self-Beliefs in the Spelling Domain: The Present Study	47
Chapter 4	The Measuring of Spelling-Specific Self-Concept	55
Chapter 5	Longitudinal Relations between Self-Concept and Achievement	65
Chapter 6	Differentiating the Construct: Error-Related Self-Estimates	71
Chapter 7	Longitudinal Relations between Test-Anxiety, Self-Concept, and Self-Esteem	79
Chapter 8	Longitudinal Relations between Self-Concept, Test Anxiety, Self-Esteem and School Attitudes	87
Chapter 9	Causal Attributions of Success and Failure in Spelling	97
Chapter 10	Summary and Conclusion	111
References		119
Appendices		155
Index		159

PREFACE

In the past decades the self-concept research in educational psychology was increasingly able to differentiate its theoretical framework and to significantly expand its empirical state of knowledge: in a multitude of analyses it could be consistently confirmed that self-perceptions of students are represented in a multidimensional and multifaceted self-concept construct. In the process, it has turned out, time and again, that the academic self-concept is composed of both mathematical and verbal components. Overall, the development of different subject-specific self-concept facets seems to be empirically well established. Within a broader nomological network with respect to the self-concept construct, it can thus be assumed that related cognitive-motivational variables (such as motivational orientations and test anxiety) are most probably, to a large extent, also more subject-specific.

Against this background, however, the spelling domain seems to have been, by comparison, only in rare cases subject to detailed analyses – which should come as a surprise in the face of its high significance in everyday school life. In general, there exists hardly any appropriate research aiming at a systematic empirical analysis of spelling-specific self-beliefs. For this reason, it has been the objective of a comprehensive series of studies to analyze, in greater detail, the spelling-specific self-concept of elementary students with regard to its relations to relevant self-belief and achievement variables.

On the basis of related preliminary studies, a longitudinal study has been conducted whose most important results are introduced. In detail, this study concerns itself with selected findings on the measurement of the spelling-specific self-concept, on the causal ordering between the spelling-specific self-concept and spelling achievement, on the relationships between the spelling-specific self-concept and causal attributions of dictation outcomes as well as on the relationships between the spelling-specific self-concept, spelling-specific test anxiety, and global self-esteem variables and on the relationships between the spelling self-concept and test anxiety, global self-esteem, and school attitude variables. Moreover, an empirical approach to further differentiate the spelling-specific self-concept and thus to analyze a more task-specific facet is documented. Altogether, these findings can provide strong evidence for a basic model of academic self-beliefs in the spelling domain. In particular, structural equation results indicate the achievement variable to be causally predominant on the self-concept variable. Further multivariate analyses demonstrate the students' test anxiety and causal attributions being significantly affected by the self-concept variable. With regard to the relations between students' global self-esteem, spelling-specific self-concept, and spelling achievement, test anxiety appears to be the mediating key variable. Some additionally conducted analyses also can provide empirical evidence for the students' general school attitudes to be significantly and differentially affected by their spelling-specific self-concept. In particular, it is the affective subcomponent of spelling-specific self-concept which substantially predicts negative perceptions of schooling and teacher behavior.

Thus, in the long term, the formation of lowered spelling-specific self-beliefs may have a critical impact on students' development beyond academic concerns. In conclusion, implications resulting from these findings for future research efforts as well as for educational interventions are discussed.

INTRODUCTION

In educational and psychological research the issue of persistent literacy difficulties always has been intensively discussed with respect to their possible impact on children's and adolescents' personality development (Ingesson, 2007; Riddick, 2010). Theoretically based on a reciprocal understanding of these relations, it can be expected that individually emerging reading and/or spelling disabilities will lead to critical emotional and social responses over time, which in turn negatively affect the ongoing learning process (Matthews, Zeidner & Roberts, 2006). From a more general perspective focusing on the longitudinal development of academic achievement, significant direct and indirect effects from prior achievement on subsequent motivation, behavior, and performance outcomes must be assumed (DiPerna, Volpe & Elliott, 2001). Thus, in most cases long-lasting cumulative failure experiences will produce negative trajectories in a wide range of students' social and emotional competencies (Bender & Wall, 1994; Bryan, Burstein & Ergul, 2004). Meanwhile, a number of empirical studies provide sound evidence for the critical consequences of learning problems in the reading and/or spelling domain. Overall, across different theoretical backgrounds and methodological approaches their results can substantiate that poor achieving students demonstrate, already in the early elementary school years, higher levels of inappropriate classroom behavior, less adaptive levels of learning strategies as well as lowered levels of motivational beliefs and attitudes (Arnold, Goldston, Walsh, Reboussin, Daniel, Hickman & Wood, 2005; Carroll, Maughan, Goodman & Meltzer, 2005; Gadeyne, Ghesquière & Onghena, 2004; Heiervang, Stevenson, Lund & Hugdahl, 2001; Mugnaini, Lassi, La Malfa & Albertini, 2009; Poskiparta, Niemi, Lepola, Athola & Laing, 2003; Solheim, 1989; Tiedemann & Faber, 1991; Undheim, Wichstrøm & Sund, 2011).

The development of these social-emotional problems must be considered in terms of the students' information processing (Lee & Shute, 2010). It is not the emergence and maintenance of poor achievement per se but rather the nature, direction, and magnitude of their individual perceptions, appraisals, and interpretations which gradually contribute to the formation of certain behavior patterns. The students' educational attainment appears to be substantially associated with their cognitive-motivational orientations as they are derived from their academic expectancies and evaluations, in particular, from their related self-estimations, task values, goal orientations, and emotions (Boekaerts, 1996; Eccles & Wigfield, 2002). As mentally represented self-schemata they reflect the students' individual experiences in academic settings (Markus, 1980). As such, they constitute a system of relatively stable self-beliefs which can refer to very specific or already more complex aspects of academic situations or requirements, respectively. Thus, the students' academic self-beliefs play a crucial role in the regulation of their learning behavior (Pintrich, 2003; Wigfield & Karpathian, 1991). In a long-term perspective, they determine the students' academic engagement as well as they, if nothing else, may influence their overall social-emotional well-being (Craven & Marsh, 2008). Within this set of personal self-beliefs the academic self-concept appears to be a processual key variable. Students with learning disabilities in a certain domain or subject mostly report lower perceptions of their own academic competencies than their normally achieving classmates do. In particular, they feel less capable to cope with the tasks and requirements in that particular domain or subject, strongly underestimate the malleability of their own skills and, therefore, tend to avoid related task situations (Chapman, 1988; Hay, Ashman & van Kraayenoord, 1998a; Licht & Kistner, 1986; Zeleke, 2004). In each individual case such avoiding strategies may be either more externalizing or more internalizing in nature. As an integrated part of a multidimensionally and hierarchically organized self-system (Shavelson, Hubner & Stanton, 1976; Marsh, 2006) the domain- or subject-specific facets of academic self-concept are well proven to explain more variance of interindividually existing achievement and behavior differences than more generalized construct operationalizations such as global academic self-concept or self-esteem can do (Byrne, 1996; Valentine, DuBois & Cooper, 2004). Accordingly, for remedial interventions it should be reasonable to target primarily the academic, in particular, the domain- or subject-specific facets of students' self-concept. Empirical research lends clear support to this assumption: educational approaches which conceptually refer to more specific self-concept variables as explanative and prescriptive constructs can claim, at least, significantly stronger effects in modifying students' self-beliefs (Elbaum & Vaughn, 2001; O'Mara, Marsh, Craven & Debus, 2006). These findings, however, do not necessarily mean to rule out students' more generalized self-beliefs from educational considerations. Rather they suggest the potential of specific self-concept facets as a mediating or moderating pathway to further motivational and behavioral constructs (Eccles, Wigfield & Schiefele, 1998; Marsh & O'Mara, 2008b; Skinner, 1995).

Against this theoretical and empirical background, the issue of students' self-beliefs in literacy and dyslexia research has been analyzed in various studies focusing on the matter of students' general self-esteem and academic self-concept deficits. Their findings, altogether, do not support the assumption of negative self-esteem levels – but mostly indicate lowered academic self-perceptions in dyslexic samples (Alexander-Passe, 2006; Burden, 2005; Humphrey, 2002b; Polychroni, Koukoura & Anagnostou, 2006; Ridsdale, 2004; Rosenthal, 1973; Solheim, 1989; Terras, Thompson & Minnis, 2009; Thomson & Hartley, 1980). Due to the cumulative failure history of dyslexic students these findings appear to be completely in line with theoretical predictions and, not least, with everyday experiences in educational practice. But with regard to the multidimensionality of the self-concept construct they do not consider self-concept variables beyond the general academic domain and suffer, to a wide extent, from a lack of domain- or subject-specific analyses – that is, they miss the opportunity to gain further differentiated and refined insights into the students' self-beliefs system e.g., by exploring its potential reading- or spelling-specific subcomponents.

In contrast, in the past decades psychological and educational research has obviously made greater efforts to fill this research gap. Various studies have successfully demonstrated the empirical separation of subject-specific self-concepts components within the academic domain (Boersma, Chapman & Maguire, 1979; Marsh, 1992; Rost, Sparfeldt & Schilling, 2007; Simpson, Licht, Wagner & Stader, 1996). Some of them have succeeded, moreover, in identifying distinguishable subcomponents of subject-specific competence beliefs – mostly concerning the students' self-perceptions as readers, but also as writers and as mathematics or foreign language learners (Chapman & Tunmer, 1999; Cloer & Ross, 1997; Henk, Bottomley & Melnick, 1996; Henk & Melnick, 1995; Lau, Yeung, Jin & Low, 1999; Nurmi, Hannula, Maijala & Pehkonen, 2003). With regard to children and adolescents struggling with literacy problems, all these studies yield strong evidence for the validity and the need for more specific approaches in related self-belief research. That way, empirical analyses seem to be promising to provide a better understanding of the cognitive-motivational orientations underlying difficult individual learning. However, it seems remarkable that relevant research for the most part has dealt with self-perceptions in reading; comparatively fewer studies have considered self-perceptions in spelling (Faber, 2007). This must come as a surprise all the more as students, in particular at elementary and lower secondary grades, perceive spelling and orthographics as important, but also as rather demanding and less popular aspects of school learning (Downing, DeStefano, Rich & Bell, 1994; Freedman-Doan, Wigfield, Eccles, Blumenfeld & Harold, 2000; Varnhagen, 2000). There is still a lack of educational research which should not only investigate whether students view themselves as good, moderate, or poor spellers, but which also should try to differentiate the spelling-specific self-concept construct by exploring its meaningful subcomponents and facets. Correspondingly, it would be worthwhile to analyze the associations between these subcomponents and facets with relevant achievement and related self-belief variables. Analyses of that kind should be able to clarify which variables contribute to the formation of positive or negative self-belief patterns and typically appear to determine students' learning in the spelling area (Martin, 2002).

For this reason, it has been the aim of a comprehensive series of studies to analyze, in greater detail, the spelling-specific self-beliefs of elementary students in the context of nomologically relevant personality and achievement variables. On the basis of related preliminary investigations, a longitudinal study with a sample of elementary fourth-graders has been conducted, the most important results of which are to be introduced here. Some of these findings have been already reported elsewhere (Faber, 2007), but most of the empirical results have not been previously published. Theoretically grounded on a multidimensional and multifaceted understanding of the academic self-belief construct, and conceptually associated with a basic model of subject-specific self-beliefs, the current research deals, in particular, with

- the construction, psychometric analysis, and validation of a questionnaire for measuring students' spelling-specific self-concept,
- the relationships between the spelling-specific self-concept and spelling achievement variables,
- the construction, psychometric analysis, and validation of a scale for measuring students' error-specific self-estimates in the spelling domain,
- the relationships between these error-specific self-estimates, spelling achievement variables, and related self-belief variables,
- the construction, psychometric analysis, and validation of a questionnaire for measuring students' causal attributions of dictation outcomes,
- the relationships between these causal attributions, spelling achievement, and related self-belief variables,
- the relationships between the spelling-specific self-concept, test anxiety, and global self-esteem variables,

- the relationships between the spelling-specific self-concept, test anxiety, global self-esteem, and school attitude variables.

In conclusion, implications resulting from these findings for future research efforts and their potential relevance for spelling instruction in educational settings will be discussed — e.g., considering related educational assessment issues and treatment approaches to enhance students' self-beliefs in the spelling domain.

Chapter 1

ACADEMIC SELF-BELIEFS

A SOCIAL COGNITIVE PERSPECTIVE ON ACADEMIC ACHIEVEMENT

Current models of academic achievement agree to regard students' personality as an important factor. It comprises, in a narrower sense, those non-cognitive traits of personality with which the academic evaluations, expectations, and orientations of the students are characterized. In detail, they can refer to their subjective perceptions, interpretations, and explanations with respect to their academic performance (Chan, 2000), and may influence their actual learning favorably or adversely, directly or indirectly, in a short-term or in a long-term manner (Lee & Shute, 2009; Rosen, Glennie, Dalton, Lennon & Bozick, 2010). As such, these academic self-beliefs are based upon a close interaction of cognitive, affective, and behavioral elements – so that they can be defined, at large, as cognitive-motivational and emotional constructs. Developmentally, they can be understood both as consequences of previous academic experiences and as antecedents of future academic outcomes (Pintrich, 2003; Wang, Haertel & Walberg, 1993). Interindividual differences in these academic self-beliefs result from relatively stable expectations of students, adopted on a longer-term basis, about the (assumed or actual) relationships between a specific situation, their own capabilities, and their outcome values in this particular situation (Heckhausen, 1977). Thus, students engage in self-reactive, self-reflective and self-monitoring processes to analyze their experiences and to verify their cognitions, emotions, and goals. In a particular situation, these expectancies and evaluations have a motivational and regulating effect on their behavior – with subjective evaluations of the outcome and/or their consequences in turn again affecting self- and/or situation-related expectancies. Depending upon the individual experiences predominating at any one time, they can be, by and by, confirmed, modified, or discarded (Bandura, 2001; Schunk, 2012; Zimmerman & Cleary, 2009).

According to this social cognitive perspective, self-beliefs are therefore assigned to play a mediating part in the process of school learning. As Helmke (2009) points out in his educational effectance model, the students' self-related cognitions, emotions, and meta-cognitive skills determine substantially their perception and adoption of current classroom activities – which, in turn, always reflect the teacher's professional competencies, educational orientations, and personality traits within a given school setting (Figure 1). To what extent such proximal instructional variables as the teacher's classroom management, the amount of available learning time, the frequency and intensity of individual learning support, or the clarity of subject-specific cues and tasks (Weinert, Schrader & Helmke, 1989) may contribute to desirable learning outcomes appears to be affected by the students' self-beliefs. They regulate to a certain degree, just as a cognitive-motivational filter, their attention, activation of prior knowledge, and on-task persistence in the classroom as well as in the homework context. In the long term, subject-specific as well as general effects of classroom instruction, then again, confirm or alter individually existing self-beliefs (Marshall & Weinstein, 1984) and thus will predispose further skill acquisition and competency development. This mediating role of students' self-beliefs, of course, does not reduce the basic importance of instructional quality (Rowe, 2003) in any way, but rather it stresses the relational functioning of teacher and teaching variables within each educational setting.

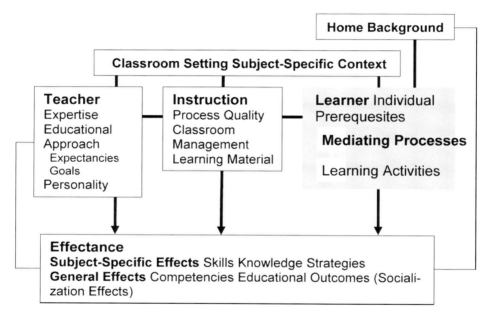

Figure 1. Determinants of educational effectance (Helmke, 2009).

The direction, frequency, and quality of learning engagement students will display in a certain academic situation depends, in particular, upon their individual assumptions

- whether a potential action outcome may already seem predetermined by the situation at hand (situation-outcome-expectancy),
- whether they may possess adequate behavioral capabilities to achieve a certain action outcome (action-outcome-expectancy),
- whether they may evaluate the respective action outcome as important or worthwhile (outcome valence),
- which foreseeable consequences they may attribute to the action outcome (outcome-consequences-expectancy),
- and how they evaluate these consequences for themselves (outcome-consequences valence).

Academic expectancies and evaluations of this nature derive from various ways of individual and social comparisons (Skaalvik & Skaalvik, 2002) and are, over time, accumulated and organized as self-related schemata in the students' long-term memory. They represent the students' mentally inferred competence and control perspectives as well as their values and thus constitute their self-belief patterns with respect to a certain type of situation (Bandura, 1986; Heckhausen, 1977; Krampen, 1988).

Theoretically, they can be described and explained as expectancy-value constructs which predict to a large extent how an academic situation is being either approached or possibly avoided (Eccles & Wigfield, 2002; Wigfield & Eccles, 2000). As such, they can refer to very specific or already more comprehensive types of academic situations. Most of the academically relevant expectancy-value constructs have been proven to develop in a domain- or subject-specific manner. In particular, with increasing age and, thereby, depending on more differentiated achievement experiences, students display distinct expectations and values across various school subjects – e.g., subject-specific competence beliefs (Möller, Pohlmann, Köller & Marsh, 2009), task values (Viljaranta, Nurmi, Aunola & Salmela-Aro, 2009), interests (Corbière, Fraccarolli, Mbekou & Perron, 2006), motivational orientations (Green, Martin & Marsh, 2007; Magson, Craven, Nelson & Yeung, 2008), and emotional responses (Goetz, Cronjaeger, Frenzel, Lüdtke & Hall, 2010).

PERCEPTIONS OF PERSONAL COMPETENCE, CONTROL, AND THREAT

Expectancy-value perspectives can be assigned to various constructs concerning academic self-beliefs in a certain educational setting (Covington, 1986; Eccles, Wigfield & Schiefele, 1998; Pekrun, 1988a; Pintrich, 2003). Conceptually as well as empirically, the most prominent constructs refer to the students' perceptions of personal competence, control, and threat:

- *Expectancies of personal competence:* they concern the expectancies having arisen subjectively against the background of previous performance experiences, to possess appropriate and sufficient competencies in order to meet the demands of an academic task in a certain situation. These competence expectancies manifest, for the most part, in the students' academic self-concept and, more specifically, in their self-efficacy beliefs.
- *Expectancies of personal control:* they concern the expectancies having arisen subjectively against the background of previous performance experiences, to be able to influence the outcome of an achievement situation in a sufficient and desired manner – that is, to be the origin of a certain outcome. These control expectancies manifest primarily in the students' academic success and failure attributions.
- *Expectancies of personal threat:* they concern the expectancies having arisen subjectively against the background of previous performance experiences, to be affected in a negative way by the consequences of an anticipated failure out-

come which, in particular, means a threat to self-esteem. These threat expectancies manifest mainly in the students' fear of failure or test anxiety.

The perceptions of personal competence, control, and threat existing in each individual case certainly do not explain exhaustively the self-beliefs of students in a given academic context – but they are substantial and sufficient. In the long term, complex interrelations between them can be assumed (Figure 2) which may in turn affect future academic outcomes in favorable or unfavorable ways (Martin & Marsh, 2006; Wigfield & Karpathian, 1991).

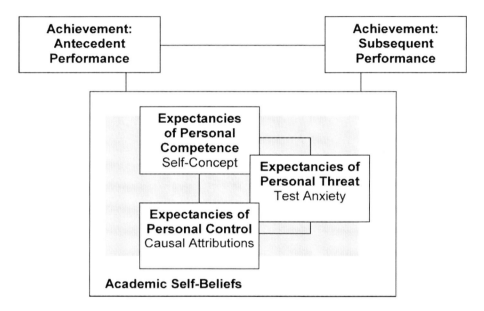

Figure 2. Academic achievement and expectancies: A preliminary framework.

ACADEMIC SELF-CONCEPT

Structural Components

With the students' academic self-concepts, their individual experiences of success and failure in academic contexts have been processed to become relatively stable competence beliefs. As such, they represent, in a subjectively significant manner, the perceived possibilities existing so as to meet academic demands, and they can influence current as well as future learning and performance behavior (Byrne, 1996; Wigfield & Karpathian, 1991). With regard to particular achievement-related aspects being individually important in the view of students, they may basically include descriptive as well as evaluative and affective elements (Skaalvik, 1997a).

Structurally, it could be demonstrated that the students' academic self-concepts are an integrated part of their self-system organized dimensionally and hierarchically in a comprehensive manner (Epstein, 1980; Shavelson, Hubner & Stanton, 1976): As self-beliefs related to one's own academic abilities and skills, associated with various non-academic and non-performance self-components and subordinate to the global feeling of self-esteem, they are again in turn composed of several subconcepts distinguishable as regards content – in particular with respect to experiencing domain- and subject-specific competencies (Figure 3). In a revised version of this structural assumption, the various components of academic self-concept are traced back to a verbal and/or mathematical factor (Marsh & Shavelson, 1985) reflecting, with a particular characteristic in each case, the general and subject-specific self-perceptions realized. However, this higher-order factors model suffers from several shortcomings and was not consistently supported in empirical studies (Koumi & Meadows, 1997). As a more recent research approach could demonstrate in a sample of secondary students (Brunner, Keller, Dierendonck, Reichert, Ugen, Fischbach & Martin, 2010), the structure of academic self-concept appeared to be more complicated as theoretically predicted. There was some evidence for a broader academic self-concept factor superordinate to all subject-specific self-concept facets – and which only indirectly represented a latent mathematics and verbal component. For more clarification, further studies are recommended which, in particular, should analyze the models' scope with regard to students' age, educational level, and the academic subjects to be considered.

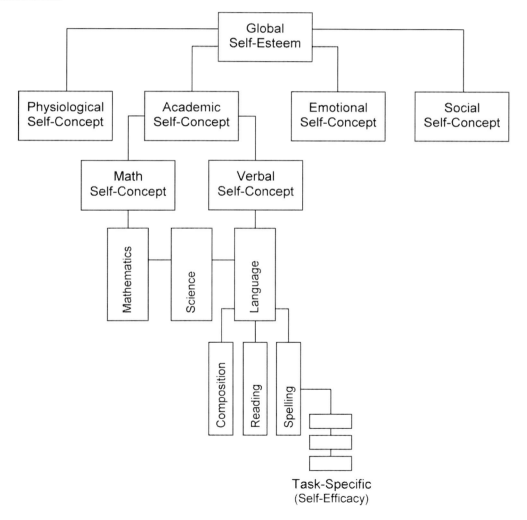

Figure 3. The structure of self-concept (sensu Marsh & Shavelson, 1985).

Similarly, another aspect of construct validation seems to be not yet sufficiently clarified. As the findings by Marsh, Craven and Debus (1999) and, more recently, by Lee and Yeung (2007) as well as by Arens, Yeung, Craven and Hasselhorn (2011) demonstrated, the multidimensional and multifaceted structure of academic self-concept did not only emerge on a cross-domain level as a matter of content. Within a certain domain or subject, respectively, academic self-concepts also could be further separated into a competence and an affect component. Within each academic domain these competence and affective components were substantially related but represented empirically distinguishable constructs. With various academic achievement measures they correlated in a domain-specific manner – in each domain the competence component being more highly associated with achievement than the affect component. The correlational pattern between these self-concept and achievement variables appeared to be invariant across gender and grade level. These findings are in line with an expectancy-value perspective of learning motivation (Eccles & Wigfield, 2002) and support several previous approaches for the development and validation of subject-specific self-concept instruments (Chapman & Tunmer, 1999; Rider & Colmar, 2005). Students' academic self-beliefs reflect both their competence perceptions and their emotional evaluations. This within-domain specification of the academic self-concept construct contributes to a refinement of the commonly held assumptions concerning the competence and affective elements in self-concept structure (Shavelson, Hubner & Stanton, 1976; Skaalvik, 1997a). Future validation research has, first of all, to replicate these results and to test their generalizability to other subjects within the math and verbal domain. Only under this condition it might be useful to discuss its possible implications for self-concept assessment and intervention.

Apart from this issue of adequate construct modeling, previous research has produced strong evidence for the subject-specific self-concept facets to correlate only to a moderate extent. According to theoretical assumptions they discriminate sufficiently (Figure 3). Within the self-system, they already take a position relatively closely pertaining to academic behavior and situation. With corresponding performance measures, these subject-specific self-concept facets are stronger associated than the students' general academic self-concept or their global self-esteem. Also with performance measures in matched domains or subjects they were stronger correlated than with performance measures in non-matched domains or subjects – thus evidently indicating their differential validity (Alsaker, 1989; Faber, 1992a; Helmke, 1997; Marsh, 1990a; Marsh & MacDonald Holmes, 1990; Rost, Sparfeldt & Schilling, 2007; Trautwein, Lüdtke, Köller & Baumert, 2009; Valentine, DuBois & Cooper, 2004). Across different theoretical orientations, methodological procedures, and sample characteristics numerous studies have repeatedly identified various subject-specific self-concept facets – as they concern a wide range of elementary and secondary school subjects such as mathematics, native and foreign languages, social studies, science, physical activities, and arts (Bauer, 2005; Brookover, Thomas & Paterson, 1964; Chanal, Sarrazin, Guay & Boiché, 2009; Faber, 2009; Frühauf, 2008; Koumi & Meadows, 1997; Marsh, 1992; Marsh, Kong & Hau, 2001; Möller, Streblow, Pohlmann & Köller, 2006; Tiedemann & Billmann-Mahecha, 2004). The formation of subject-specific self-concept facets appears to set in already during the early elementary years and then tends to gradually increase (Marsh, Craven & Debus, 1998; Poloczek, Karst, Praetorius & Lipowsky, 2011).

Moreover, these subject-specific self-concept facets can be further differentiated with regard to distinguishable subcomponents (Figure 3). Several studies have succeeded in identifying such subcomponents within a certain domain or subject – mostly concerning the students' self-perceptions as readers but also as writers and as mathematics or foreign language learners. In particular, empirical findings demonstrated the native language facet to be subdivided into several subcomponents such as perceptions of reading competence, perceptions of reading difficulties, attitudes and feelings toward reading (Chapman & Tunmer, 1995; Rider & Colmar, 2005). The Reader Self-Perception Scale as presented by Henk and Melnick (1995) includes, along with other subscales more tapping relevant teacher feedback and affective value, two reading-specific competence scales about one's own performance within the classroom context and one's own achievement progress (Mata, Monteiro & Peixoto, 2009; Melnick, Henk & Marinak, 2009). The same subcomponents have been confirmed in an analogously built questionnaire for measuring students' self-perceptions as a writer (Bottomley, Henk & Melnick, 1997; Henk, Bottomley & Melnick, 1996). A more comprehensive approach to analyze the structure of the reading motivation construct revealed a broad set of subscales also including a distinct competence component (Baker & Wigfield, 1999). In the context of foreign language learning, the subject-specific self-concept could be further differentiated with regard to distinct subcomponents referring to the perception of listening, speaking, reading, and writing performance (Holder, 2005; Lau, Yeung, Jin & Low, 1999). Likewise, in the mathematics domain several studies identified some factorially separated components of students' subject-specific self-perceptions. They appeared to represent, however, various aspects of the subject-specific construct rather than its achievement-related subcomponents. Anyhow, some of these scales seem to confound different construct perspectives and deserve further attention with regard to their theoretical rationale and their psychometric properties (Cretchley, 2008; Hannula, Maijala & Pehkonen, 2004; Nurmi, Hannula, Maijala & Pehkonen, 2003; Roesken, Hannula & Pehkonen, 2011). Beyond that, empirical findings also exist which could demonstrate distinct subcomponents in students' musical self-concept (Vispoel, 2003) as well as in students' and young athletes' physical self-concept (Marsh, 2002; Tietjens, Möller & Pohlmann, 2005).

Beneath that level of subject-specific self-concepts and their various subcomponents, students' competence beliefs can be further differentiated with respect to particular tasks and demands in a given domain or subject (Figure 3). With the strongest degree of specificity they typically manifest as self-efficacy beliefs concerning the individually perceived confidence to master a task – e.g., to correctly solve a certain number of subtraction problems in mathematics or to correctly use verb tenses in writing a short story (Bong & Skaalvik, 2003; Marsh, Walker & Debus, 1991; Pajares & Schunk, 2001). Self-efficacy beliefs are, thus, expectations of task-specific success or failure in a concrete and well-known situation. They depend less on social comparison than on intraindividually accessible information such as own emotional states, received feedback, vicarious experiences, and, most of all, own mastery experiences (Joët, Usher & Bressoux, 2011; Usher & Pajares, 2009). In the long term, they might cumulatively operate as precursors of more aggregated self-concept levels. Conversely, they might just as well be affected by students' more past-oriented and stable self-concepts. In the latter case, past outcome experiences and evaluations as aggregated on the subject-specific self-concept level might predetermine students' self-efficacy beliefs (Ferla, Valcke & Cai, 2009). However, bottom-up and top-down processes of this nature are not yet thoroughly analyzed. There is still a need for future research which should take into account possible differences by age, gender, prior achievement, school level, and academic domain (Marsh & Yeung, 1998). Taken altogether, according to the assumption of a multidimensional and multifaceted construct perspective, the domain- or subject-specific differentiation of academic self-concept appears to be well proven. As such, numerous studies, including the most diverse student samples and with regard to the most different school subjects, have been able to demonstrate that the subject-specific self-concepts are in each case substantially higher correlated with performance measures within the same subject than across other subjects – thus, indicating their convergent and discriminant validity (Möller, Pohlmann, Köller & Marsh, 2009; Valentine, DuBois & Cooper, 2004).

Dimensional Comparison Effects

The formation of academic self-concepts can essentially be explained by individual information processing, in particular by the use of social, dimensional, and criterion-related information. That is, domain- or subject-specific self-perceptions develop by social comparisons of one's own achievement with the outcomes of classmates (Dijkstra, Kuyper, van der Werf, Buunk & van der Zee, 2008), by dimensional comparisons of one's own academic achievement in a certain domain or subject with the own outcomes in other domains or subjects, and by criterion-related comparisons of one's own academic achievement with decisive outcome standards in a specific domain or subject (Skaalvik & Skaalvik, 2002). Social and dimensional comparisons can also both be realized in a temporal perspective by considering one's own current or past achievement (Butler, 1998). In that way, individual changes across time as well as individual differences across subjects can also serve as more ipsative comparison information.

Leaving aside such temporal comparisons, the internal/external frame of reference model as presented by Marsh (1984a, 1986a) provides a theoretical framework that explains and predicts the impact of social (external) and dimensional (internal) comparison processes on the formation of domain- or subject-specific self-concepts in academic settings (Figure 4). It assumes that the students' academic competence beliefs in a particular domain or subject are primarily affected by social comparison – that is, by perceiving their classmates mainly displaying worse, equal, or better outcomes. This social comparison shall lead to a substantially positive relationship between achievement and self-concept in a certain domain or subject. Moreover, students draw self-related conclusions from dimensional comparisons – that is, by perceiving their outcomes across various domains or subjects as equal or different. This dimensional comparison can be made upward to an intraindividually stronger subject and will then result in a relatively lower self-concept, or it can be made downward to an intraindividually weaker subject and will then result in a relatively higher self-concept. Provided that the students really perceive their outcomes in various subjects as different (Rost, Sparfeldt, Dickhäuser & Schilling, 2005; Skaalvik & Rankin, 1992), this dimensional comparison shall lead to a substantially negative relationship between the achievement in a weaker subject and the self-concept in a stronger subject – and vice versa. This seems paradoxical because, at first glance, theoretically inexplicable negative associations between academic achievement and self-concept variables can be traced back to dimensional comparison processes.

In the past two decades empirical research has been able to largely support the predictions of the internal/external frame of reference model, which originally refers to the relations between verbal and math constructs. Across a wide range of age groups, school grades and educational settings there was consistent evidence for the subject-specific self-concepts of students to be dependent on social as well as dimensional comparison effects, thus also confirming the cross-cultural generalizability of the model's predictions (Möller, Pohlmann, Köller & Marsh, 2009; Rinn, Plucker & Stocking, 2010). The validity of the model was also supported in a 4-year longitudinal study which revealed small but significant negative effects from prior achievement on subsequent self-concept variables across the mathematics and verbal domain (Möller, Retelsdorf, Köller & Marsh, 2011). Mainly, the research on the internal/external frame of reference model dealt with student samples at the secondary school level, but significant contrasting effects between achievement and self-concept measures across the mathematics and verbal domain already had been found in upper elementary grades (Faber, 1992a; Marsh, Smith, Barnes & Butler, 1983; Lohrmann, Götz & Haag, 2010; Tiedemann & Billmann-Mahecha, 2004). One single study reported substantial negative relations across both domains even in a sample of second-graders (Zeinz, 2006). However, most of the studies testing the internal/external frame of reference model used regression analysis or structural equation modeling approaches. Their results were correlational in nature and could not clarify the direction and magnitude of dimensional comparisons. Until now, only a few experimental studies have addressed this issue. According to the model's assumptions, their results achieved to confirm the impact of cross-domain contrasting effects on students' self-concepts (Dickhäuser, Seidler & Kölzer, 2005; Möller & Köller, 2001; Pohlmann & Möller, 2006). This contrasting effect was found to be stronger for students who believed in a relative interdependence of domain-specific abilities (Möller, Streblow & Pohlmann, 2006). Moreover, there was also evidence from post hoc analyses in the educational setting that students with moderate achievement scores in a certain subject tended to prefer downward comparisons with the intraindividually weaker subject to enhance their self-concept (Pohlmann & Möller, 2009).

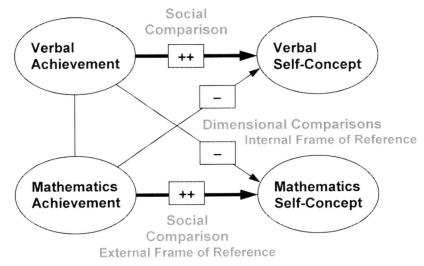

Figure 4. Dimensional comparison effects: The internal/external frame of reference model (Marsh, 1984a).

The consistently replicated pattern of empirical findings raises the question of whether the model's conceptual scope can be extended to other academic domains or subjects – that is, whether the internal/external frame of reference model is able to explain the relations between achievement and self-concept variables in other than the verbal and math domains or subjects. Altogether, the studies testing such extensions yielded somewhat mixed results. Thus, several structural equation modeling approaches revealed significant negative path coefficients between sports and mathematics (Streblow, 2004), between various competency areas within the physical activities domain (Tietjens, Möller & Pohlmann, 2005), and between physical activities, mathematics and verbal achievement (Chanal, Sarrazin, Guay & Boiché, 2009). In contrast, studies that included additional subjects within a certain domain mostly failed to verify any dimensional comparison effects. They rather pointed out that the achievement and self-concept variables between similar subjects were likely to correlate in a significantly positive manner, thus indicating small assimilative comparison effects (Dickhäuser 2005a; Dickhäuser, Reuter & Hilling, 2005; Möller, Streblow, Pohlmann & Köller, 2006; Rost, Sparfeldt, Dickhäuser & Schilling, 2005).The results from a study of Taiwanese eight graders must be read accordingly (Jen & Chien, 2008). They reported small but significant negative path coefficients between achievement and self-concept measures in mathematics and science. However, this finding does not necessarily seem to be contradictory to the relevant research line because in this study science-related achievement and self-concept indicators have been used which, to a considerable extent, include verbal competency operationalizations (Garden & Smith, 2000). In this respect, a cross-cultural analysis of the relations between self-concept and achievement in science and mathematics helps to draw a more differentiated picture. Across the wide range of countries from the TIMSS study, it demonstrated varying degrees of contrasting or assimilative comparison effects and, therefore, indicated the impact of cultural differences on students' academic perceptions or ability beliefs (Chiu, 2008). In particular, within the verbal domain some studies also analyzed the issue of dimensional comparison effects between the native (L1) and foreign (L2) language. Basically, there is no reason to rule out the possibility that students might perceive the academic tasks and outcomes, respectively, in the L1 and L2 in a different manner – because, e.g., oral skills are assigned more importance in the L2 context and thus the students' competence beliefs in both language subjects might reflect fairly different competence experiences (Horwitz, 2001; MacIntyre, Dörnyei, Clément & Noels, 1998). However, the whole current self-concept research on internal comparison processes within the verbal domain only yielded few and inconsistent findings. Those studies in which the relations between achievement and self-concept variables in the L1 German and the L2 English were considered mostly showed no significant path coefficients between self-concept and achievement across both languages (Dickhäuser, 2003; Möller, Streblow, Pohlmann & Köller, 2006; Pohlmann, 2005; Rost, Sparfeldt, Dickhäuser & Schilling, 2005). In another research context significant negative path coefficients between achievement and self-concept in Chinese (as a native language) and English (as a foreign language) have been repeatedly reported, but this result appeared to be very plausible in view of the fundamental differences between these two languages. Thus, the students' self-perceptions might have largely emphasized the very contrasting nature of classroom requirements and achievement outcomes (Marsh, Kong & Hau, 2001; Xu & Marsh, 2009). Just recently, in a longitudinal investigation of preadolescent students' achievement and self-concepts in German and French, significant negative relations between prior achievement and later self-concept variables have been found indicating that the formation of language-specific self-concepts is affected by the dimensional comparison processes (Brunner, Keller, Dierendonck, Reicher, Ugen, Fischbach & Martin, 2010). This result evidently serves to clarify the question of dimensional comparison effects within the verbal domain. But it cannot claim to substantiate such effects with regard to the native versus foreign language issue because, in the Luxembourgian school system where the study has been conducted, German and French both are already taught simultaneously as official languages on the elementary school level. Nevertheless, this result underlines the need for further research on the individual and contextual determinants of emerging contrasting effects between similar language subjects.

Furthermore, some studies have investigated the extension of the model to other cognitive-motivational constructs such as academic emotions, motivations, and interests – assuming that these constructs can be expected to be strongly associated with the students' academic self-concepts and therefore will also get involved in dimensional comparison processes (Pohlmann & Möller, 2006; Skaalvik & Rankin, 1995). The results of these studies showed significant negative path coefficients between the achievement, self-concept, and interest measures in mathematics and biology as well as between self-concept and interest measures in English, mathematics and physics – thus indicating dimensional comparison effects only to be apparent between strongly different, but not between similar school subjects (Daniels, 2008; Nagy, Trautwein, Baumert, Köller & Garrett, 2006; Pohlmann, 2005). With regard to academic emotions, one single study demonstrated significant negative path coefficients between mathematics and verbal achievement and related test anxiety ratings (Marsh, 1988a), though this result could not be confirmed by other research findings (Streblow, 2004; Schilling, Sparfeldt & John, 2005). Also, with regard to the students' learning enjoyment, significant negative path coefficients between achievement and enjoyment across several subjects were found which considerably decreased in magnitude after controlling related self-concepts (Goetz, Frenzel, Hall & Pekrun, 2008). A similar finding had been previously reported with a regard to the test anxiety construct (Faber, 1993a). These results recommend attention to the conceptual issue, whereby an extension of the internal/external frame of reference model by adding other cognitive-motivational constructs definitely must take into account the mediating role of academic self-concept.

A few studies had also analyzed the extension of the internal/external frame of reference model to an observer's perspective. Their results, in sum, could not reveal any evidence for dimensional comparison effects to influence peers', parents', or teachers' perceptions. Instead, they were more likely to use social comparison information for inferring students' abilities or self-beliefs (Dai, 2002; Pohlmann, Möller & Streblow, 2004). Obviously, in everyday situations within an educational setting, people do not appreciate intraindividually existing differences in another person's competencies. But once provided with the achievement information necessary for dimensional comparison, they performed more contrasting assumptions of students' self-concept across various domains (Dickhäuser, 2005b) – that is, if parents or teachers obtain salient information about students' achievement differences, they will change their estimates of students' self-beliefs and, foreseeably, change their own perceptions and expectancies. Further research still has to clarify the educational consequences and implications of this issue.

Social Comparison Effects

Another line of comparison process significantly affecting the formation of academic self-concept relates to the proximal learning environment, in particular to the perceived achievement level of reference groups or selected classmates in a given educational setting (Dijkstra, Kuyper, van der Werf, Buunk & van der Zee, 2008). Students commonly compare their own academic outcomes with their peers' outcomes. This social comparison will lead either to a contrast effect negatively influencing their self-evaluation or to an assimilation effect positively influencing their self-evaluation (Cialdini & Richardson, 1980; Wheeler & Suls, 2005). However, when comparing to more able peers in a high ability setting, their self-perceptions will be relatively lowered – and when comparing to less able peers in a moderate or low ability setting, their self-perceptions will be relatively heightened. This big-fish-little-pond effect (Marsh, 1987) assumes the students' self-concept to be dependent not only on their individual achievement but also on the average achievement level of their academic context. It is then expected to correlate positively with their individual outcome level, and negatively with the average outcome level of a certain learning environment (Figure 5). As a contrasting result of social comparison, the big-fish-little-pond effect may refer both to an average school- or classroom level. Principally, it may operate in a domain- or subject-specific manner indicating an individual student to be a 'big fish in a little math pond' and a 'little fish in a big reading pond' as well (Marsh & Craven, 2002). Moreover, it seems to be specific to general and subject-related self-concept inasmuch as more task-related self-efficacy measures barely reflect social comparison information (Bong & Skaalvik, 2003; Seaton, Marsh & Craven, 2010). Likewise, it does not apply to explain any differences in non-academic self-concept variables (Marsh, 2006).

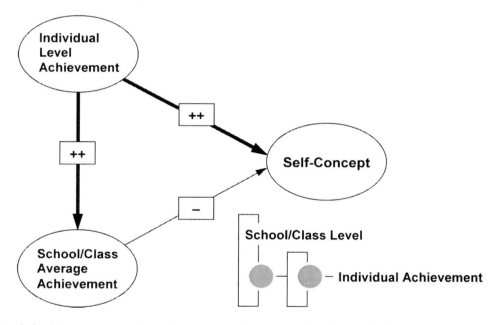

Figure 5. Social comparison effects: The big-fish-little-pond effect (Marsh, 1987).

Previous empirical research on the big-fish-little-pond effect has produced a wide range of findings which lend robust support to its validity across various student samples, contextual level characteristics of educational systems, cultural diversities, and research designs (Marsh & Hau, 2003; Seaton, Marsh & Craven, 2009). According to its theoretical predictions, students' academic self-concepts were negatively associated with the average achievement level of their school or classroom setting. Thus, students in high-ability schools or classes reported substantially lower academic self-concepts than equally achieving students in mixed- and low-ability schools or classes. Altogether, there was not any consistent evidence for a positive assimilation effect of school- or class-average achievement level on students' self-concept (Trautwein, Lüdtke, Marsh, Köller & Baumert, 2006). Several studies could contribute to differentiate and extend the conceptual scope of the big-fish-little-pond model. With regard to various academic subjects, the average school- or classroom level of ability negatively affected secondary school students' self-concepts in the mathematics and verbal domain as well as in the science and the physical domain. Furthermore, with regard to other self-belief constructs, subject-specific anxiety mediated the strength of the negative contrast effect by high-anxious students reporting more decreased self-concepts than their low-anxious classmates (Chanal, Marsh, Sarrazin & Bois, 2005; Nagengast & Marsh, 2011; Trautwein, Gerlach & Lüdtke, 2008; Seaton, Marsh & Craven, 2010). Due to the close negative association between test anxiety and self-concept scores (Faber, 2007; Meece, Wigfield & Eccles, 1990), it remains unclear whether high-anxious students would be more prone to a negative contrast effect – or whether a negative contrast effect would additively depress their already lowered self-concepts. In terms of different frames of reference, the negative big-fish-little-pond effect was demonstrated either using an average school ability level, the within-class position in a certain academic subject or the placement in a high- versus low achieving learning course within a certain educational track. When considering both the school- and the class-average achievement level, and thus controlling for their interrelation, only the more proximal class-average achievement level negatively correlated with the students' self-concept (Ireson, Hallam & Plewin, 2001; Manger & Eikeland, 1997; Trautwein, Lüdtke, Marsh, Köller & Baumert, 2006; Trautwein, Lüdtke, Marsh & Nagy, 2009; Wouters, Germeijs, Colpin & Verschueren, 2011). Within a given classroom, the students' perceived class position mediated the relation between classmates' achievement and self-concept which, in turn, was primarily affected by the achievement of same-gender classmates. But controlling for students' perceived standing in class rendered the negative big-fish-little-pond effect nonsignificant, thus confirming the crucial role of a proximal frame of reference (Huguet, Dumas, Marsh, Régner, Wheeler, Suls, Seaton & Nezlek, 2009; Thijs, Verkuyten & Helmond, 2010). Especially in highly selective school systems and, therein, after the students' transition from elementary school to secondary educational tracks, the negative big-fish-little-pond effect appeared to be stronger in magnitude (Jerusalem, 1984; Marsh & Hau, 2003). Similar results were reported from analyses in gifted student samples. The academic self-concept of gifted students was substantially higher in mixed ability classrooms than in special classroom settings. Social comparison within a high ability environment led to significantly decreased competence beliefs. Moreover, the girls' self-concept was negatively influenced by gender-ratio in the classroom, that is, their self-concept slightly decreased with a higher proportion of boys in class (Preckel, Zeidner, Goetz & Schleyer, 2008; Zeidner & Schleyer, 1999). However, a recent study revealed contradictory results. In a sample of gifted fifth-graders, higher class-average ability led to lower math self-concepts, thus indicating a negative contrast effect. But at the same time, class type had a counterbalancing positive influence on math self-concepts, thus indicating a positive assimilation effect in favor of those students being placed in a special class setting (Preckel & Brüll, 2010). Though this result might be partially traced to several measurement and sample characteristics of this study, further research still has to replicate and explain this coincidence of both a contrast and an assimilation effect. As most of the research dealing with the big-fish-little-pond effect on academic self-concept took place at the upper secondary school level, some analyses also could prove its validity for elementary school samples. In a longitudinal approach, third- and fourth-graders' subsequent mathematics self-concept was negatively affected by prior class average achievement (Tiedemann & Billmann-Mahecha, 2004). Similar results were found in a study with second- and third-graders which, additionally, could substantiate a negative big-fish-little-pond effect on their participation in classroom activities. Students from classrooms with a moderate- or lower-average achievement level displayed a significantly higher frequency of participation than students from classrooms with a high-average achievement level (Köller, Zeinz & Trautwein, 2008). This finding must be handled with caution, though, because for the assessment of students' classroom behavior teachers were asked to use a single rating item which, however, might have been seriously biased due to their self-fulfilling expectancies and contextually influenced perceptions (Tiedemann, 2002; Tiedemann & Billmann-Mahecha, 2007).

To further clarify possible determinants or mediators of the big-fish-little-pond effect, one study analyzed the role of teachers' frame of reference. In particular, it was expected that teacher behavior emphasizing individual improvement and support instead of stressing social comparison and differences (Rheinberg, Vollmeyer & Burns, 2000) would reduce the negative contrast effect on students' mathematics self-concept – and thus would weaken the negative relations between self-concept and class-average achievement. The results from a secondary school sample could demonstrate a significant positive relation between individualized teacher behavior and students' self-concept but did not confirm the hypothesized decrease of the big-fish-little-pond effect on students' self-concept (Lüdtke, Köller, Marsh & Trautwein, 2005). Although experiencing a more individualized and supportive classroom setting, the students continued to use a within-class ranking order to compare their academic competencies. Not surprisingly, educational efforts to reduce negative contrast effects of social comparison need to consider the whole complexity of an academic setting rather than trying to alter a single environmental factor.

Nevertheless, besides the broad and seemingly overwhelming evidence for the negative big-fish-little-pond effect, several studies also found empirical support for a positive assimilation effect of social comparison processes on students' self-beliefs and performance. In line with the results from relevant methodological research which pointed out the positive consequences of social comparison as a function of their implicit versus explicit nature (Stapel & Suls, 2004), an assimilation effect occurred when students explicitly compared themselves with classmates having only slightly better grades (Huguet, Dumas, Monteil & Genestoux, 2001). When explicitly choosing a small peer group as target, this moderate upward comparison was positively associated with the students' subsequent self-perception and performance in a physical ability setting – albeit the negative contrast effect of class-average level was still existing (Chanal & Sarrazin, 2007). Similar results have been reported elsewhere and provided additional evidence of an upward assimilation effect. In particular, they demonstrated that at all achievement levels students were likely to choose slightly better performing peers for comparison, and that they felt very similar to them despite objectively remaining ability differences. They also demonstrated a comparison with an individual target to positively correlate with class average ability. Hence, students' choice of a similar target or target group depends on the contextually characterizing achievement level (Huguet, Dumas, Marsh, Régner, Wheeler, Suls, Seaton & Nezlek, 2009; Marsh, Seaton, Kuyper, Dumas, Huguet, Régner, Buunk, Manteil & Gibbons, 2010). Theoretically, these findings might emphasize an integration perspective on social comparison because various frames of references simultaneously affect students' self-beliefs. However, against the negative contrast effect of class-average achievement, the positive assimilation effect of target comparison appears to be relatively small in magnitude even though it obviously contributes to somewhat reduce the power of an existing contrast effect. On the other hand, an experimental study with third- and fourth-graders revealed contradictory results. In particular, those children with unexpected poor outcomes mostly preferred upward comparisons with better achieving classmates which, however, significantly lowered their self-concept after a mathematics exam. Downward comparisons with worse achieving classmates enhanced their self-concept. Methodologically, this study differed from similar approaches using self-concept items without any socially comparative content (Dickhäuser & Galfe, 2004). In sum, current research on assimilation effects reveals important and incremental insights into the complexities of social comparison processes in educational settings, but it has yet to overcome some methodological problems – e.g., concerning the probable impact of various self-concept instruments on its findings. It has, moreover, to analyze the longitudinal consequences of both implicit and explicit social comparisons on students´ self-beliefs, as well as to replicate the determination of assimilation effects in other academic domains and student samples. It must further clarify to which extent students (beyond an experimentally forced choice) really use social comparison with a target or small target group in a natural school setting.

Gender Differences

The formation of academic self-concepts depends not only on the students' achievement and their comparative processing of achievement information but also on their gender – thus leading to more or less pronounced differences between males and females in a certain domain or subject.

Empirically, the superiority of males in the mathematics and science domain has been well documented throughout the past decades. Males mostly achieved better outcomes and reported higher self-concepts than females did. Although this gender gap in mathematics and science achievement has apparently decreased in the meantime (Lindberg, Hyde, Petersen & Linn, 2010; Ma, 2010), self-concept differences favoring the males are to be found further on. Across various sample characteristics and research designs there is strong evidence for the boys to report significantly higher self-concepts in the math and science domain (Freedman-Doan, Wigfield, Eccles, Blumenfeld, Arbreton & Harold, 2000; Hergovich, Sirsch & Felinger, 2004; Marsh, 1989b; Nagy, Watt, Eccles, Trautwein, Lüdtke & Baumert, 2010; Skaalvik & Skaalvik, 2004; Wilgenbush & Merrell, 1999; Wilkins, 2004). Even when achievement differences were statistically controlled for and, thus, when equally performing boys and girls were compared, boys consistently reported higher self-concept scores in math and science (Bornholt, Goodnow & Cooney, 1994; Frenzel, Pekrun & Goetz, 2007; Hargreaves, Homer & Swinnerton, 2008; Manger & Eikeland, 1998; Rustemeyer & Fischer, 2005; Schilling, Sparfeldt & Rost, 2006). A number of studies could demonstrate that this gender-specific pattern in students' self-concepts already appeared to emerge in the early elementary grades (Ehm, Duzy & Hasselhorn, 2011; Herbert & Stipek, 2005) and to level off in the course of the elementary school (Dickhäuser & Meyer, 2006; Faber, Tiedemann & Billmann-Mahecha, 2011; Frühauf, 2008; Köller, Zeinz & Trautwein, 2008; Meelissen & Luyten, 2008; Tiedemann & Faber, 1995). Despite their comparable or even better math and science performance, girls had significantly lower self-perceptions and were, in general, more likely to develop less adaptive competence beliefs and academic emotions (Kurtz-Costes, Rowley, Harris-Britt & Woods, 2008; Stipek & Gralinski, 1991). The occurrence of gender-dependent self-concept differences, therefore, cannot not be completely explained by mere achievement differences.

Compared with this, gender differences in the verbal domain are less clear. Though empirical research findings across various age levels and educational tracks mostly could evidence females to display significantly higher verbal competencies and, in particular, to achieve better reading scores than males, these differences strongly varied in magnitude and often turned out rather small (De Fraine, Van Damme & Onghena, 2007; Gambell & Hunter, 1999; Hay, Ashman & van Kraayenoord, 1998b; Kurdek & Sinclair, 2001; Marsh, 1989a; Schilling, Sparfeldt & Rost, 2006; Steinmayr & Spinath, 2008; Tiedemann & Faber, 1994; Winkelmann & Groeneveld, 2010). However, this advantage does not appear to be consistently associated with higher verbal self-concepts in female learners. Whilst some studies reported higher self-concepts for females (Brunner, Hornung, Reichert & Martin, 2009; Byrne & Shavelson, 1987; Hay, Ashman & van Kraayenoord, 1998b; Hergovich, Sirsch & Felinger, 2004; Jacobs, Lanza, Osgood, Eccles & Wigfield, 2002; Marsh, 1989b; Schilling, Sparfeldt & Rost, 2006; Wilgenbusch & Merrell, 1999), other studies could not demonstrate any gender-dependent differences in verbal self-concepts (De Fraine, Van Damme & Onghena, 2007; Faber, 2003; Skaalvik & Skaalvik, 2004). Moreover, when statistically controlled for verbal achievement, the self-concept differences between males and females in some cases substantially remained (Ehm, Duzy & Hasselhorn, 2011), in other cases they completely diminished (Faber & Billmann-Mahecha, 2012; Schilling, Sparfeldt & Rost, 2006) or they apparently increased in favor of the boys despite their lower reading and writing outcomes (Frühauf, 2008; Treutlein & Schöler, 2009). To some extent, these mixed and even contradictory results might be traced back to the various grade levels and educational tracks analyzed in each study. Furthermore, with regard to foreign language learning there are similar findings in L2 research. Some studies reported self-concept differences favoring females (Dörnyei & Clément, 2001; Heinzmann, 2009; Henry, 2009), other studies failed to demonstrate any gender-dependent differences in self-concept – even when the female students clearly outperformed their male classmates (Daniels, 2008; Faber, 2009; Helmke, Schrader, Wagner, Nold & Schröder, 2008; Holder, 2005).

Altogether, research on gender differences provides evidence for a typically biased pattern in students' academic self-concepts. As existing achievement differences do not seem to lead to corresponding self-concept differences, these findings indicate a tendency for the males to overestimate and for the females to underestimate their competencies (Bornholt, Goodnow & Cooney, 1994; Cole, Martin, Peeke, Seroczynski & Fier, 1999; De Fraine, Van Damme & Onghena, 2007; Yoon, Eccles & Wigfield, 1996). Some studies lent additional support to this perspective of a gender bias. They could show that girls perceived themselves more defensively and thus discounted their competencies (Stetsenko, Little, Gordeeva & Oettingen, 2000; Stipek & Gralinski, 1991), and that boys tended to maintain more ego-enhancing self-evaluations than girls did (Hattie & Marsh, 1996; Skaalvik & Skaalvik, 2004). According to traditional gender stereotypes, elementary school boys from first grade on identified with math-gender stereotypes more strongly than girls. As the children's gendered views of mathematics as a male domain, moreover, were typically acquired before their domain-specific self-concepts emerged, pertinent socialization effects prior to school entry must be assumed (Cvencek, Meltzoff & Greenwald, 2011).

Thus, as one important determinant of emergent gender differences in academic self-concepts, parental socialization effects must be considered. Parents are to be seen as an important source of information children draw on to form their self-perceptions. Long before school entry, they usually act as significant others by modelling and affecting their children's academic gender stereotypes. As relevant empirical analyses pointed out, parents' gender-stereotyped beliefs appeared to be closely and longitudinally associated with their children's self-concepts and, to a lesser degree, with their domain-specific attainment as well (Bleeker & Jacobs, 2004; Frome & Eccles, 1998; Meece, Glienke & Askew, 2009). In particular, parents of elementary school students commonly viewed the mathematics domain as a more male and the verbal domain as a more female subject (Räty, Kasanen & Kärkäinen, 2006). Therefore, they expected their sons to achieve stronger and their daughters to achieve weaker outcomes in mathematics (Herbert & Stipek, 2005; Mösko, 2010; Tiedemann, 2000a). Accordingly, parents also were more likely to attribute the boys' success to their ability and the girls' success to their effort (Räty, Vänskä, Kasanen & Kärkkäinen, 2002; Yee & Eccles, 1988). With regard to the daily homework situation, it was also demonstrated in a small exploratory study that parents of secondary students communicated their own math stereotype beliefs in particular to their daughters and, thus, affected their self-perceptions (Bhanot & Jovanovic, 2005).

Another important determinant of emergent gender differences in academic self-concepts is, of course, the existing school setting – including the stereotyping effects of teacher expectancies, classroom interactions, and peer influences (Meece, Glienke & Askew, 2009). Teacher perceptions and expectancies concerning the nature of academic subjects, student abilities and developmental processes constitute an educational belief system which plays a crucial role in forming and communicating typical gender stereotypes. There is strong evidence for teacher expectations being biased by gender. Longitudinal analyses in math classrooms at the secondary level could demonstrate that teachers perceived the boys to be more talented than the girls even though there were no gender differences in their academic outcomes. Accordingly, teachers assumed that the girls would try harder than the boys in mathematics (Jussim, 1989; Jussim & Eccles, 1992). In a predominantly female sample of elementary school math teachers, similar and somewhat more differentiating results were found. Teacher perceptions were consistent with gender stereotypes. In general, the teachers believed girls to be less logical than equally achieving boys. Therefore, they rated mathematics as more difficult for average achieving girls and attributed unexpected failure more to low ability and less to lack of effort. Interestingly, these findings held valid for average and low achieving but not for high achieving students – indicating teachers' gendered views to be substantially moderated by students' performance (Tiedemann, 2000b, 2002). Teachers' gender stereotypes of students' abilities and behaviors, thus, should contribute to different interactions and treatment during classroom lessons. For example, expecting less competence in girls may lead teachers to assign easier tasks to them, to attribute their failure outcomes more to low ability, and to give them less supportive feedback (Georgiou, Christou, Stavrinides & Panaoura, 2002) – which altogether will, in turn, generate self-fulfilling prophecy processes that weaken their self-concept and undermine their learning progress. Correspondingly, in the course of daily classroom interaction various gender-dependent differences could be observed. Boys received more attention from teachers and participated more in classroom activities. In particular, they were given more time to talk during classroom lessons, they received more acknowledgement, approval, encouragement and corrective feedback than girls (Jovanovic & King, 1998; Meece, Glienke & Askew, 2009; Sadker, Sadker & Klein, 1991; She, 2000). However, due to various contextual structures and sample characteristics, the differences observed varied considerably across all studies and were rather small in magnitude (Brophy, 1985; Parsons, Kaczala & Meece, 1982). Research on gender differences in teachers' and students' classroom behavior must, therefore, proceed in a more contextualized manner. It still suffers from a lack of analyses which are able to clarify the long-term consequences of gender stereotypes on students' academic self-beliefs and learning outcomes in different domains, at different age levels, and in different educational tracks. In particular, there is a need for studies to integrate cognitive-motivational self-belief approaches and behavioral observations of relevant classroom interactions. These studies should also consider the role of teacher-student relations as well as the impact of peer pressure in the classroom which obviously may contribute to the strength of gender-dependent achievement differences (Van de gaer, Pustjens, Van Damme & De Munter, 2006).

But beyond the impact of relevant teacher and classroom factors, gendered perspectives will also be inferred by students and will affect their self-beliefs in that way. As a study with third- and fourth-graders could show, girls reported lower math self-concepts than equally achieving boys. Though teacher evaluations of children's competencies did not differ across gender, girls perceived them as lower in magnitude than boys. Girls' and boys' self-concepts were more closely related to inferred teacher evaluations than to grades. Hence, academic gender stereotypes were already present in students' cognitive-motivational orientations and significantly mediated the relation between achievement and self-concept (Dickhäuser & Stiensmeier-Pelster, 2003). This finding, in particular, underlines the overlap of various socialization effects in and outside school and, thus, illustrates that students' gender stereotypes already acquired will significantly affect current educational processes in the classroom. Especially academic test situations in which negative gender stereotypes become salient might substantially contribute to impair students' self-beliefs and performance by triggering stereotype threat (Croizet, Désert, Dutrévis & Leyens, 2001; Kiefer & Shih, 2006; Steele, Spencer & Aronson, 2002).

To summarize, parent and teacher stereotypes must be seen as crucial sources of gender differences in students' academic self-concepts and contribute to support or hinder the acquisition of individual skills and competencies in a certain domain (Linver & Davis-Kean, 2005; Stevenson & Newman, 1986; Turner, Stewart & Lapan, 2004). Self-concept research has already produced important knowledge about this issue, but it has yet to advance and to unravel the developmental and educational complexities of its underlying processes.

Causal Ordering

Although educational research has produced widespread and convincing evidence for substantial relations between academic self-concept and academic achievement variables, empirical findings concerning their causal ordering appear to be less unambiguous. For a while, this issue has been widely influenced by two contrasting theoretical perspectives: the self-enhancement perspective considers prior self-concept to determine subsequent achievement, whereas the skill development perspective considers prior achievement to determine subsequent self-concept (Calsyn & Kenny, 1977). Hence, the self-enhancement perspective stresses the motivational role of self-concept to influence further learning activities and achievement outcomes – also including an individually strong motive to maintain or protect one's self-worth which can lead to biased self-estimates of own academic competencies (Covington, 1984). The skill development perspective focuses the dependence of self-concept formation upon antecedent learning processes and achievement outcomes in a given academic environment – also being affected by relevant dimensional and social comparison processes (Green,

Nelson, Martin & Marsh, 2006). Undeniably, both perspectives offer each an essentially important approach to direct and explain the relationship between self-concept and achievement, but they surely cannot claim to exclusively reflect this complex relationship. From the viewpoint of developmental and learning theories, academic self-concept and achievement must be needfully seen more likely as mutually reinforcing constructs (Wigfield & Karpathian, 1991). In the long term, self-concept will be either a cause or a consequence of achievement (Figure 6) – thereby, it also will mediate prior outcome experiences to subsequent learning outcomes. Consequently, the causal ordering between academic self-concept and achievement should be reciprocal in nature rather than unidirectional (Marsh, 1990b, 2006).

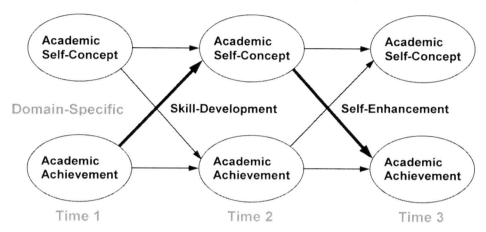

Figure 6. Causal ordering of academic self-concept and achievement: The reciprocal effects model (Marsh, 1990b).

Empirically, the reciprocal effects perspective has been mostly supported. Whereas earlier studies in the field typically suffered from various theoretical and methodological limitations and, thus, produced somewhat mixed and less defensible results (Byrne, 1986; Marsh, 1988b; Marsh, Byrne & Yeung, 1999; Newman, 1984; Shavelson & Bolus, 1982), more recent studies yielded sound evidence for the reciprocal effects models' validity. A meta-analysis of longitudinal analyses could demonstrate both significant effects from prior achievement to subsequent self-concept variables and the other way around. Standardized regression coefficients were larger for academic than for either subject-specific or global self-belief measures, but there was no difference with regard to the achievement measures used in each study. Furthermore, neither student age nor time interval between longitudinal measurement points had an impact on effect size. However, due to the various diversities of studies under consideration, all effect sizes turned out rather small in magnitude (ranging from $\beta = .05$ to $\beta = .18$) and could have underestimated the strength of relations in several aspects (Valentine & DuBois, 2005). Therefore, a closer look on relevant studies particularly taking into account their operationalization of self-concept and achievement constructs, their number and type of variables analyzed, and the grade level of their student samples may draw a more differentiated picture.

Remarkably, despite the academic self-concept being well evidenced as a multidimensional and multifaceted construct, a reasonable number of studies had analyzed the causal ordering of relations between self-concept and achievement using general academic self-concept measures and correspondingly aggregated achievement measures (such as grade point average or similar composite scores). Across various cultural contexts, grade levels, research designs, and measurement procedures, for the most part they could basically substantiate a reciprocal pattern in the relations between self-concept and achievement variables. In particular, effects appeared to be statistically significant but mostly small or moderate in magnitude. Within each reciprocal pattern of relations between constructs, in studies from lower (elementary) grades, standardized regression coefficients from prior achievement to subsequent self-concept tended to be slightly stronger than from prior self-concept to subsequent achievement – in studies from higher (secondary) grades the opposite was true (Guay, Marsh & Boivin, 2003; Hoge, Smit & Crist, 1995; Marsh, 1990b; Marsh, Hau & Kong, 2002; Marsh & O'Mara, 2008b; Mujis, 1997; Pekrun, 1987; Pinxten, De Fraine, Van Damme & D'Haenens, 2010; Satow & Schwarzer, 2000; Van Damme, Opdenakker, De Fraine & Mertens, 2004). Moreover, one single study could clearly demonstrate a different pattern of relations depending on students' grade level. As the relations between self-concept and achievement in a third-grade sample lend support to the causal predominance of achievement, in a seventh-grade sample a truly reciprocal relationship was found (Skaalvik & Hagtvet, 1990). Especially this result contributes to confirm the assumption of developmental changes in the relation between academic self-concept and achievement. Further research should, therefore, pay more attention to this issue. However, with regard to their theoretical validity and empirical generalizability, all these findings appear to be subject to one important restriction. Based on general self-concept and achievement measures, they always seem to be at risk for leveling or even masking potentially existing differences in construct relations due to various academic domains or subjects which only can be explored by means of a subject-specific research approach.

Studies on domain- or subject-specific construct relations in secondary school samples could, for the most part, support the reciprocal effects perspective. With regard to several subjects (such as math, science, English) and various grade levels, results consistently reported comparable strong relations between prior achievement on subsequent self-concept variables – and vice versa. In some of these studies the basic causal ordering approach was extended by adding other motivational constructs such as subject-specific interest or general self-esteem. Neither for interest nor for self-esteem, substantial or even incremental effects could be found. In particular, when statistically controlled for subject-specific self-concept, the weak relations between self-esteem and achievement diminished, thus indicating the mediating role of self-concept (Helmke, 1992; Marsh, Trautwein, Lüdtke, Köller & Baumert, 2005; Marsh & Yeung, 1997; Trautwein, Lüdtke, Köller & Baumert, 2006). However, there were also contradictory results clearly supporting the skill development perspective. In two cohorts of advanced secondary students the effects from prior achievement on subsequent self-concept in the math and verbal domain concordantly turned out to be stronger than the other way around. Moreover, there were also significant path coefficients from prior achievement to subsequent motivation, but no mediating effect of subject-specific self-concepts ((Skaalvik & Valås, 1999). Another analysis concerning the longitudinal relations between math achievement, self-concept, and intrinsic value could report quite similar results (Yoon, Eccles & Wigfield, 1996). And finally, one single study did offer a more detailed but also somewhat confusing view on the causal ordering of achievement and self-concept variables in mathematics. In two cohorts differing by age for both seventh-grade boys and girls, the reciprocal effects perspective at the first measurement time and the skill development perspective at the second measurement time could be supported. For ninth-grade boys and girls, the results appeared to be very mixed. Whereas they confirmed for boys, again, a clear reciprocal pattern of relations at the first measurement time, for girls they showed a clear self-enhancement pattern of relations. Unfortunately, no multiple group analyses were calculated to test for significant differences between male and female structural equation models (Antunes & Fontaine, 2007). Consistent with a more dynamic understanding of self-concept development, these findings point out possible invariances of causal ordering analyses across age and gender – indicating the influence of gender stereotypes on girls' prior self-beliefs as well as on their subsequent learning behavior.

At the elementary school level, distinctly fewer research activities on domain- or subject-specific construct relations must be noted. Relevant studies could, for the most part, support the skill development perspective. Prior achievement significantly affected later self-concept in math and reading, whereas the relations between prior self-concept and subsequent achievement were relatively weak and insignificant (Aunola, Leskinen, Onatsu-Arvilommi & Nurmi, 2002; Chapman & Tunmer, 1997; Helmke & van Aken, 1995; Skaalvik & Valås, 1999). However, within the course of first grade, the self-enhancement perspective was supported demonstrating only significant path coefficients from prior self-concept on subsequent achievement. Viewed developmentally, this finding can be expected as first-graders' self-beliefs still cannot reflect individually sustained achievement experiences. Furthermore, the same study reported cross-lagged path coefficients between achievement and self-concept being weak and statistically not significant when analyzing construct relations from first to second grade (Kammermeyer & Martschinke, 2006). Possibly, this null pattern may be interpreted in terms of a developmentally determined shift in causal ordering relations between both constructs – but only further research might clarify this issue. Also at the elementary school level, one single study reported an interesting extension of the basic causal ordering approach analyzing the longitudinal relations between physical abilities and self-concept. Their results lend clear support for the reciprocal effects perspective which could be generalized over age and gender (Marsh, Gerlach, Trautwein, Lüdtke & Brettschneider, 2007).

Empirical analyses on the causal ordering of achievement and self-concept has been more or less reductive as they focused the longitudinal relations between both constructs within a certain domain or subject. Hence, they completely neglected the social and dimensional comparison perspective of self-concept formation across domains or subjects. As an integrative approach to overcome this conceptual and empirical shortcoming, Möller, Retelsdorf, Köller and Marsh (2011) concluded to integrate the reciprocal effects model and the model of internal/external frame of reference model. As their longitudinal results could demonstrate, consistent with the reciprocal effects perspective in both the math and verbal domain there were significant cross-lagged relations between prior achievement and subsequent self-concept as well as between prior self-concept and subsequent achievement. Furthermore, consistent with the prediction of dimensional comparison effect there were negative cross-lagged relations between achievement and self-concept across domains. Prior self-concepts did not strongly affect subsequent achievement in the non-corresponding domain – thus dimensional contrasting effects in subject-specific self-concepts were longitudinally apparent but did not generalize across domains. Over time, reciprocal effects between achievement and self-concept mainly occurred within a certain domain or subject.

Taken altogether, causal ordering results concerning subject-specific achievement and self-concept variables are less consistent. Depending on the school level of student samples, relevant studies reveal rather different lines of findings. At the secondary school level, analyses mostly supported the reciprocal effects perspective, at the elementary school level they mostly supported the skill development perspective. This difference in causal ordering patterns seems to be plausible from a developmental point of view. As younger students' self-concepts still are in the process of emerging, they will stronger reflect academic appraisal and feedback within a certain educational setting and, therefore, intensely incorporate and process information about their own competencies. Over time, then, the motivational role of self-concept will increase and lead to more reciprocal effect lines between achievement and self-concept (Hattie, 1992; Wigfield & Karpathian, 1991). At both school levels, however, some findings are hardly to interpret and need further clarification. This certainly applies to the issue of age and gender differences in causal ordering patterns. Apart from that, analyses of the causal ordering between achievement and self-concept should be further elaborated in terms of potential mediator variables which possibly might influence the relations between constructs (Helmke, 1992; Marsh & Martin, 2011) – e.g. subject-specific causal attributions, test anxiety, task values, goal orientations, motivational orientations, and academic engagement (Barker, Dowson & McInerney, 2005; Chouinard, Kassenti & Roy, 2007; Green, Nelson, Martin & Marsh, 2006; Mägi, Lerkkanen, Poikkeus, Rasku-Puttonen & Kikas, 2010; Skaalvik & Skaalvik, 2006; van Kraayenoord & Schneider, 1999). There still exists a considerable lack of causal ordering studies additionally incorporating such cognitive-motivational variables. The analysis of more complex models will challenge self-concept research in several ways. Theoretically it must integrate various similar cognitive-motivational constructs which are conceptually separable but will empirically overlap. Furthermore, this integration work must be founded on a well-defined theory or theoretical framework, at least, which should able to clarify and predict the relations and causal ordering perspectives among domain- or subject-specific constructs. Methodologically it must, therefore, handle several problems in sound modeling of construct relations – e.g., the problem of multivariate multicollinearity effects and inappropriate fitting of structural equation models when using conceptually less distinguishable constructs (Kline, 2011).

CAUSAL ATTRIBUTIONS

Students' academic self-attributions refer to their subjective beliefs about the causes of their performance outcomes which are drawn on, both for the explanation of past and the prediction of future performances. Dependent on the experience of individually persistent success or failure, they immediately provoke favorable or un-favorable emotional responses as well as they, in the long term, contribute to subsequently adaptive or maladaptive learning behaviors (Diener & Dweck, 1978). The causal dimensions subjectively preferred reflect the students' control expectations to influence academic task requirements and classroom situations – hence, they crucially account for the extent students will feel and act as "pawns" or "origins" in a given educational setting (deCharms, 1977; Ryan & Grolnick, 1986).

Following the well-known classification scheme originally introduced and onwardly elaborated by Weiner (2010), academic self-attributions can relate to causes located within or without the individual student and refer to the dimension of internality vs. externality. These causes can also be seen as more or less consistent over time and refer to the dimension of stability vs. variability. Each attribution of an individual outcome thus will inevitably reflect a certain cause being internal (or external) and stable (or variable) which furthermore appears more or less controllable (Figure 7). If a failure outcome is predominantly assigned to a cause which cannot be sufficiently influenced then, in the course of time the student will gradually experience feelings of uncontrollability and helplessness in the face of critical requirements. As such, students' individually cumulated explanations of success and failure in a certain academic domain should increasingly lead to the development of attribution tendencies sustainably reflecting their corresponding control expectations (Abramson, Garber & Seligman, 1980; Weiner, 2005).

| | Internal || External ||
	Stable	Unstable	Stable	Unstable
Controllability Low	Ability	Mood	Task Difficulty	Luck
Controllability High		Effort		Help From Others

Global ◄► Specific

Figure 7. Dimensions of causal attributions (Weiner, 2005).

The formation of causal attributions turns out to be crucially dependent upon the students' processing of ipsative and social comparison information – in particular, with regard to the perceived consistency, consensus, and distinctiveness of an academic outcome (Heckhausen, 1987; Kelley & Michela, 1980). If students perceive their outcome being intraindividually consistent with prior performance, they will be more likely attributed to stable causes – if they perceive their outcome being intraindividually inconsistent with prior performance, they will be more likely attributed to variable causes. Concurrently, if they perceive their outcome being interindividually comparable with their classmates' outcomes, they will be more likely attributed to external causes – if they perceive their outcome being interindividually less comparable with their classmates' outcomes, they will be more likely attributed to internal causes. Eventually, this information may covary with the perception of task-specific effects. If the current outcome is experienced as distinct to a high degree, i.e. depending upon special features with respect to the task, then students will tend more toward external explanations. Accordingly, a student who achieves a much better outcome than the majority of classmates will explain his or her result with internal ability or effort. Conversely, a student who achieves an outcome equally bad as the majority of classmates will explain his or her result with external bad luck or task difficulty. However, due to the complexity of academic performance situations, reference information of this nature cannot be developed in a new unit of time for each individual outcome in all aspects. Rather, it should be assumed that the students' previous experiences of consistency and consensus in particular are already represented cumulatively by self-related cognitions – and that the expectancies with respect to performance and competence available in this way should be reflected essentially in the students' academic self-concept. Thus, the attribution pattern students individually prefer should be largely affected by their competence beliefs, and therefore to a lesser degree solely explained on the basis of academic performance (Chapman & Lawes, 1984; Faber, 1990; Frieze, 1980). As students' academic self-concepts are domain- or subject-specific in nature, it also must be expected that the relationships between self-concept and attributions turn out, correspondingly, to be domain- or subject-specific – meaning that, for the purpose of explaining individual success and failure in a certain academic domain, subject-specific control beliefs will be formed as well. Furthermore, the attributional pattern students will individually prefer with regard to a certain subject may principally turn out in two different ways. Students might use explanations in order to protect or enhance their self-esteem and thus perceive themselves more responsible for success than for failure. On the other hand, contrary to that attributional bias perspective, students might use explanations in order to draw a realistic picture of their competencies and thus perceive themselves equally responsible for success and failure (Whitley & Frieze, 1985; Zuckerman, 1979). Whether they tend to explain their outcomes in a self-serving manner or not will substantially depend on their processing of attributionally relevant information – in particular, to the extent they are motivated to selectively overemphasize external rather than internal causes for failure against apparently available consistency and consensus cues. Therefore, it must be assumed that the use of self-serving or counterdefensive attributions of unfavorable outcomes will be crucially moderated by students' psychosocial beliefs and needs. Hence, the assumption of self-serving attribution tendencies per se must come as an oversimplification (Bradley, 1978; Ickes & Layden, 1978).

In the past decades, the taxonomy of Weiner earned merit as a fruitful heuristics conceptually approaching students' outcome explanations and control beliefs; however, empirical research also worked out its limitations and shortcomings. As qualitative studies by means of content analysis repeatedly could demonstrate, children and adolescents reported more diverse and differentiated causal categories than conceptually predicted. In particular, they divided internal as well as external explanations into various proximal subcategories (Little, 1985; Flammer & Schmid, 2003; Gipps & Tunstall, 1998; Normandeau & Gobeil, 1998). Similarly, quantitative studies using attribution questionnaires which included causal factors beyond the classic taxonomy could show that students generally were able to use more causal ascriptions than the original four factors – e.g., emotional mood, subject-related interest, task familiarity, use of learning strategies, peer and teacher support, and quality of classroom instruction (Bar-Tal & Darom, 1979; Connell, 1985; Frieze & Snyder, 1980; Jopt, 1978; Pekrun, 1983; Mok, Kennedy & Moore, 2011; Raviv, Bar-Tal, Raviv & Bar-Tal, 1980; Skaalvik, 1994). Altogether, across conceptually and methodologically very different approaches to assess students' attributions (Hau & Salili, 1993), there was strong evidence for a broad range of success and failure explanations which, nevertheless, always included the original factors of ability, effort, task difficulties, and luck. Moreover, in both research lines significant age effects were found. In particular, older children's control beliefs were found to be more closely related to their individual personality and aptitude characteristics (Skinner, Zimmer-Gembeck & Connell, 1998). According to developmental findings on children's emerging abilities to understand the compensatory relation between ability and effort, students' causal attributions became more refined with increasing age (Nicholls & Miller, 1983; Stipek & DeCotis, 1988).

Subject to this age effect, various field studies analyzing students' causal attributions regarding different school subjects could, at least in some aspects, demonstrate the subject-specific validity of academic attribution measures. Due to methodological features especially concerning the format of attribution items as well as the type and number of causal factors, their findings appear less comparable and consistent. However, in several studies from secondary and elementary samples, subject-specific differences in students' attributions were found. In particular, they indicated internal attribution scores (mainly concerning ability and effort) in the verbal domain being more strongly associated with students' verbal self-concept and in the math domain being more strongly associated with students' math self-concept, but less strongly associated across domains. A similar correlational pattern could be found with regard to academic achievement variables. In particular, ability and effort attributions for success and failure were more strongly correlated to performance scores within the same subject than across different subjects. With regard to external causes, the findings produced less clarity. In some studies they did not correlate to criterion measures, in other studies they equally correlated to criterion measures across subject areas (Faber, 1996, 2002a; Marsh, 1984b; Marsh, Cairns, Relich, Barnes & Debus, 1984; Moreano, 2004; Licht, Stader & Swanson, 1989; Ryckman, Peckham, Mizokawa & Sprague, 1990; Vispoel & Austin, 1995; Watkins & Gutierrez, 1989). Thus, the issue of subject-specificity of causal attributions needs further research which should analyze students' explanations by the means of theoretically representative and methodologically adequate procedures – also taking into consideration possible attributional differences within a certain subject (Hiebert, Winograd & Danner, 1984).

Though several studies could substantiate low achieving students' tendencies to attribute failure outcomes externally (Skaalvik, 1994; Whitley & Frieze, 1985), other studies could show primarily high achieving students' attributions being self-serving (Licht, Stader & Swanson, 1989; Marsh, 1986b; Vispoel & Austin, 1995). Furthermore, a number of empirical findings demonstrated students' attribution patterns being less biased by self-serving preferences. However, this result held mainly for ability attributions, whereas the findings with regard to the remaining causal dimensions appeared less consistent. This fact should, not least, be the result of diversities in the self-belief and performance measures applied. With this reservation, the empirical research hitherto existing strongly supports the occurrence of typical attribution tendencies congruently depending upon academic self-concept and achievement level: students with rather poor performance and low self-concept scores are undergoing more critical experiences of loss of control and helplessness by primarily explaining failure with stable internal causes (with a lack of academic ability) and, mostly to a lesser degree, also with variable internal causes (with a lack of effort). On the other hand, they cannot explain success with the same level of conciseness, but they definitely rule out the possibility of their own ability acting as a causal factor. In contrast, students with rather high performance and high self-concept scores explain success predominantly with stable internal causes (with their own academic ability), and frequently also with variable internal causes (with their own effort). Failure is traced back by them, primarily, to a lack of effort or to environmental constraints (Bell, McCallum, Bryles, McDonald, Park & Williams, 1994; Butkowsky & Willows, 1980; Diener & Dweck, 1980; Faber, 1996, 2002a; Helmke, 1992; Jacobsen, Lowery & DuCette, 1986; Nicholls, 1979; Pekrun, 1983). In particular, poor achieving students who perpetually attribute their failure to a lack of own ability and their success to external relief are strongly at risk to strengthen deep expectations of failure and increasingly to experience resignation and helplessness. Likewise, they are prone to display reduced engagement in critical or demanding tasks (Stipek & Mason, 1987) and to develop self-handicapping orientations and strategies (Martin, Marsh, Williamson & Debus, 2005). In the long-term, this will impede their individual perspective to alter maladaptive learning behaviors and to actively reach for improved learning outcomes (Abramson, Garber & Seligman, 1980; Skinner, Zimmer-Gembeck & Connell, 1998).

According to relevant findings of self-concept research, in particular to the well proven influence of stereotypes, some studies also reported considerable gender differences in causal attribution patterns. These differences could be already substantiated in the elementary years. In the math domain, boys were less likely to explain failure with a lack of ability than girls and more likely to explain success with own ability than girls. In the verbal domain, no significant gender differences could be found – thus, once again, indicating the subject-specificity of attributional preferences (Dickhäuser & Meyer, 2006; Mok, Kennedy & Moore, 2011; Ryckman & Peckham, 1987; Stipek, 1984; Stipek & Gralinski, 1991; Tiedemann & Faber, 1995).

Those studies having concurrently analyzed the relations of self-concept and academic achievement with causal attributions revealed clear evidence that differences in the students' subject-specific control beliefs could be explained more profoundly by the corresponding self-concept variable rather than by achievement. Individual preferences in causal explanations for success and failure appeared to be strongly dependent on self-related competence beliefs – hence, students' domain- or subject-specific self-concepts will play an important mediating role in the formation of their academic attributions (Bandalos, Yates & Thorndike-Christ, 1995; Butkowsky & Willows, 1980; Faber, 1996, 2002a; Marsh, 1986b; Marsh, Cairns, Relich, Barnes & Debus, 1984; Moreano, 2004; Nicholls, 1979; Watkins & Gutierrez, 1989). For clarifying its constitutive antecedents and determinants, empirical analyses of students' academic attributions should, therefore, principally consider not only relevant achievement but also related self-concept variables.

Empirical investigations of subject-specific causal attributions in general, and of the relationships between subject-specific self-concepts and attribution tendencies in particular, have so far been conducted primarily on the basis of cross-sectional data. For further analyzing developmental, especially causal ordering aspects, longitudinal research in this field has, to a large extent, still to be undertaken. Only few studies do exist which point to the long-term risks of unfavorable attributional tendencies and control beliefs with respect to the students' overall psychosocial development. But there is still a strong need for more prospective investigations in which the relations between the subject-specific self-concept, attribution, and achievement variables can be longitudinally explored (Boggiano, Main, Flink, Barrett, Silvern & Katz, 1989; Fincham, Diener & Hokoda, 1987; Fincham, Hokoda & Sanders, 1989; Harter & Connell, 1984; Kurtz-Costes & Schneider, 1994; Nolen-Hoeksema, Girgus, & Seligman, 1986, 1992).

TEST ANXIETY

Test anxiety defines the students' individual disposition to perceive certain academic demands, especially related to evaluative situations, as personal threat (to their self-worth or self-esteem) because they fear not to master the task at hand and to experience inevitable failure. These threat perceptions are commonly associated with strong negative feelings and physiological arousal which may negatively affect the students' behavioral responses and, in turn, detrimentally influence their academic performance (Zeidner, 1998).

With regard to its development, processing, and consequences, test anxiety has to be seen as a multidimensional construct being determined by complex relations between various psychological components. Recent theoretical conceptualizations largely agree on the crucial role of cognitive processes which can be further differentiated into cognitive-attentional and cognitive-motivational aspects. Cognitive-attentional aspects of the test anxiety construct refer to the impact of students' threat perceptions on their information processing before and during task completion – in particular concerning their lowered level of task-related attention and their impaired retrieval of learned contents (Sarason & Sarason, 1987; Wine, 1982). Cognitive-motivational aspects of the test anxiety construct refer to various types of failure-related expectancies and valence beliefs – in particular concerning the uncontrollability of a failure outcome and its negative consequences (Pekrun, 1988a). Likewise, predominating expectations of failure and uncontrollability may also be considered as appraisals which might trigger individual reactions of distress – that is, test anxiety means a stressful psychological state (Jerusalem, 1993; Lazarus & Folkman, 1984). Cognitive-motivational aspects also refer to the motive of self-worth enhancement or protection – in particular concerning the tendency to reinterpret failure outcomes or to avoid failure experiences (Covington, 1992). All these aspects are assumed to work in a mutually reinforcing way.

As none of the theoretical conceptualizations seem capable to completely account for the complex and multidimensional feature of test anxiety, therefore, their specific contributions to describe and to explain the construct might be fruitfully combined within a broader framework of a transactional model (Zeidner, 1998). It seeks to include the antecedents or determinants, the phenomenological components and processing stages as well as the consequences of test anxiety (Figure 8).

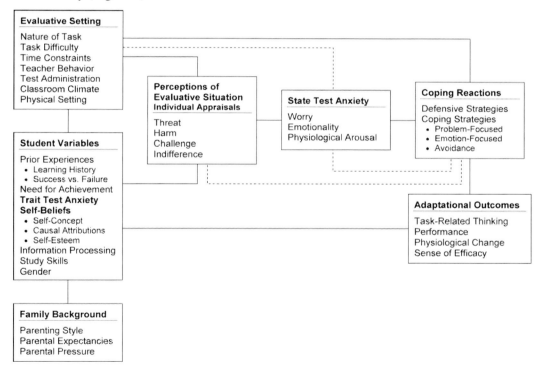

Figure 8. A transactional model of test anxiety determinants, processes, and consequences (sensu Zeidner, 1998).

The central antecedent variable for the development of test anxiety, first of all, is the evaluative setting in a certain educational context. In particular, the characteristics of the academic task, time available for task completion, and the modalities of test administration may be more or less perceived as threatening cues that initiate students' fear of failure. Evaluative situations may be either written or oral examination procedures in a certain subject. Especially in the latter case, students' test-related feelings will be strongly confounded with an increased degree of public self-awareness which may additionally evoke social anxiety responses. As an essential part of the evaluative setting, of course, teacher behavior and classroom climate are relevant factors that may contribute to students' test-anxious reactions. As various empirical studies could demonstrate, the use of less structured teaching methods, high teacher pressure for achievement, a more competitive classroom climate, and a negative relation to teachers were associated with students' heightened test anxiety level. However, there were marked differences among classrooms. Somewhat unexpected, teachers' intense use of instructional time also appeared to correlate positively to students' anxiety – indicating that strong instructional density in the classroom could possibly have overextended the cognitive-attentional capacities of high-anxious students. Similarly, the relationship between perceived climate and teacher variables with test anxiety can also reflect high-anxious students' selective attentional and motivational bias and, thus, must be considered as bidirectional in nature (Bossong, 1994; Helmke, 1988; Pekrun, 1985).

Another central antecedent of students' test anxiety is evidently their individual learning history, namely their prior experiences of academic success and failure. Students who have consistently experienced failure outcomes in evaluative settings are more prone to emerge test-anxious expectancies (Dusek, 1980). Therefore, the individually already existing degree of test anxiety appears to play a crucial role in students' perceptions of evaluative situations. As accumulated failure experiences become more salient by social comparison processes within the classroom and students' views of their academic standing become more differentiated over time, the negative impact of previously acquired test anxiety on their current coping with evaluative situations will increase with age (Wigfield & Eccles, 1989). Against this background of their individual learning history, students will have developed correspondingly lowered self-beliefs. There is sound evidence that high-anxious students display strongly lowered competence and control beliefs. In various studies they reported more negative academic self-concepts (Abu-Hilal, 2000; Britner & Pajares, 2006; Faber, 1995a; Helmke, 1999; Krampen, 1991; Meece, Wigfield & Eccles, 1990; Newbegin & Owens, 1996; Putwain, Woods & Symes, 2010) as well as more internal-stable failure attributions and more external success attributions (Bandalos, Yates & Thorndike-Christ, 1995; Faber, 1995a; Leppin, Schwarzer, Belz, Jerusalem & Quast, 1987). Even more, as a result of enduring failure experiences and failure-oriented self-perceptions, their global self-esteem also appeared to be strikingly depressed. Across various grade levels and sample characteristics, students' test anxiety scores were negatively correlated with general self-esteem or self-worth measures – indicating the personality impairing effect of test anxiety beyond academic concerns (Faber, 1995a; Many & Many, 1975; Pekrun, 1983; Skaalvik, 1997b). Furthermore, due to persisting failure experiences and more pessimistic self-beliefs, high-anxious students will also have developed more improper cognitive skills, e.g. biased information processing, and maladaptive study strategies (Covington, 1985; Tobias, 1992). As academic development considerably depends on students' gender or gender stereotyping processes within a given educational setting, the formation of test anxiety also will. According to the findings of self-concept and attribution research, empirical analyses of test anxiety could demonstrate modest, but significant gender differences in test anxiety scores. Male students mostly reported lower anxiety scores than female students (Cassady & Johnson, 2002; Hembree, 1988; Rouxel, 2000; Schwarzer, Seipp & Schwarzer, 1989). However, this difference does not mean that boys in general will be less anxious but rather that they are more defensive and hesitant to admit personal threat (Hill & Sarason, 1966). Overall, with regard to students' actual test anxiety responses in an evaluation situation, their already existing academic experiences, self-beliefs, and strategies must be seen as important mediating variables – which substantially contribute to activate and strengthen individual threat expectancies.

However, from a developmental perspective, high-anxious students' academic experiences, self-beliefs, and strategies are not merely the result of individual pathways. Rather, they always appear to be directly and indirectly influenced by certain home environmental variables. There is some empirical evidence that children experiencing both a more authoritarian or a more overprotective parenting style reported higher levels of test anxiety. Especially, a family setting being less supporting and more aversive against the child's feelings and activities must be seen as a serious environmental risk factor for emerging test anxiety – in particular, if parents continuously use overcontrolling strategies and harsh punishment, place high pressure on their child to succeed, and fail to establish a more cohesive family climate (Dinnel, Brittain, Johnson, King, Pust & Thompson, 2002; Hock, 1992; Krohne, 1992; Putwain, Woods & Symes, 2010; Sideridis & Kafestsios, 2008).

Being confronted with a certain evaluative situation, high-anxious students will immediately produce perceptions and appraisals that primarily focus on their failure expectancies which, in turn, will trigger strong feelings of threat and harm. This may happen either by real confrontation or by mental anticipation. Only low-anxious students will perceive the evaluative situation as a challenge or, at least, as less important. Whether an evaluative situation will lead to subjective threat appraisals will interindividually vary to some extent. Depending on their individual failure experiences and self-beliefs, some students might be threatened by certain conditions, other students might not. In any case, those students appraising the situation as a more failure-prone and thus threatening event will suffer from marked state test anxiety – which commonly manifests as strong worry cognitions, emotionality reactions, and physiological arousal. The worry component of anxiety reactions refers to the students' thinking concerning the expected failure outcome and its negative consequences, whereas the emotionality component of anxiety reactions refers to the students' feelings of tenseness, nervousness and distress. The physiological component of anxiety reactions refers to the students perceptions of bodily symptoms (Morris, Davis & Hutchings, 1981; Deffenbacher, 1980; Hagtvet, 1976). In some construct conceptualizations, the emotionality component implies the physiological component; other conceptualizations further differentiate or extend these components (Cassady & Johnson, 2002; Gjesme, 1981; Sarason, 1986; Schwarzer, 1984; Schwarzer & Quast, 1985). Across a wide range of student samples, empirical research could demonstrate these components being distinguishable but mutually reinforcing. Thus, high-anxious students being aware of their arising affective stress and physiological reactions in an evaluative situation might be increasingly worried and self-concerned – and vice versa. However, the worry component in particular turned out to be more strongly correlated with academic performance measures than the emotionality or the physiological component (Deffenbacher, 1980; Faber, 2000; Hembree, 1988; Pekrun, 1983).

The debilitating effects of worry cognitions on high-anxious students' performance are mainly caused by self-focused and task-irrelevant information processing before and during task completion. High-anxious students are extremely attentive or even sensitive and, thus, biased in their perception of threatening cues within an evaluative setting. They have more and stronger thoughts which interfere with the process of task completion. In particular, high-anxious students were demonstrated to think more frequently about expected failure and its negative consequences. Also, they suffered more strongly from self-doubts to cope with the task at hand and therefore produced more escape cognitions (Campbell, Rapee & Spence, 2001; Schwarzer, 1996; Zeidner, 1998). In sum, high-anxious students' attention and cognitions appear to be more self-focused than task-focused. As a result, their attentional and cognitive resources are to be seen preoccupied and thus, with regard to the task, notedly reduced (Dusek, 1980; Wine, 1982) – especially concerning their working memory capacities. Various empirical studies could consistently substantiate this cognitive-attentional deficit. High-anxious students showed poorer memory performance and were less able to retrieve previously learned contents or knowledge (Ashcraft & Kirk, 2001; Hadwin, Brogan & Stevenson, 2005; Hopko, Ashcraft, Gute, Ruggiero & Lewis, 1998; MacLeod & Donnellan, 1993; Richards, French, Keogh & Carter, 2000; Sarson & Sarason, 1987). However, there was also some evidence that a cognitive blockage effect of test anxiety did not appear per se. Rather, it could be determined by interaction with the level of individual study skills. For high-anxious students who reported poor study skills, no blockage effect could be found (Covington & Omelich, 1987). At least, this result indicates the complexity of psychological processes involved. Due to methodological constraints, these studies can only yield approximative insights. There is still need for further analyses to clarify the impact of interfering processes on cognitive performance that would use academically more valid and curriculum-based performance measures. Likewise, there is still a need for analyses of interfering processes with regard to different academic domains or subjects.

While perceiving strong worry cognitions, emotional stress and physiological arousal, high-anxious students will tend to use less adaptational coping strategies. Due to their pessimistic or even helpless competence and control beliefs, they primarily anticipate a negative outcome which they, moreover, cannot prevent. Therefore, they react cognitively and behaviorally in a more emotion-focused or problem-avoiding rather than in a problem-focused manner (Zeidner, 1998). In particular, they prefer coping strategies such as anxiety repression, anxiety control or situation control. Anxiety repression seeks to direct attention away from threatening situation cues. Anxiety control seeks to actively reduce the extent of individual threat feelings. Situation control seeks to directly influence the threatening situation by cheating or avoiding. Another coping strategy, danger control, refers to the intention of being well prepared and thus to approach the mastery of the task at hand – but it would not work well during actual task completion (Rost & Schermer, 1989). Within an evaluative situation, these coping strategies will neither contribute to essentially reduced feelings of threat and uncontrollability, nor will they readily facilitate mastery of the academic demand. They will not improve high-anxious students' learning skills but instead lead to less desirable performance outcomes which, in turn, will confirm their failure expectancies. Hence, when compared with their low-anxious classmates, high-anxious students will mostly achieve poorer results. In the long term, if students would repeatedly experience heightened states of test anxiety in an evaluative situation and thus would predominantly display high personal threat reactions and self-focused coping strategies, they will be strongly at risk to habitualize their anxious cognitions, emotions, and behaviors. Their state of anxiety then will become a more stable disposition of trait test anxiety (Spielberger, 1975). From a transactional perspective, the emergence of trait test anxiety crucially contributes to establish a self-reinforcing circle of negative anxiety-outcome relations.

High-anxious students' academic achievement commonly appears to be lowered. Empirical findings could consistently demonstrate significant negative correlations between test anxiety scores and academic outcome measures – indicating the worry component to correlate more strongly with academic achievement (Cassady & Johnson, 2002; Faber, 1995a, 2000; Haferkamp & Rost, 1980; Hembree, 1988; Ma, 1999; Pekrun, 1983; Pintrich & De Groot, 1990; Schwarzer, Seipp & Schwarzer, 1989). However, these relations were moderate in average and differed across various grade levels and subject matters. This finding might reflect the subjective nature of test anxiety because not only poor achieving but also moderate achieving students will experience personal threat in evaluative settings. In particular, those studies using general measures across domains or subjects might have leveled and thus underestimated the relations between constructs. Furthermore, according to the transactional process model, the impact of prior achievement on subsequent test anxiety will be substantially mediated by academic self-beliefs. Empirical research consistently lends broad support to this assumption. With regard to various grade levels and student samples, the relations between test anxiety and self-belief variables turned out to be stronger than the relations between test anxiety and achievement variables – even more, there was also evidence for the impact of students' study skills on their test anxiety being mediated by their competence beliefs (Faber, 1995b; Hackett, 1985; Hodapp, 1989; Jain & Dowson, 2009; Krampen, 1991; Meece, Wigfield & Eccles, 1990; Schilling, Sparfeldt & John, 2005; Seaton, Marsh & Craven, 2010; Streblow, 2004; Wigfield & Meece, 1988).

Against the background of earlier personality and, in particular, more recent self-belief research, theoretically and methodologically sound conceptualizations of test anxiety have to reflect its multidimensional and multifaceted nature (Becker, Schneider & Schumann, 1975; Zuckerman, 1976; Goetz, Cronjaeger, Frenzel, Lüdtke & Hall, 2010; Marsh & Yeung, 1996). Test anxiety measures assessing worry and emotionality reactions only on a generalizing construct level must seriously fail to reveal situation- or domain-specific differences among students – and thus are principally at risk for less valid results. Much rather, as students' individual competence and control expectancies will be processed in a domain- or subject-specific manner, their test anxiety responses also will (Everson, Tobias, Hartman & Gourgey, 1993; Hodapp, 1989; Krampen, 1991; Schwarzer & Jerusalem, 1992). Meanwhile there is strong empirical support for this assumption. As a number of studies could consistently show, different subject-specific measures of test anxiety were only moderately correlated and could be sufficiently separated from measures of general test anxiety. They could explain more interindividual variance in achievement measures than general anxiety. Moreover, subject-specific measures of test anxiety correlated most strongly with self-belief and achievement measures in the matched subject (Dew, Galassi & Galassi, 1984; Faber, 1995a; Gottfried, 1982; Hembree, 1990; Jacobs, 1982; Lukesch, 1982; Marsh, 1988a; Morris, Kellaway & Smith, 1978; Sepie & Keeling, 1978; Skaalvik, 1997b; Shores & Shannon, 2007; Wigfield & Meece, 1988). Further differentiating the construct, some studies also could demonstrate distinguishable test anxiety facets within a certain domain (Cheng, 2004; Cheng, Horwitz & Schallert, 1999; Pajares & Urdan, 1996; Plake & Parker, 1982; Rounds & Hendel, 1980; Suinn & Edwards, 1982; Wigfield & Meece, 1988). However, in these studies only few subjects had been analyzed – that is, mostly in the mathematics domain. There is still a need for extended analyses – especially concerning such domains or subjects being relevant for engendering threat experiences and test anxiety (Britner, 2010; Brozo, Schmelzer & Spires, 1983; Zbornik & Wallbrown, 1991). Also, many studies under consideration suffer from several limitations in scale validation. Mostly, they had considered several test anxiety, achievement or self-belief variables in one or at least two concurrent subjects. Only in rare cases, comprehensive analyses of relevant within- and between-construct relations had been realized (Sparfeldt, Schilling, Rost, Stelzl & Peipert, 2005).

Beyond cross-sectional validation research, the issue of causal ordering between test anxiety, self-belief and achievement constructs appears to be less clear. Following existing theoretical approaches and empirical findings from self-belief research, it can be assumed that test anxiety and achievement variables would be reciprocally related over time – and thus be substantially mediated by self-belief variables. However, relevant longitudinal studies yielded only fragmentary results. They could mostly demonstrate the direct causal effects from prior achievement to subsequent test anxiety being small to moderate in magnitude, but comparatively stronger than the other way around. According to theoretical predictions, the relations between competence beliefs and test anxiety were markedly stronger in magnitude (Ma & Xu, 2004; Pekrun, 1991; Satow & Schwarzer, 2000; Schwarzer & Cherkes-Julkowski, 1982). Thus, empirical analyses cannot confirm a reciprocal effects perspective; rather they support a mediating modeling approach. There is still a need for more complex research designs which should systematically clarify the longitudinal relations among subject-specific achievement, self-belief and test anxiety variables across various grade levels and school subjects. They should, in particular, stepwise extend and refine their basic assumptions and also explore the contribution of cognitive and behavioral coping variables as well as the role of more general personality constructs such as self-esteem (Fincham, Hokoda & Sanders, 1989; Helmke, 1997; Jerusalem & Schwarzer, 1989; Marsh & Yeung, 1998).

A BASIC RESEARCH MODEL OF ACADEMIC SELF-BELIEFS

Viewed in general, the various theoretical conceptualizations and empirical findings on academic self-beliefs appear to complement one another in some ways, as well as overlap and corroborate in other ways. They all attempt to define and specify a distinct cognitive-motivational perspective on students' self-related and self-regulating information processing with regard to academic concerns, in particular to learning outcomes and achievement within a certain educational setting – and thus correspondingly refer to the key element of students' competence expectancies (Eccles, Wigfield & Schiefele, 1998; Pintrich, 2003). Hence, for clarifying and explaining academic self-beliefs with regard to their manifold structures and multiple interrelations, a more integrative research line would be worthwhile (Dweck & Wortman, 1982; Green, Nelson, Martin & Marsh, 2006). The close relationships among students' self-concepts, causal attributions, and test anxiety are empirically well documented. Principally, they can be seen as correlating and mutually reinforcing constructs. However, from the viewpoint of ontogenetic development it seems to be plausible that individually emerging control and threat expectancies will essentially depend on individual competence expectancies. Therefore, in terms of individual self-belief formation, academic self-concept will affect causal attributions and test anxiety (Boggiano, Main, Flink, Barrett, Silvern & Katz, 1989) – and therefore will figure as a core variable among self-belief constructs. Individual success or failure experiences will be first reflected in the students' self-concepts and will then be mediated to their causal attributions and test anxiety (Hattie, 1992; Helmke, 1992).

Due to the multidimensional and multifaceted nature of cognitive-motivational variables, another common feature of construct conceptualizations in self-belief research is that, in the meantime, they take a more detailed domain- or subject-specific look on students' self-concepts, causal attributions, and test anxiety. These domain- or subject-specific components of constructs will be, in turn, typically associated with implicit beliefs about the malleability of individual competencies, the type of task requirements, the ways of knowledge acquisition, and the process of learning (Blackwell, Trzesniewski & Dweck, 2007; Buehl & Alexander, 2009; Dweck & Legett, 1988; Schunk, 1995). Overall, they are to be considered integrated parts of a nomologically complex network including within- and between-relations among self-belief and achievement constructs (Marsh & O'Mara, 2008a; Martin, 2007; Pekrun, 1983).

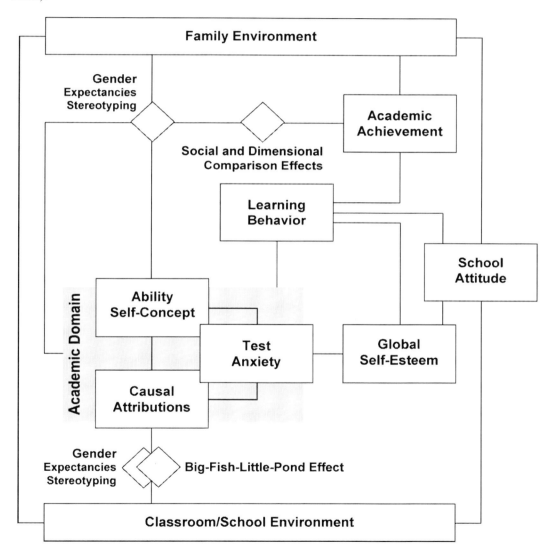

Figure 9. A basic research model of academic self-beliefs.

Against that background in particular, an approach to integrate the various self-belief constructs into a basic research model has to be, first of all, domain- or subject-specific. With regard to a certain domain or subject the students' self-concepts are assumed to play a crucial role because they subjectively reflect and interpret the students' academic experiences to a large extent and, thus, substantially contribute to their individually emerging control and threat expectancies. More specifically, academic self-concepts will affect causal attributions and both, in turn, will affect test anxiety (Figure 9). Directly as well as indirectly, the formation of these academic self-beliefs will be depend on prior achievement and thus, will be already individually shaped by relevant social and dimensional comparison processes as well as by other influences of the home and school setting – e.g., by gender stereotyping expectancies from parents, teachers, and peers (Schunk, Pintrich & Meece, 2008). In the long term, students with more positive self-concepts, more mastery-oriented attributions, and low test anxiety will be able to cope with academic demands more adequately – whereas students with more negative self-concepts, more helpless attributions, and high test anxiety will be more strongly at risk for further academic failure (Jerusalem & Schwarzer, 1989; Martin, 2002). Theoretically, according to a reciprocal effects perspective, students' self-concepts, causal attributions and test anxiety will be either consequences of prior achievement or antecedents of subsequent achievement. As cognitive-motivational antecedents of individual outcomes they will hardly act directly rather than they will be mediated by individual learning behaviors, in particular by task orientation and academic self-regulation strategies (Mantzicopoulos, 1990; Phan, 2010; Skaalvik & Skaalvik, 2006; Skinner, Wellborn & Connell, 1990; Tuckman, 1999). With regard to a certain academic task, it is the individually preferred level of information processing and self-instruction which appears to be largely predisposed by academic self-beliefs which, in turn, will be decisive for successful or failing task completion (Pintrich & Zusho, 2002; Zimmerman, 2000).

Although this modeling approach is assigned domain- or subject-specific on the level of relevant achievement and self-belief constructs, it will not get by without various conceptual extensions. From a developmental perspective, it can be reasonably assumed that students' academic achievement and self-beliefs will also impact their overall psychosocial development – especially concerning their global self-esteem which must be seen as an important resilience factor over the life span (Harter, 1990; Heinonen, Räikkönen & Kelikangas-Järvinen, 2005; Rosenberg, Schooler, Schoenbach & Rosenberg, 1995; Wigfield & Karpathian, 1991). According to the predictions of bottom-up effects within the cognitive-motivational self-system (Marsh & Yeung, 1998; Trautwein, Lüdtke, Köller & Baumert, 2006; Wagner & Valtin, 2004), interindividually existing differences in students' subject-specific self-concepts, causal attributions, and test anxiety will be substantially associated with corresponding self-evaluations in general. In the long term, thus, students' general self-esteem or sense for self-worth (Covington, 1992; Rosenberg, 1979) will depend on their subject-specific self-beliefs, but will also affect their academic behaviors. Empirical research has revealed sound evidence for significant negative relations between academic failure, attributional perceptions of uncontrollability and test anxiety with self-esteem variables (Faber, 1995a; Many & Many, 1975; Pekrun, 1983; Skaalvik, 1997b). Within the present modeling approach in particular, the effects of academic self-concepts and attributions on general self-esteem will be predicted as mediated, to a large extent, by self-derogating test anxiety.

Furthermore, another extension beyond domain- or subject-specific constructs refers to the students' overall school attitude. Conceptually, this variable appears to subsume a wide range of various perceptions concerning their liking of school, sense of belonging, school involvement, school attachment or teacher relations (Libbey, 2004) – which on the level of construct operationalizations and scale development are, in particular, seriously confounded with self-related expectancy and task- or subject-related value components (Dolan, 1983; Holfe-Sabel & Gustafsson, 2005; Marjoribanks, 1992; Suldo, Shaffer & Shaunessy, 2008; Voelkl, 1996). Empirical findings are, therefore, contradictory and vary considerably across different methods and sample characteristics. However, there is some evidence for positive relations between school attitudes, academic self-beliefs and outcomes. Students with moderate or high achievement scores and moderate or high self-concepts reported more positive attitudes to school as students with poor achievement scores and lower self-concepts. Similarly, subject-specific test anxiety was positively correlated with negative school attitudes (Alban Metcalfe, 1981; Alves-Martin, Peixoto, Gouveia-Pereira, Amaral & Pedro, 2002; Chapman & Boersma, 1979; Connolly, Hatchette & McMaster, 1998; Faber, 1995a; Fend, H., Knörzer, W., Nagl, W., Specht, W. & Väth-Szusdziara, 1976; Goodenow, 1993; Heaven, Mak, Barry & Ciarrochi, 2002; Ireson & Hallam, 2005; Valeski & Stipek, 2001). For clarifying the effects of domain- or subject-specific self-beliefs on students' overall personality development, the variable of school-related attitudes is conceptualized here in the most general sense as their liking of school – that is, as their evaluative perceptions and feelings towards school and schooling, respectively. Thus, school attitude will be largely affected by subject-specific self-beliefs and general self-esteem. Students with more positive and mastery-oriented self-beliefs in a certain academic domain or subject and, therefore, with a strong sense of self-worth, will display a higher level of positive school attitude. On the other hand, students with more negative and failure-oriented self-beliefs in a certain domain or subject and, therefore, with a lesser sense of self-worth, will display a lower level of positive school attitude. In the long term, school attitude will positively or negatively contribute to the students' learning behavior and academic performance. With regard to their interrelation and function in cognitive-motivational processing, general self-esteem and school attitude are assumed to correlate moderately. Though both constructs are assigned to reflect academically relevant evaluations and feelings on a general trait level, they are assumed to differ in cognitive-motivational functioning: whereas general self-esteem will operate more internalizing, school attitude will operate more externalizing. Hence, domain- or subject-specific self-beliefs will affect both personal and environmental evaluations on conceptually distinctive ways.

However, this basic model does not yet make any prediction with regard to structural characteristics of the constructs included. As the structural feature of self-belief constructs will considerably depend on conceptual assumptions, grade level and subject matter this issue must be reserved to detailed validation analyses of the various construct operationalizations applied – e.g., concerning the number and type of empirically separable subcomponents within the domain- or subject-specific self-concept or causal attributions variable (Arens, Yeung, Craven & Hasselhorn, 2011; Faber, 1992b; Mok, Kennedy & Moore, 2011).

Similarly, the model assumes the relations among constructs being principally influenced by gender differences which will mainly emerge as a result of stereotyping expectancies communicated by significant others (Kling, Hyde, Showers & Buswell, 1999; Skaalvik, 1986a,b; Skaalvik & Skaalvik, 2004; Zeidner, 1998). The direction and size of gender differences will almost vary across certain constructs, academic domains, and grade levels. Therefore, no overall predictions can be made. Instead the impact of gender must be particularly analyzed with respect to specific construct perspectives.

In sum, this basic model of domain- or subject-specific self-beliefs is, first of all, designed to integrate various cognitive-motivational conceptualizations from the field of relevant research and, thus, will offer a more comprehensive as well as a more differentiating perspective on academic development. It does not claim to capture the complex phenomenon of academic self-beliefs in an exhaustive way. Rather it might serve as a preliminary theoretical framework for empirical analyses and should further be extended, completed and refined. Principally, all relations among the constructs involved must be understood as reciprocal or transactional in nature. Ultimately, only empirical analyses will be able to clarify possible directions of construct relations with respect to the domain or subject matter under consideration – and thus to test the models' scope for different grade levels and educational tracks (Hattie, 1992; Marsh, 1993, 2006; Pekrun, 1983; Zeidner, 1998).

Chapter 2

EMPIRICAL ANALYSES OF ACADEMIC SELF-BELIEFS IN THE SPELLING DOMAIN

REVIEW OF EMPIRICAL RESEARCH FINDINGS

Across all grade levels and educational tracks, a certain number of students always appears to struggle with the acquisition of spelling skills and displays lowered outcomes over time. Likewise, they perceive spelling or orthographics as a rather demanding and less positively valued domain or subject (Downing, DeStefano, Rich & Bell, 1984; Freedman-Doan, Wigfield, Eccles, Blumenfeld, Arbreton & Harold, 2000; Varnhagen, 2000). In the case of accumulated failure experiences, these students are assumed to be strongly at risk for negative trajectories in social-emotional and motivational development which, in turn, might seriously impair their further learning and academic attainment.

Therefore, over the past decades a multitude of empirical research has investigated the relations between students' social-emotional and motivational characteristics and their spelling competencies, most notably under the aspect of individually consistent literacy problems or dyslexia, respectively (Pollak, 2009; Riddick, 2010; Ridsdale, 2004). However, all research efforts obviously suffered from a general lack of domain- or subject-specific construct operationalizations. Instead, students' social-emotional and motivational characteristics are being analyzed by means of various scales or questionnaires for measuring global self-esteem or self-worth, general academic self-perceptions (Keith & Bracken, 1996), general causal attributions or control orientations, and state or trait test anxiety. In some studies, only single item formats were used to assess students' self-beliefs. Overall, the empirical findings were quite mixed and could not evidence consistent trait differences between students with low versus high spelling achievement. For the most part, they could demonstrate poor spelling students to report somewhat lowered academic competence beliefs and heightened anxiety levels at least. However, these differences often were small or moderate in magnitude (Alexander-Passe, 2006; Burden, 2005; Finkbeiner & Isele, 1974; Frederickson & Jacobs, 2001; Humphrey, 2002a,b; Kershner, 1990; Rosenthal, 1973; Solheim, 1989; Terras, Thompson & Minnis, 2009; Thomson & Hartley, 1980; Valtin, 1972). Due to the assessment of more general self-beliefs, students' responses might have reflected their perceptions across several academic domains and, therefore, might have been potentially leveled or even biased. For instance, in each individual case the evaluation of own academic competencies might be anchored on the subject matter best or worse – or on a somehow inferred composite estimate. Hence, a poor spelling students' response to an item measuring general academic self-concept may refer to his or her weak spelling performance, to his or her better math performance or to a subjectively built average impression. As this individual decision making cannot be reconstructed or controlled a posteriori, the sum scores of general self-belief scales will be confounded with students' implicit preference or importance perspectives. Of course, this problem will not appear if students achieve equally poor or well across domains or subjects. With this reservation, however, the administration of general self-concept items might have masked the subject-specific variance of self-belief responses in relevant studies. Additionally, a number of studies had investigated highly selective student samples from special remedial settings (Burden, 2008; Burden & Burdett, 2005; Humphrey, 2002b; Pollak, 2009). Their results might have been considerably affected by statistical regression to mean and the institutional endeavor for educational support. In sum, the use of highly inferent self-belief instruments as well as the selectivity of student samples might have been important reasons for less clear findings in the research field. With regard to existing spelling difficulties, these studies failed to demonstrate definite cognitive-motivational correlates or consequences (Burden, 2005).

Accordingly, there still is a need for empirical knowledge concerning the basic cognitive-motivational structures, mechanisms, and processes – which should be foremost investigated in samples from educationally regular, more diverse settings rather than from already preselected, e.g. clinical or dyslexic student samples. Furthermore, against the background of the multidimensional and multifaceted nature of academic self-beliefs, relevant analyses should use construct operationalizations that are most differentiated and typically can reflect the various task and situation features in the area of spelling learning and achievement. Nevertheless, the empirical analysis of students' spelling-specific self-beliefs turns out to be a largely neglected research line. The number of previous studies dealing with the issue of self-concept, causal attributions, and test anxiety in the spelling domain appears to be relatively small.

With regard to the self-concept construct, Boersma, Chapman and Maguire (1979) had successfully presented a very early approach for scale development and validation in a sample of third-, fourth-, fifth- and sixth-graders. Among five academic areas their "Student's Perception of Ability Scale" included a spelling-specific subscale. For scale interpretation however, only a composite score consisting of spelling- and reading-related items was available. As both competence areas can be individually experienced as relatively independent from one another (Hay, Ashman & van Kraayenoord, 1997; Polychroni, Koukoura & Anagnostou, 2006), a selected and valid measure of spelling-specific self-perception is not warranted. Similarly, in the longitudinal study Helmke (1997) conducted in elementary grades 2 through 4, spelling-related self-perceptions were included. Though assessed separately, they were only used as part of a composite score for indicating students' verbal self-concept. The "Student Rating System" repeatedly used as research instrument by Meltzer and colleagues (Meltzer, Katzir-Cohen, Miller & Roditi, 2001) was designed to assess students' competence beliefs in several academic areas and also included a spelling subscale. Unfortunately, the previously published scale documentations did not provide any further information concerning relevant psychometric and validation analyses. Some progress seems to have been made with the self-concept scale of Vincent and Claydon (1996). As a supplement to their "Diagnostic Spelling Test" for elementary school children, this instrument contained ten rating items concerning the students' self-perceptions of spelling achievement which referred to both social comparison and ipsative perspectives. The total sum score of this scale was demonstrated to substantially correlate with various performance measures. Students with lower spelling outcomes reported more negative self-perceptions as students with average or better outcomes. Though, more broadly designed validation results concerning relevant within- and between-construct relations were missing. Hence, the construct validity of the scale can ultimately only be suspected. Another approach concerning students' self-perceptions in the spelling domain dealt with the self-efficacy construct (Rankin, Bruning & Timme, 1994; Rankin, Bruning, Timme & Katkanant, 1993). Based on Bandura's conceptualization (1986), students from an university sample as well as from elementary and secondary school levels were asked to estimate the subjective probability they could successfully complete various spelling tasks. These tasks, in particular, tapped relevant situations in which spelling competence might be important as well as the orthographic difficulty of words to be written – e.g., correctly spelling words in a letter or correctly spelling words that are not spelled the way they sound. A principal-components analysis led to the formation of a highly reliable spelling-specific scale with eight items. Looking closer on their wording however, the spelling items evidently referred to a more aggregated task understanding and thus represent an intermediate level of self-efficacy (Phan & Walker, 2000). Conceptually, this raises the question whether this construct operationalization might rather indicate a subject-specific self-concept than a task-specific self-efficacy measure. At least, it might reflect the interface between self-concept and self-efficacy components within the academic self-system (Figure 3). In both studies the sum scores of this scale substantially correlated with spelling test performance. Students with higher spelling achievement reported more positive self-perceptions than students with poorer spelling achievement. No other validation results were available. For the use in educational research which will comprehensively analyze students' spelling-specific self-beliefs, the scale's items or spelling tasks should be further extended by regarding more school-related task features and situations. Franklin-Guy (2006) also reported an investigation of spelling-related self-beliefs using the "Thoughts on Spelling Questionnaire" which had been developed by Wasowicz and colleagues (Wasowicz, Apel, Masterson & Whitney, 2004). This questionnaire was designed to assess beliefs about one's spelling abilities and spelling in general. Its items mostly referred to students' self-reported strategies and reactions to ensure most wanted spelling outcomes. Only a few items tapped more or less the issue of spelling-specific self-concept. Consequently, empirical validation results demonstrated the scale's sum score not being substantially correlated with spelling performance. Despite the purpose it was designed for, this questionnaire cannot be considered as a valid instrument for measuring the spelling-specific self-concept. Wilson and Trainin (2007) had developed and empirically analyzed a conceptually and methodologically more sophisticated instrument. Their "Early Literacy Motivation Scale" consisted of three separate subscales assessing young elementary children's perceived competence, self-efficacy expectancies, and internal attributions in early reading, writing, and spelling. As theoretically predicted, the distinction of these constructs appeared to be well supported by confirmatory factor analyses. The item responses in reading, writing, and spelling were summed up to composite scores with regard to each latent construct – e.g., the competence beliefs subscale all related reading, writing, and spelling items. All subscales could claim acceptable reliabilities. Structural equation modeling results could demonstrate the self-concept to correlate significantly with self-efficacy, internal outcome attributions, and literacy achievement. Thus, no differentiation between literacy areas was made. Being designed to follow a more holistic approach, this instrument does not allow a straight measure of spelling-specific self-beliefs. Compared with this, the self-concept measures developed and evaluated by Frühauf (2008) consisted of three separate subscales for the assessment of elementary third-graders' self-perceptions in mathematics, reading, and spelling. Confirmatory factor analyses could demonstrate the model with three latent domain factors to achieve the best fitting solution. The spelling-specific subscale comprised 13 rating items and appeared to be highly reliable. The items reflected, in particular, a wide range of spelling situations which can be typically encountered in the educational or instructional setting. However, they exclusively referred to the students' self-perceptions by social comparison with their classmates. Across different domains, the scale's sum score correlated somewhat stronger with achievement measures in spelling and reading and evidently weaker with achievement measures in mathematics. Mostly, these correlations were statistically significant but small in magnitude. The subject-specific validity of this subscale could thus only receive limited support and should deserve further attention. For the measurement of early elementary first-graders' self-concepts, Poloczek and colleagues (Poloczek, Greb & Lipowsky, 2009; Poloczek, Karst, Praetorius & Lipowsky, 2010) had developed a multidimensional research instrument. Confirmatory factor analyses led to a solution with three subject-specific subscales in mathematics, reading, and spelling. The spelling-specific subscale consisted of four rating items and, therefore, showed a somewhat lowered reliability value. However, validation results concerning the scale's relations to relevant cognitive-motivational and performance measures are not yet available.

With regard to the causal attribution construct, the state of research on spelling-specific operationalizations up to now turns out to be rather deficient in all respects. Only a few analyses of students' relevant attributions for spelling success and failure exist. Unfortunately, in most studies general control beliefs or general attributional factors were assessed and related to spelling achievement. Across various measurement methods and sample characteristics, they produced less consistent results and could, at best, demonstrate rough trends. In particular, they repeatedly found that students with rather poor spelling performance were more likely to perceive their outcomes as less controllable – as they explained failure outcomes internally with a lack of own ability and success outcomes externally with favorable circumstances (Biermann, 1992; Dodds, 1994; Frederickson & Jacobs, 2001; Humphrey & Mullins, 2002; Krampen & Zinßer, 1981; Petkovic, 1980; Stipek, 1984). Conceptually, these findings do not allow for subject-specific interpretations and, thus, cannot contribute to clarify the domain- or subject-specificity of relations among attribution and achievement variables. In particular, they suffer from a lack of spelling-specific operationalizations of relevant causal factors. For instance, in the spelling domain students' understanding of own ability and effort might reflect other cognitive and behavioral perspectives than in the mathematics domain. Against this, only the studies of Bruning and colleagues (Rankin, Bruning & Timme, 1994; Shell, Colvin & Bruning, 1995) used a somewhat closer approach for assessing students' attributions of spelling outcomes. They administered a questionnaire including effort, ability, luck, ease, help and enjoyment as causal factors. The item wording for each factor explicitly referred to the spelling task – e.g., being a good speller, trying hard to spell correctly, having easy words to spell. Across several grade levels however, correlational results failed to demonstrate any substantial association between attribution and performance variables, whereas the associations between attribution and self-perception variables appeared to be statistically significant but moderate in magnitude. This latter result, once again, lends support to the mediational role of domain- or subject-specific competence beliefs. Another reason to consider previously reported results with caution is methodological in nature. As various studies used attribution scales or questionnaires with forced choice items, they could have simplified or biased students' attributional preferences and thus probably reduced the empirical variance of their responses.

And finally, with regard to the test anxiety construct, the research findings hitherto existing cannot be based upon theoretically and methodologically appropriate analyses either. Apparently none of these studies had recognized the multidimensional and multifaceted nature of the construct and thus had used a specific measure of test anxiety. Instead they all had investigated the relations between students' spelling achievement and general test anxiety. Overall, their results could demonstrate poor spelling students to report a higher degree of academic anxiety or fear of failure, respectively. However, the strength of correlations or differences varied considerably across measurement methods and sample characteristics – e.g. due to the use of diverse comprehensive questionnaires or single item scales, the investigation of regular or dyslexic samples, and the wide range of sample size (Bäcker & Neuhäuser, 2003; Carroll & Iles, 2006; Finkbeiner & Isele, 1974; Knabe, 1973; Riddick, Sterling, Farmer & Morgan, 1999; Schneider, 1980; Tsovili, 2004; Valtin, 1972). As all studies had analyzed general test anxiety variables, their results cannot be interpreted in terms of subject-specificity. Methodologically none of them can decompose the variance of test anxiety into its spelling-specific and general contents. Only in cases where students will achieve equally low or high outcomes as well as display equally low or high competence beliefs across all domains or subjects, this issue would not come as a problem. Accordingly, in subsamples of dyslexic students, an accumulated process of generalizing test anxiety or threat expectancies might have emerged. Therefore, in terms of individual development, the formation of spelling-specific anxiety could have been already masked, though these assumptions are speculative in nature and should be tested empirically by research approaches which are able to analyze both general and specific test anxiety constructs.

As the research on students' spelling-specific self-beliefs basically suffers from various theoretical and methodological shortcomings, it should, first of all, try to get a more appropriate conceptual framework and instrumentation. In particular, further research in this field should realize the multidimensional and multifaceted nature of constructs under consideration. From this perspective, consistent modeling approaches should be developed which will be able to describe, explain and predict relevant construct relations. They should include important theoretical references and reflect empirical findings – e.g. concerning the role of social and dimensional comparison effects or the reciprocal and transactional processing among self-belief and achievement constructs. Further analyses should, therefore, be based on elaboratively designed measurements which will allow for straightforward spelling-specific interpretations of research data. Hence, there is a strong need for suitable measurements which should empirically be well evaluated. Likewise, there is still a strong need for empirical investigations which should clarify the role of spelling-specific self-beliefs within the nomological network of relevant motivational, behavioral and achievement constructs – e.g., with regard to the relations among spelling-specific and general academic constructs or the causal ordering of self-beliefs and outcomes in the spelling domain (Van Aken, Helmke & Schneider, 1997).

For this purpose, the research field has, in the first instance, to develop and evaluate psychometrically sound measurement methods. They should be properly designed for the assessment of spelling-specific operationalizations of the self-concept, attribution, and test anxiety construct and thus comprehensively reflect typically appearing spelling tasks and situations – which, in particular, should also be differentiated with respect to various grade and track levels. Consequently, well developed self-belief scales should not only consist of more or less simple statements of competence, control, and threat expectancies – e.g. using items like "I am good in spelling". Instead they should unfold the spelling domain with respect to a wider range of learning and achievement aspects. Furthermore, they should not only focus on self-perceptions via social comparison, but also incorporate ipsative perspectives of students' perceptions and feelings in the domain. Though substantially affected by social comparison in the classroom, the students' self-beliefs will also represent individual competence experiences and expectancies. Consequently, well developed self-belief scales should not only consist of mere comparisons with classmates – e.g. using items like "I can spell words better than others". Once developed, these measurement methods should then be tested carefully for construct validity. One central issue of this validation work will refer to their relations with discriminant and convergent variables within the spelling domain and across other domains – likewise across various related constructs. Only these analyses will clarify the structural position and processual role of the spelling-specific constructs within the academic self-system. In particular, relevant analyses should investigate whether the spelling-specific self-concept appears to be empirically separable from other subject-specific self-concepts, and to which extent it might be further differentiated into several subcomponents (Figure 3). Of course, the same procedure will apply to the causal attributions and the test anxiety variable. Subsequent analyses then should enlighten the complex relations between spelling-specific self-beliefs and other relevant constructs and thus contribute to gradually evaluate the nomological network of a basic self-belief model in the spelling domain (Figure 9).

PREVIOUS OWN RESEARCH RESULTS

In view of the various shortcomings in the field, it has been the objective of an own research project to successively analyze the spelling-specific self-beliefs in elementary school samples. Conceptually rooted in a multidimensional and multifaceted understanding of constructs and referring to the basic model of academic self-beliefs as presented before (Figure 9), the studies conducted up to now dealt with several aspects of scale development and validation as well as with the analysis of relevant construct relations – e.g. concerning dimensional comparison effects across the spelling and mathematics domain or the mediating role of self-concept with regard to individually perceived level of test anxiety within the spelling domain. Data were gathered in several independent samples of elementary third- and fourth-graders and were for the most part cross-sectional in nature.

In particular, first of all a questionnaire for measuring the students' spelling-specific self-concept was developed and analyzed. Principal components analysis led to the formation of three subscales relating to "Perceived Learning and Performance Problems", "Perceived Coping with Classroom Dictations", and "Negative Affective Evaluations" (Faber, 1991). Interestingly, the latter subscale was in line with findings from other studies which years after also lend support to an affective component in academic self-concept (Marsh, Craven & Debus, 1999; Arens, Yeung, Craven & Hasselhorn, 2011). All scales had sufficient reliabilities. As theoretically predicted, the sum scores of all subscales and a total composite score appeared to correlate with various achievement and self-belief measures in a subject-specific manner

(Faber, 1991, 1993b, 1994). The spelling-specific self-concept scales were more strongly associated with the students' spelling than with their math outcomes. They also could explain more variance in spelling outcomes than the general academic self-concept measure (Figure 10). Hence, this questionnaire could claim preliminary construct validity, at least.

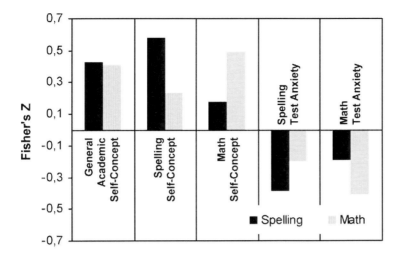

Figure 10. Correlations between various self-beliefs and academic achievement in spelling and mathematics.

According to the structural perspectives of self-concept modeling (Figure 3), the spelling-specific self-perceptions could further be differentiated. As more task-related construct operationalizations, students' error-specific self-estimates were analyzed. They concerned, in particular, the individual estimations to make certain spelling errors more or less frequently – e.g. omitting letters, adding letters, or confusing letters (Faber, 1989b, 1992b). Principal components analyses repeatedly revealed a one factor solution and led to a scale including all items. Beyond the spelling-specific self-concept variables, their sum score could incrementally explain additional variance in spelling outcomes. Within the self-system, these error-specific self-estimates could be demonstrated to pinpoint below the subject-related construct level and nearest to the achievement variables. Across all error-specific self-estimates however, students with poor performance significantly tended to underestimate their spelling errors (Faber, 1989c). Especially this finding indicated educationally important implications as it could stress the need for enhancing the veridicality in poor spellers' task-related self-perceptions (Klassen, 2002).

Additional multivariate analyses were conducted to investigate the subject-specific nature of relations among self-concept and achievement variables. In particular, they aimed at testing the scope of the internal/external frame of reference model (Marsh, 1986a) for its generalizability to the spelling domain in elementary grades. Analyses included self-concept and performance variables in spelling and mathematics as well as a general academic self-concept and a global self-esteem variable (Faber, 1992a). Empirical results could show the subject-specific self-concepts were best predicted by matched performance measures – thus clearly indicating the subject-specific validity of spelling-specific self-concept construct (Figure 11). According to the predictions of the internal/external frame of reference model, significant negative path coefficients across subjects were found. In this way, contrasting effects of students' dimensional comparisons could be substantiated already in elementary grades. Moreover, effects from spelling and math achievement on the general academic self-concept were mediated by subject-specific self-concepts. Students' global self-esteem could be directly predicted only by their general academic self-concept. Altogether, the predictions of the internal/external frame of reference model could not only be supported but also extended and refined.

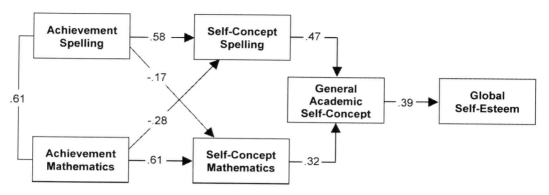

Figure 11. Relations among achievement and self-belief variables across different subjects: zero-order correlation and standardized regression weights (Faber, 1992a).

Another study referred to the validation of a newly developed instrument for measuring students' spelling-specific test anxiety. This short scale consisted of 13 rating items assessing students' worry and emotionality in the spelling domain. However, principal components analyses consistently could not separate these two components and led to an overall scale format. This scale appeared to be sufficiently reliable. As theoretically expected, their sum scores were most strongly correlated with self-beliefs rather than with achievement variables. Moreover, they turned out to correlate more strongly with spelling-specific than with math-specific or general academic self-belief variables. Also in line with conceptual assumptions, spelling-specific anxiety scores were quite strongly associated with the global self-esteem variable. High-anxious students reported significantly lower self-esteem scores than low-anxious students – thus supporting the negative impact of spelling-specific test anxiety beyond academic concerns (Faber, 1993b, 1995a,b). Moreover, multivariate analyses could demonstrate the mediational role of spelling-specific self-concept to explain interindividually existing differences in self-specific test anxiety. It was not merely the students' spelling achievement which most strongly affected their anxiety rather than their self-concept (Figure 12).

These findings could be further differentiated and extended by additional analyses. Using scales for separately assessing spelling-specific worry and emotionality scores could show only the worry component of spelling-test anxiety being strongly associated with related achievement and self-concept variables as well with negative school attitudes – whereas both components appeared to equally correlate with the global self-esteem variable (Faber, 2000, 2002b). Though highly overlapping, both components differently contributed to the validation variables. Therefore, they evidently reflected unique cognitive-motivational processes within the relations among constructs. The results of variance analyses could also demonstrate that not only students with poor achievement but also students with moderate and high achievement reported heightened anxiety scores – thus confirming the relational feature of academic test anxieties (Faber, 2000).

Also relating to the test anxiety construct, the findings from two independent samples outlined teachers' difficulties to adequately assess students' individual levels of spelling-specific worry and emotionality. They consistently could demonstrate that teachers' perceptions of student anxiety were mainly affected by their individual achievement level (Faber, 1994, 2001) – and thus could replicate similar results from an earlier study (Faber, 1988). In particular, teachers assumed students with poor spelling achievement to be more anxious than students with moderate or high spelling achievement. Their judgments were highly inferential in nature and misleading. They were unable to recognize that also students with sufficient spelling performance would probably suffer from anxious feelings with regard to spelling-specific evaluation situations. Overall, these findings underline the well documented difficulty of teachers to perceive and evaluate the motivational orientations of students within an educational setting (Argulewicz & Miller, 1985). For warranting more valid assessments, appropriate diagnostic tools should be available (Faber, 2006b).

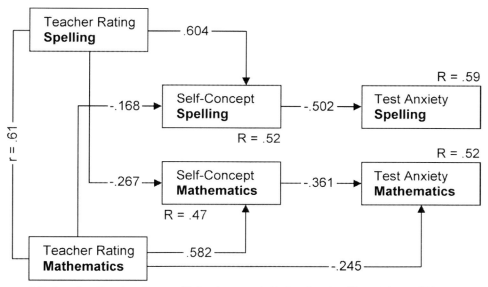

Figure 12. Relations among achievement, self-concept and test anxiety variables across different subjects: standardized regression weights and multiple regression cofficients (Faber, 1993a).

Another line of research concerned the development and validation of an instrument for measuring students' spelling-specific attributions. Based on Weiner's basic classification scheme (Weiner, 2010), students were asked to rate the importance of ability, effort, task difficulty, and luck to explain own success and failure in a dictation outcome. As the results from two independent student samples could show, the ability attributions for success and failure as well as the luck at-tributions for success correlated more strongly with spelling-specific than with math-specific achievement variables (Faber, 1996, 2002a). For all other attributions, these correlations appeared to be nonsignificant. Variance analyses could only partially demonstrate different attribution patterns – mostly determined by significant main effects of the self-concept variable. Students with poor spelling achievement and a low spelling-specific self-concept were more likely to attribute success to good luck, and failure to a lack of own ability than students with moderate to high spelling achievement and a moderate to high spelling-specific self-concept. However, one particular finding was theoretically unexpected and turned out to be somewhat perplexing. Especially students with a low spelling-specific self-concept explained failure not only with a lack of own ability but also with a lack of own effort. Though realizing their lack of spelling ability, they blamed themselves for less appropriate practicing. Against the background of learning helplessness theory, this finding appeared to be contradictory. Data from both samples did not allow for further clarification – e.g. with regard to a compensatory relation between students' ability and effort attributions (Heckhausen, 1987). Apart from that, these less clear findings might also be traced back to the causal factors used in both studies. Therefore, subsequent analyses of students' attributions should be based on a broader and more differentiated range of spelling-related causes (Mok, Kennedy & Moore, 2011; Pekrun, 1983).

Finally, students' spelling-specific self-beliefs were also controlled for relevant gender differences. With regard to the self-concept variable, only boys' negative affective evaluations turned out to be significantly stronger (Faber, 1991). With regard to the anxiety variable, no significant gender differences could be found (Faber, 1993b, 1995a). An additional multivariate analysis with gender and spelling achievement as independent factor variables revealed small differences favoring the girls' achievement whereas in the self-concept variable no significant gender differences occurred. Overall, students' spelling-specific self-concept could be best predicted by spelling achievement – without any impact of the students' gender (Faber, 2003).

To summarize, these previous research findings could contribute to essentially enhance empirical knowledge about the nature and role of spelling-specific self-beliefs in elementary school samples. In particular, this research project led to the development and validation of psychometrically sound instruments for measuring students' self-concept and test anxiety in the spelling domain which can further be used in subsequent analyses. However, it also outlined the limited usability of classic attributional causes and thus could stress the need for a more differentiated operationalization of the construct.

Chapter 3

ACADEMIC SELF-BELIEFS IN THE SPELLING DOMAIN: THE PRESENT STUDY

OVERALL BACKGROUND AND CONCEPTUALIZATION

Based on the previous own research results, the present study aims at a threefold purpose. Firstly, the validation findings concerning the instruments for measuring students' spelling-specific self-concept, error-specific self-estimates, and spelling-specific test anxiety shall be replicated and refined. Secondly, for the measurement of spelling-specific attributions a revised instrument including a more differentiated set of causal factors shall be developed and evaluated. Thirdly, the complex relations among all spelling-specific and general constructs shall be unraveled with regard to particular theoretical assumptions. Therefore, a structurally and processually modified version of the originally presented modeling approach (Figure 9) is hypothesized. It explicitly focuses on the spelling domain and is assigned to predict the associations between spelling-specific self-beliefs and general variables (Figure 13).

Though this modeling approach cannot claim to exhaustively reflect students' cognitive-motivational orientations in the spelling domain, it will be capable of reflecting the most important constructs and relations at least. Conceptually it refers to relevant theoretical considerations and empirical results and, thus, partially seeks to integrate expectancy-value perspectives on academic motivation (Eccles, Schiefele & Wigfield, 1998), the structural and processual perspectives on the multifaceted nature of self-concept (Marsh, 2006), the attributional perspective on learned helplessness (Abramson, Garber & Seligman, 1980; Dweck & Wortman, 1982), and the transactional perspective on test anxiety (Zeidner, 1998).

Against that background, the present study pursues the following research objectives in detail:

- With regard to its factorial structure and psychometric properties, a somewhat revised version of the questionnaire for measuring students' spelling-specific self-concept shall be examined and validated. In particular, this analysis refers to the replication of the originally built subscales across different measurement times.
- The causal ordering of relations between spelling-specific self-concept and achievement shall be longitudinally analyzed. In particular, this analysis refers

to the relative strength of relations across constructs and measurement times and shall clarify whether they will display a more skill-dependent, self-enhancing, or reciprocal pattern.
- With regard to its factorial structure and psychometric properties, a slightly revised version of the scale for measuring students' error-related self-estimates shall be examined and validated. In particular, this analysis refers to the replication of the originally used instrument for assessing students' more task-related competence perceptions.
- Additionally, the relations of error-related self-estimates with relevant self-concept and achievement variables shall be further clarified. In particular, this analysis refers to their structural position within the self-beliefs system concerning a most concrete differentiation of students' spelling-specific self-perceptions.

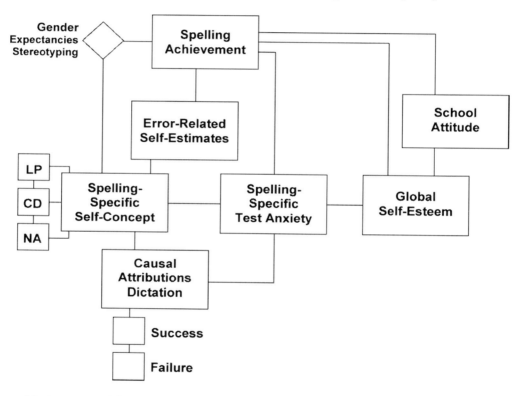

Figure 13. A conceptual framework of the present study: relations among achievement and self-belief constructs in the spelling domain.

- Moreover, a newly developed instrument for measuring students' causal attributions of positive and negative dictation outcomes shall be examined. In particular, this analysis refers to the factorial structure and psychometric properties of a success and a failure attribution scale as well as to their relations with relevant self-belief and achievement variables.
- With regard to possible consequences of spelling-specific self-beliefs on students' general self-esteem, a partial structural model including the relations between achievement, self-concept, test anxiety, and the self-esteem variable shall

be tested. It is hypothesized that spelling-specific test anxiety will be affected primarily by prior self-concept and, in turn, will predict subsequent self-esteem. In particular, this longitudinal analysis refers to the mediational role of self-concept in determining interindividually existing differences in students' test anxiety as well as to the mediational role of test anxiety in determining interindividually existing differences in students' self-esteem.

- Similarly, the possible consequences of spelling-specific self-beliefs on students' general school attitude shall be investigated. Again, a partial model including the relations among self-concept, test anxiety, self-esteem, and attitude variable shall be tested. It is hypothesized that the spelling-specific self-concept will predict subsequent test anxiety which will, in turn, predict self-esteem and school attitude. In particular, this analysis refers to the mediational role of spelling-specific test anxiety in determining interindividually existing differences in students' self-esteem and school attitude. As it is assumed that self-esteem will act more internalizing and school attitude will act more externalizing, both constructs are expected to be predicted differently.

All analyses will be based on both cross-sectional and longitudinal data. Principally, for all relevant variables their change over time will be also considered. For testing partial models which sequentially predict the direction of construct relations, primarily longitudinal data will be used.

SAMPLE CHARACTERISTICS AND PROCEDURE

All empirical analyses have been conducted with a sample of elementary fourth-graders from 17 different classes at eight schools, located in larger German cities in the majority of cases. The student sample consisted of N = 284 children (145 girls and 139 boys). Due to missing data in certain variable sets, a final sample size of N = 188-274 could be analyzed. The average age of the children was 9 years and 11 months (SD = 6 months) at the beginning of the school year. Their participation took place on a volunteer basis and only with explicit consent of their parents and teachers. The average participation rate per class amounted to 78 percent.

In the process, all relevant self-belief and achievement data were gathered at the beginning and at the end of the school year. In each classroom, this required two two-hour lesson periods and took place in the absence of the responsible teachers with two specially instructed study conductors. They gave systematically standardized assistance to those children that exhibited difficulties while answering the questions presented to them in written form. As the study conductors were not informed of the exact study objectives, the risk of exerting an undue expectancy effect should have been minimized from the beginning. The instruction of the study conductors took place in two two-hour sessions. In these sessions, essential methodical aspects of the instruments employed were dealt with, in particular questions concerning proper behavior in the assessment situation. In the case of arising difficulties, adequate and particularly comparable coping strategies were provided, tested, and modified as necessary.

For assessing the students' latest marks and various competence aspects, teachers being responsible for spelling instruction in each particular classroom were asked to complete brief questionnaires at both measurement times.

MEASUREMENT OF SELF-BELIEF AND ACHIEVEMENT VARIABLES

Spelling Achievement

The students' spelling achievement was assessed at both measurement times using three indicators: first, a standardized spelling test had to be taken. At measurement time 1, an abridged combination of the two parallel forms of the Diagnostic Spelling Test for Third-Graders by Müller (1983) was administered. It contained 30 word dictation items, the difficulty of which ranges at intermediate level (mean item difficulty: P = 58.2). The test results were scored with respect to the sum of correctly spelled words. At measurement time 2, another spelling test was administered whose 42 items were primarily drawn from the spelling tasks Glogauer (1980) had presented. Average item difficulty was at an intermediate level (mean item difficulty: P = 60.3). Here as well, the sum of correctly spelled words was scored. At both measurement times, the reliability of these tests proved to be sufficient (Table 1). Secondly, teacher ratings of the students' current spelling achievement level were assessed. For this purpose, a six-point rating item was used. High scores indicate a high level of spelling achievement. With the spelling test scores, these teacher ratings proved to correlate as expected (at measurement time 1 r = .75, p ≤ .001, and at measurement time 2 r = .62, p ≤ .001). Additionally, the students' latest dictation marks were assessed. High scores indicate poor performance results (ranging from 1 = very good to 6 = very bad). For all statistical analyses, their scoring was inverted. At measurement time 1, their correlation a-mounted to r = .87 (p ≤ .001) with the teacher ratings and r = .67 (p ≤ .001) with the test scores. At measurement time 2, their correlation amounted to r = .88 (p ≤ .001) with the teacher ratings and r = .64 (p ≤ .001) with the test scores. And finally, with respect to particular validation analyses the students' participation in special remedial spelling instruction outside the classroom setting was assessed. Higher scores indicated their longer lasting participation (0 = no remedial instruction, 1 = remedial instruction for at least six months, 2 = remedial instruction for at least 12 months, 3 = remedial instruction for at least 18 months, 4 = remedial instruction for more than 18 months).

Performance in Other Subject Matters

As discriminant achievement variables, the students' performance in mathematics (Table 1), German language, and general subjects were considered at both measurement times. In German elementary schools general subjects refer to a combination of social studies and natural science matters. These informations were gathered by means of corresponding teacher using a six-point rating item Here as well, high scores indicated high performance levels.

Spelling-Specific Self-Concept

For the purpose of measuring the spelling-specific self-concept, an especially developed questionnaire (Faber, 1991), modified for this particular analysis, was used which consists of three factor-analytically derived subscales: as such, the scale "Perceived Performance and

Learning Problems" consisted of 10 four-point self-ratings and outlines the students' subjectively experienced difficulties in meeting academic spelling demands. The scale "Perceived Coping with Classroom Dictations" consisted of 8 four-point self-ratings and outlines the students´ experienced confidence and competence with regard to coping with classroom dictations. And the scale "Negative Affective Evaluations" consisted of 6 four-point self-ratings and outlines the students' reported extent of refusal and/or devaluation of spelling-specific demands. The internal consistencies for all scales turned out to be sufficient throughout (Table 1).

Error-Related Self-Estimates

As a more task-specific measure of students' spelling-specific self-perceptions, a scale concerning the relative frequency of various spelling errors was used. In particular, 7 four-point rating items referred to concrete misspellings students had individually experienced – e.g. omitting letters, adding letters, or confusing letters (Faber, 1989b, 1992b). These error categories should explicitly reflect students' mastering experiences and thus were worded in the most phenomenological manner. Hence, they could not claim to represent linguistically or psychologically sound error classifications but were descriptive in nature (Zingeler-Gundlach, Langheinrich & Kemmler, 1973). As such they can be considered as conceptually naïve error types.

Spelling-Specific Test Anxiety

The spelling-specific worry and emotionality cognitions were measured using an especially developed short scale (Faber, 1993b, 1995a). It consisted of 13 four-point self-ratings. Sample item: "Prior to class dictations, I am often worried about forgetting everything I have been practicing." As previous studies had repeatedly shown that the spelling-specific worry and emotionality cognitions could not be separated by factor analyses, an overall scale format had been devised. Students with high scores reported a strong degree of spelling-specific test anxiety. The internal consistencies of this scale turned out well (Table 1).

Causal Attributions of Dictation Outcomes

The spelling-specific causal attributions were measured separately, for success and failure, using 14 respective four-point rating items. They contained a series of internal and external causes to explain a good and a poor dictation result – particularly with respect to the students' personal characteristics and endeavors as well as influences depending upon classroom instruction. For each causal factor, the students had to estimate to what extent it might have contributed to the good or poor dictation result. Overall, the internal consistencies for the relevant scales still turned out to be sufficient (Table 1).

General Academic Self-Concept

As concurrent validation variable, the students' general academic self-concept across domains or subjects was assessed. The scale consisted of 10 four-point self-ratings. They originate from relevant instruments by Pekrun (1983) and Wagner (1977a). Sample item: "I am a bright and apt student." Students with high scores report a high level of general academic self-concept. Principal components analyses of data at measurement time 1 and 2 revealed one common factor and led to an overall scale. Its internal consistencies at both measurement times appeared to be sufficient (Table 1).

General School Attitudes

Based on the questionnaire by Wagner (1977b) 10 four-point self-ratings were used. They referred to the students' negative perceptions of schooling, school climate and teacher behavior in the classroom. Students with high scores were indicated to have strong negative attitudes. Sample item: "I don't like to go to school." Principal components analyses of data at measurement time 1 and 2 revealed one common factor and led to an overall scale. Its internal consistencies for this scale at both measurement times also turned out to be sufficient (Table 1).

Table 1. Descriptive statistics and internal consistencies of the achievement and self-belief measures (AD = arithmetic mean, SD = standard deviation, α = Cronbach's alpha, 1,2 = measurement time)

Variable/Measures	AM1	SD1	α1	AM2	SD2	α2
Spelling Achievement						
Spelling Test	17.6	7.2	.91	25.3	7.9	.89
	Range: 2-30			Range: 4-42		
Teacher Rating	4.1	1.1		3.9	1.2	
Latest Dictation Mark	3.9	1.3		4.0	1.4	
Math Achievement						
Teacher Rating	4.3	0.9		4.3	1.0	
Spelling Specific Self-Concept						
Performance Problems	20.5	6.6	.87	19.9	6.4	.85
Coping with Dictations	21.7	5.6	.84	20.8	6.1	.87
Affective Evaluations	13.9	4.8	.79	15.6	4.9	.81
Self-Perceptions of Spelling Task Mastering						
Error Estimates	14.5	4.0	.85	13.8	4.0	.83
Spelling-Specific Worry and Emotionality Cognitions						
Test Anxiety	28.8	9.2	.87	27.6	9.8	.90
Causal Attributions of Dictation Outcomes						
Success Internal	11.7	3.6	.74	10.3	3.6	.77
Success External	19.8	4.5	.75	18.9	4.7	.77
Failure Internal	9.2	3.5	.76	9.4	3.7	.78
Failure External	16.3	4.8	.77	16.5	4.9	.79
General Academic Self-Concept						
Academic Self-Concept	29.0	6.0	.87	28.6	6.3	.87
General School Attitudes						
Negative Perceptions of Schooling and Teacher Behavior						
	25.0	9.1	.93	28.1	8.2	.89
Global Self-Esteem/Self-Worth						
Self-Esteem	31.6	6.3	.84	32.2	6.3	.85

Global Self-Esteem

For the purpose of measuring the students´ global self-esteem, 9 four-point self-ratings of the relevant subscale from the self-concept questionnaire by Wagner (1977a) were used and complemented with one item from the relevant research instrument by Pekrun (1983). Students with high scores report strong feelings of self-worth and perceive their emotional state as well as their social situation overall rather more positively. Sample item (scoring reversed): "I am always fouling up things." Principal components analyses of data at measurement time 1 and 2 revealed one common factor and led to an overall scale. Its consistencies at both measurement times turned out to be sufficient (Table 1).

Gender

Additionally, the students' gender was taken into account for some analyses as an academically and cognitive-motivationally interesting moderating variable (dummy coding: 1 = male, 2 = female).

STATISTICAL ANALYSES

Though not completely reported in all analyses, basic descriptive statistics for items or tasks under consideration were calculated in a very first step.

For the purpose of scale construction, principal components analyses of data from both measurement times were used – including varimax rotation if necessary (Bryant & Yarnold, 1995). In particular, for the identification of factorial dimensions theoretical as well statistical criteria were treated to be equally decisive. Beyond initial screen tests (Cattell, 1966) especially the relative proportion of item variance being explained by a certain latent factor relative to its communality was determined – thus identifying marker items following the criteria by Fürntratt (1969). For determining internal scale consistencies, Cronbach's alpha and part-whole corrected item-total correlations were calculated (Cortina, 1993).

For clarification of relations as a first step among constructs zero-order correlations as well as multiple regression analyses and analyses of variance were conducted. The direction and magnitude of variables' change over time was tested by means of analyses of variance with repeated-measure designs. For all analyses the SPSS software was used (Field, 2009).

As a second step for further clarification of construct relations, the method of structural equation modeling was used by means of the AMOS software (Arbuckle & Wothke, 1999; Byrne, 2010). Based on maximum likelihood estimations of covariance matrices, the structural equation modeling procedure compares the relations among empirically gathered data with the structure of theoretically predicted relations. Thus, it allows to calculate standardized path coefficients for weighting the direct effects between exogenous and several waves of endogenous model variables across both measurement times. Structural models may include either manifest or latent variables. Latent variables can be indicated by single manifest items or item parcels. Item parceling has been demonstrated to yield several advantages as it contributes to enhance the parsimony of structural models and thus may lead to better fitting solutions. However, entering item parcels into structural equations absolutely requires a unidimensional and reliable set of items (Bandalos, 2002; Little, Cunningham, Shahar & Widaman, 2002). Otherwise, item parceling will provoke biased or even invalid modeling results. A theoretically predicted model of structural relations was considered as being confirmed by covariances among the empirical variables when the overall model fit appeared to be acceptable, at least. As goodness-of-fit indices, in particular, the relative chi-square value χ^2/df, the Tucker-Lewis Index TLI, the Normed Fit Index NFI, and the Root Mean Square Error of Approximation RMSEA were used (Kline, 2011). In the present study, an acceptable model fit was assumed if the χ^2/df value was equal to or lower than 3, the TLI value was equal to or higher than .90, the NFI value was equal to or higher than .90, and the RMSEA value was equal to or lower than .08 (Marsh, Balla & Hau, 1996). The structural equation modeling procedure in AMOS, moreover, automatically compensates missing data by means of the full information maximum likelihood method. In simulation studies, this method has been demonstrated to produce unbiased and more efficient results than other methods (Enders & Bandalos, 2001).

Chapter 4

THE MEASURING OF SPELLING-SPECIFIC SELF-CONCEPT

SCALE DEVELOPMENT AND RESEARCH OBJECTIVES

Based on previous findings (Faber, 1991), in the present study the item pool for operationalizing the construct had to be revised and extended. As it was supposed to assess the spelling-specific self-concept in the most differentiated way possible, the items should reflect a broad range of specific task and situation features in the area of spelling learning and achievement. For that purpose, an item pool was generated which could map the students' perceptions to master relevant spelling demands. Accordingly, students with high competence beliefs were assumed to display sufficient knowledge and successful strategies so as to minimize their error rates in the domain. In contrast, students with low competence beliefs were assumed to display a lack of knowledge and less effective strategies – which should lead to repeated failure experiences in the domain.

As to their content, competence belief items primarily referred to three typical aspects of relevant learning and performance: firstly, they should relate to the writing of class dictations or spelling tests. These evaluative situations must be considered as key events per se with respect to the spelling domain. Mastering these situations will require both spelling competencies and test-taking skills. Hence, the measurement of the spelling-specific self-concept should include a set of items which focuses on the students' coping with evaluative situations. Secondly, learning and performance in the spelling domain would be more strongly dependent on students' intensive and continuous practice than on other subjects. The students' self-perceptions will, therefore, always substantiate their individually perceived efficacy of own effort. Hence, the measurement of the spelling-specific self-concept should also include a set of items which focus on the students' perceived contingencies between prior learning and subsequent outcomes. And thirdly, due to the affective value of success or failure experiences in the spelling domain, students will always perceive relevant tasks and outcomes as more or less pleasant and, thus, will always display more positive or negative feelings against spelling requirements. Hence, the measurement of the spelling-specific self-concept should also include a set of items which focuses on the students' affective evaluations. In particular, competence perceptions and affective evaluations were considered to operate mutually reinforcing. Students with high competence beliefs should be more likely to report positive affective evaluations – whereas students with low competence beliefs should be more likely to report negative affective evaluations. Moreover, students who would experience accumulated failure in the spelling domain and, thus, would have extremely lowered competence beliefs, should be prone to developing avoiding strategies over time. Conceptually, these affective evaluations always should influence the students' motivational orientations concerning academic spelling situations and therefore might be understood as indirectly self-related or even self-defining beliefs, at least (Arens, Yeung, Craven & Hasselhorn, 2011; Marsh, Craven & Debus, 1999).

Against the background of these considerations, a pool of 23 items operationalizing the spelling-specific self-concept had been analyzed in a pilot study (Faber, 1991). The results of the principal components analysis provided three subscales. They referred to the spelling-specific self-beliefs with respect to the perceived performance problems and efficacy of learning efforts (subscale 1), with respect to the perceived coping with classroom dictations or similar evaluative situations (subscale 2), and with respect to the students' affective evaluations of spelling in general, as well as regards writing dictations and the homework situation (subscale 3). All three subscales were sufficiently reliable and substantially interrelated, as could be conceptually expected. Their relations with nomologically relevant self-belief and achievement variables turned out to confirm theoretical predictions. In particular, they were correlated most strongly with the students' general academic self-concept and to a lesser degree with their global self-esteem. They appeared to correlate to a lesser degree with students' self-perceptions in mathematics. Similarly, with students' test anxiety scores in spelling they were evidently more strongly correlated than in mathematics. Moreover, with regard to relevant achievement variables, the subscales were more strongly correlated with spelling than with mathematics outcomes. Taken altogether, validation results could clearly demonstrate a subject-specific pattern of relations among the subscales for measuring students' spelling-specific self-concept and various self-belief or achievement variables – and, thus, they could preliminarily indicate the scales' construct validity.

The objective of the present study was, first of all, to replicate and refine these findings. Using a revised pool of 32 items, the dimensional structure underlying these items should be tested at two measurement times – thus also examining its stability over time. In particular, it was hypothesized to identify three latent factors which would repeatedly lead to three subscales concerning the students' perceived learning problems, coping with classroom dictations and affective evaluations. Validation analyses at both measurement times should clarify the scales' associations with relevant self-belief and achievement variables (Table 1) and evidence the conceptually predicted pattern of subject-specificity of relations. Hence, it was expected that the subscales would be most strongly related to spelling-specific variables and less strongly related to discriminant or general variables – e.g. to math performance or global self-esteem.

RESULTS

Dimensional Analyses and Scale Formation

Due to descriptive statistics at both measurement times, 5 of the originally generated 32 items had to be deleted eventually because of inappropriate distribution and variance characteristics. The remaining 27 items were subject to principal components analyses with varimax rotation, separately calculated for each measurement time. According to previous findings, a three factor solution was hypothesized a priori. At both measurement times, the results of principal components analyses consistently revealed a pattern of factor loadings that clearly could identify three latent dimensions (Table 2).

Table 2. Principal components analyses of spelling-specific self-concept items at measurement time 1 and 2 (a = factor loading, h^2 = communality)

Item	Measurement Time 1 a_1	a_2	a_3	h^2	Measurement Time 2 a_1	a_2	a_3	h^2
01	**.489**	-.249	.267	.372	.374	-.383	.446	.486
02	**.645**	-.308	.111	.524	**.526**	-.287	.206	.402
05	**.588**	-.306	.125	.495	**.547**	-.288	.042	.384
06	**.529**	-.462	.116	.507	**.504**	-.555	.201	.602
08	**.640**	-.235	.164	.492	**.496**	-.360	.312	.474
13	**.536**	-.198	.132	.345	**.569**	-.054	.178	.358
16	**.530**	-.227	.048	.335	**.570**	-.376	-.011	.466
17	**.547**	-.430	.174	.514	**.684**	-.372	.076	.613
18	**.615**	-.287	.029	.462	**.656**	-.356	.127	.574
21	**.485**	-.333	.062	.350	**.669**	-.297	-.049	.538
23	**.568**	-.016	.294	.410	**.626**	-.117	.176	.437
25	.603	-.013	.112	.377	.475	-.009	.482	.458
30	**.591**	-.048	.044	.353	**.501**	-.041	.161	.279
04	-.251	**.713**	.076	.578	-.312	**.690**	-.062	.577
10	-.203	**.710**	-.113	.559	-.319	**.736**	-.187	.679
11	-.104	**.683**	-.164	.505	-.221	**.632**	-.079	.455
12	-.399	**.658**	-.204	.634	-.309	**.734**	-.306	.733
14	-.076	**.534**	-.291	.376	-.025	**.542**	-.070	.300
19	-.155	**.589**	-.041	.373	-.195	**.678**	-.079	.505
24	-.258	**.520**	-.251	.400	-.152	**.712**	-.066	.535
31	-.184	**.643**	.007	.448	-.166	**.603**	-.054	.394
09	.455	-.118	**.482**	.453	-.234	.215	**.691**	.578
15	-.188	.339	**-.595**	.702	.366	-.106	**-.726**	.673
20	-.053	.199	**-.768**	.633	.209	-.073	**-.735**	.589
22	.289	-.001	**.620**	.468	.013	.294	**.594**	.440
27	.236	-.037	**.711**	.563	.064	.162	**.657**	.462
28	.030	.069	**-.728**	.535	.058	.087	**-.662**	.449

Item List: Appendix A

At measurement time 1, this solution could explain 46.4%, at measurement 2 49.7% of the total item variance. At both measurement times, all items included could be typically considered as marker variables (Fürntratt, 1969) – insofar as their factor loadings turned out to be sufficiently high (a ≥ .40) and, furthermore, as their loadings could proportionally specify at least half of their communality (a^2/h^2 ≥ .50). As such, on the first factor those items were loading high at both measurement times which referred to the students' perceived difficulties in spelling learning and performance. This factor accounted for 18.5% at measurement time 1 and for 17.4% at measurement time 2 of the rotated item variance. On the second factor, those items were loading high which referred to the students' perceived confidence and mastery of classroom dictations. This factor accounted for 16.3% at measurement time 1 and for 18.8% at measurement time 2 of the rotated item variance. And finally, on the third factor those items were loading high which referred to the students' negative affective evaluations. This factor accounted for 11.6% at measurement time 1 and for 13.5% at measurement time 2 of the rotated item variance. However, as the factor loadings of items 01, 06, and 25 did not allow for consistent interpretations across both measurement times, these items were excluded from further analyses (Table 2). Similar objections did also exist with respect to item 09 at measurement time 1. It was nevertheless retained, though, due to the considerable portion of specific variance factorially explained at measurement time 2.

On the basis of these results, 24 items (Appendix A) could eventually be drawn on for the final formation of three subscales:
- The subscale "Perceived Learning and Performance Problems" (LPprob) consisted of 10 items. It measured the students' competence beliefs as related to their individually experienced learning difficulties and failure outcomes. In particular, students with high sum scores perceived their spelling-specific efforts as unsuccessful and strongly displayed symptoms of resignation and helplessness.
- The subscale "Perceived Coping with Classroom Dictations" (copDIC) consisted of 8 items. It measured the students' self-confidence with respect to master classroom dictations. From the outset, students with high sum scores perceived classroom dictations as a situation which might be favorably influenced by them by the means of own competencies or additional practice efforts. In particular, they expected to cope with the situational demands posed in a foreseeable way.
- The subscale "Negative Affective Evaluations" (negAFF) consisted of 6 items. It measured the students' negative affective reactions towards spelling. Students with high sum scores perceived academic and/or home spelling requirements as unpleasant and less useful. In particular, they were more likely to exhibit emotional disassociation strategies and avoidance cognitions.

With regard to the interval between both measurement times, the retest coefficients for all three subscales turned out to be relatively high in magnitude. Therefore, all three subscales could yield reasonably stable measurements over time (Table 3). Theoretically, as expected, they did not represent independent components of the spelling-specific self-concept. Rather their sum scores were substantially correlated – and thus could be considered as theoretically distinctive but empirically overlapping components of the spelling-specific self-concept construct.

Validation Results

The relations of all three subscales with relevant self-belief and achievement variables turned out largely as theoretically predicted. As such, all three subscales appeared to correlate more strongly with various achievement measures in spelling than with the mathematics achievement measure. As the teacher ratings in spelling and mathematics overlapped to a considerable degree (r = .56 at measurement time 1, r = .54 at measurement time 2, p ≤ .001) zero-order correlations were considered to reveal only confounded results and to mask a subject-specific pattern of relations.

Table 3. Intercorrelations, stabilities, and correlations of the spelling-specific self-concept scales with students' achievement, self-beliefs, and gender (at measurement time 1 and 2)

Validation Variables	LPprob	copDIC	negAFF
LPprob 1		-.63***	.48***
2		-.65***	.41***
copDIC 1			-.40***
2			-.38***
Stability 1-2	.76***	.72***	.59***
Spelling Test 1	-.49***	.50***	-.15*
2	-.49***	.57***	-.22***
Spelling Rating 1	-.63***	.59***	-.24***
2	-.62***	.57***	-.28***
Math Rating 1	-.43***	.38***	-.02
2	-.43***	.40***	-.04
Test Anxiety 1	.78***	-.50***	.37***
2	.83***	-.56***	.37***
Academic Self 1	-.60***	.75***	-.32***
2	-.64***	.73***	-.28***
Self-Esteem 1	-.61***	.38***	-.23***
2	-.64***	.39***	-.28***
Gender 1	-.10	.09	-.13*
2	-.11	.04	-.14*

Significance: *p ≤ .05, ***p ≤ .001
LPprob = Perceived Learning and Performance Problems, copDIC = Perceived Coping with Classroom Dictations, negAFF = Negative Affective Evaluations

Therefore, regression analyses were calculated additionally with the teacher ratings as concurrently entered predictor variables. They could draw a clearer picture of relations across subject matters. Additionally calculated regression analyses could draw a clearer picture. When statistically controlling for the overlap of teacher ratings, all three subscales of spelling-specific self-concept could be significantly and strongly explained by the spelling achievement, but only to an evidently lesser degree or not at all by the mathematics achievement variable (Table 4). However, the low but significant contribution of teachers' math ratings to the students' negative affective reactions might indicate a broader understanding of this subscale's meaning or validity, respectively. At least, it might reflect not only spelling-specific but to a lesser degree also more general aspects of students' affective evaluations of academic concerns.

Table 4. Relations between spelling-specific self-concept and concurrent achievement measures: Results of multiple regression analyses (at measurement time 1 and 2)

Achievement Variables	Spelling-Specific Self-Concept		
	LPprob	copDIC	negAFF
	Standardized Regression Coefficients		
Spelling Rating 1	-.561***	.568***	-.318***
Math Rating 1	-.107	.048	.164*
Adjusted R^2	.391	.351	.060
Spelling Rating 2	-.549***	.577***	-.374***
Math Rating 2	-.121	.072	.176*
Adjusted R^2	.386	.380	.089

Significance: *$p \leq .05$, ***$p \leq .001$
LPprob = Perceived Learning and Performance Problems, copDIC = Perceived Coping with Classroom Dictations, negAFF = Negative Affective Evaluations

With respect to the various self-belief variables, the relations of the three subscales turned out to show a differential pattern (Table 3). The subscale for measuring students' perceived learning and performance problems appeared to correlate most strongly with their spelling-specific test anxiety, and to slightly lesser degree, with their general academic self-concept and their global self-esteem. By comparison, the subscale for measuring students' perceived coping with classroom dictations appeared to correlate with their spelling-specific test anxiety to a somewhat lesser degree, but most strongly with their general academic self-concept. The subscale for measuring students' negative affective evaluations turned out to correlate with all other self-belief variables to an evidently lesser degree – with the strongest relation to the spelling-specific test anxiety variable. And finally, only in the case of the affective evaluations subscale interindividually existing differences in students' spelling-specific self-concept scores could be explained by gender (Table 3). Therefore, boys reported negative affective evaluations against the spelling domain to a somewhat higher degree than girls.

For further validation analysis, the structural equation modeling method was used to test a more complex model of longitudinal relations among spelling-specific self-concept, general self-concept variables, and spelling achievement. According to the hierarchical and multidimensional feature of the self-concept construct (Figure 3), it was hypothesized that the spelling-specific self-concept would be most closely related to the achievement variable and, in turn, to moderately predict the general academic self-concept. The general academic self-concept should be predicted by the achievement variables to a lesser degree and, moreover, most strongly predict the global self-esteem variable. For all unidimensional latent constructs, measurement models with two item parcels were used. In the case of the spelling-specific self-concept the 10 items of the subscale for measuring perceived learning and performance problems and the 8 items of the subscale for measuring coping with dictations were included as manifest indicators – in order to get more accurate estimations of error variances and, thus, to provide a more precise control for the overlap between both item sets. Due to the interrelations between all subscales (Table 3), the items sets of these two subscales appeared to more typically represent the spelling-specific self-concept construct than the items of the subscale for measuring the negative affective evaluations. Therefore, with regard to most straightforward results, the use of a reduced measurement model seemed to be defensible. As the structural equation analysis could demonstrate, the latent spelling-specific self-concept variable could be strongly predicted by spelling achievement. It could also directly and significantly affect the general self-concept variable as theoretically expected. Furthermore, the global self-esteem variable was significantly predicted only by the general academic self-concept variable. Overall, this partial self-belief model had an acceptable model fit and thus could adequately confirm the hypothesized relations among variables (Figure 14).

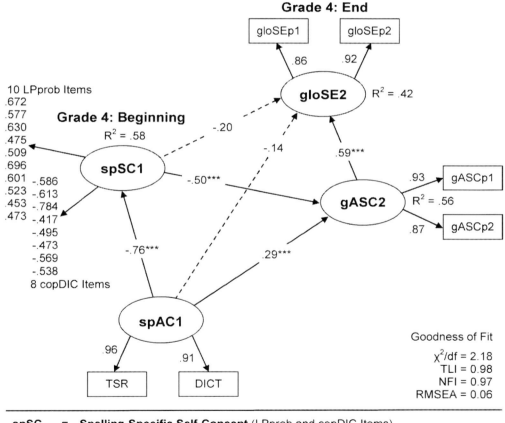

Figure 14. Longitudinal relations among achievement and self-belief variables: results of structural equation modeling.

Change Over Time

With regard to possible changes across both measurement times, the sum scores of all three self-concept subscales were compared by means of analyses of variance with repeated-measure design. In order to get most differentiated results, the students' spelling performance as assessed by individual teacher ratings and their gender were additionally used as independent factor variables. Thus, for each self-concept variable a 2 (measurement time) x 3 (teacher spelling ratings) x 2 (gender) way analysis was calculated. For the most part, the results could not demonstrate any substantial changes over time in any of the three performance groups. With one single exception, all main effects as well as interaction effects appeared to be non-significant (Table 5). Only for the subscale concerning students' perceived coping with classroom dictations a small, but significant interaction effect between the within subjects factor and the spelling performance could be found. It indicated the girls' self-perceptions with poor spelling outcomes to apparently decline over time (Figure 15).

Table 5. Change over time in spelling-specific self-concept: Analyses of variance with repeated measurement design

Subscale **Perceived Learning and Performance Problems**					
Within Subjects	Wilks λ	F	df	p	Eta²
MT	1.000	0.046	1,217	.831	.000
MT × TSR	0.996	0.438	2,217	.646	.004
MT × Gender	1.000	0.008	1,217	.930	.000
MT × TSR × Gender	0.982	1.965	2,217	.143	.018
Between Subjects					
TSR		82.208	2,217	.000	.434
Subscale **Coping with Classroom Dictations**					
Within Subjects	Wilks λ	F	df	p	Eta²
MT	1.000	0.028	1,217	.867	.000
MT × TSR	0.968	3.630	2,217	.028	.032
MT × Gender	0.987	2.863	1,217	.092	.013
MT × TSR × Gender	0.985	1.679	2,217	.189	.015
Between Subjects					
TSR		75.910	2,217	.000	.405
Subscale **Negative Affective Evaluations**					
Within Subjects	Wilks λ	F	df	p	Eta²
MT	1.000	0.038	1,217	.845	.000
MT × TSR	0.998	0.173	2,217	.841	.002
MT × Gender	0.997	0.565	1,217	.453	.003
MT × TSR × Gender	0.990	1.134	2,217	.324	.010
Between Subjects					
TSR		9.084	2,217	.000	.077

MT = Measurement Time, TSR = Teacher Rating of Spelling Performance

However, taken altogether the students' spelling-specific self-concepts remained considerably stable across all performance levels. Furthermore, interindividually existing differences in students' spelling-specific self-concepts could be best explained by differences in spelling performance between subjects.

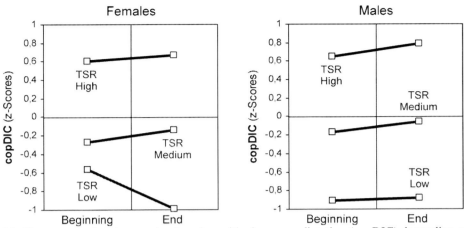

Figure 15. Change over time in perceived coping with classroom dictation (copDIC) depending on spelling achievement (TSR) and gender.

DISCUSSION

To summarize, the findings of this study could largely confirm previous research results. Dimensional analyses of the revised item pool led at both measurement times to three subscales for measuring students' spelling-specific self-concept. All three subscales could display sufficient psychometric properties. Due to their relations with relevant self-belief variables, they could claim construct validity – in particular, their sum scores could be demonstrated to most strongly correlate with spelling achievement. Moreover, the empirically substantiated formation of a subscale for measuring the students' negative affective evaluations was in line with similar research findings reported elsewhere (Arens, Yeung, Craven & Hasselhorn, 2011; Marsh, Craven & Debus, 1999; Wigfield, Eccles, Yoon, Harold, Arbreton, Freedman-Doan & Blumenfeld, 1997).

With all this, the correlation between the subscale for measuring students' perceived learning and performance problems and the global self-esteem variable appeared to turn out reasonably high. This particular finding which could replicate previous results (Faber, 1991) might stress the personal importance of accumulated failure experiences in the spelling domain. According to theoretical assumptions, strongly lowered competence beliefs and feelings of helplessness always have a negative impact on the students' self-evaluations beyond academic concerns. From a developmental perspective, this effect potentially indicates an educational and psychosocial risk factor for students' further coping with academic demands. Its occurrence will be dependent on students' grade level as the personal centrality of academic attainment might decrease over time (Wigfield & Eccles, 2002). Though structural equation results could show this relation between spelling-specific self-concept and global self-esteem being mediated by general academic self-concept (Figure 14), this particular issue undoubtedly renders the modeling perspectives on self-concept structure with regard to students' age and academic domain. Here, much more multivariate research is still needed to analyze the relations between subject-specific self-beliefs and global self-esteem or self-worth (Marsh, 1993; Marsh & Yeung, 1998).

Chapter 5

LONGITUDINAL RELATIONS BETWEEN SELF-CONCEPT AND ACHIEVEMENT

RESEARCH CONTEXT AND OBJECTIVES

Theoretically, the causal ordering of relations between academic self-concept and achievement constructs can be considered from a skill development or a self-enhancement perspective (Calsyn & Kenny, 1997). In the long term, however, these relations should be reciprocal in nature rather than unidirectional (Marsh, 2006). Instead, causal ordering research in elementary school grades mostly could support the skill development perspective – in particular when analyzing subject-specific constructs in reading or mathematics. Prior academic achievement had a stronger direct effect on subsequent achievement than the other way around (Aunola, Leskinen, Onatsu-Arvilommi & Nurmi, 2002; Chapman & Tunmer, 1997; Helmke & van Aken, 1995; Skaalvik & Valås, 1999). Developmentally, these findings appear to be plausible. As younger students' self-perceptions are in the process of emerging, they will more strongly reflect academic experiences within a given educational setting. Over time, the motivational role of self-concept will increase and lead to more reciprocal effect lines (Hattie, 1992; Wigfield & Karpathian, 1991).

With regard to the causal ordering of spelling-specific constructs, few relevant research exists. Due to the various conceptual and methodological shortcomings in the field, empirical studies concerning the role of academic self-beliefs were largely interested in cognitive-motivational differences between poor and normally achieving students on a more general level and, in particular, had mostly analyzed cross-sectional data. In the past decades, only one single study investigated the causal ordering of constructs in the spelling domain (Van Aken, Helmke & Schneider, 1997). In a sample of elementary school children it could demonstrate the causal predominance of spelling achievement over spelling-specific self-concept. Structural equation modeling results revealed stronger path coefficients from the achievement variable in grade 2 on the self-concept variable in grade 3 as well as from the achievement variable in grade 3 on the self-concept variable in grade 4. Unfortunately, the self-concept scale used in this study did obviously measure rather various literacy than pure spelling aspects and thus might have provoked somewhat confounded results. Moreover, and most interestingly, when structural equation analyses were separately calculated for different achievement measures, the findings became more mixed. Based on the students' spelling test performance, the structural modeling results could confirm the skill development perspective on causal ordering, based on spelling grades they evidently lent support for the self-enhancement perspective. Hence, the structural model best fitting the longitudinal data varied across different measurement methods. Teacher ratings or grades seemingly reflected other achievement information than the outcomes of standardized tests – and thus both methods played different roles in the students' cognitive-motivational processing.

In principle, it might be assumed that teacher ratings or grades would yield educationally more proximal information and therefore would more strongly affect the students' self-perceptions. According to similar results reported elsewhere (Marsh, 1990b; Pinxten, De Fraine, Van Damme & D'Haenens, 2010), these findings suggest to clarify the causal ordering of longitudinal construct relations with regard to different achievement indicators being analyzed separately, at least.

As previous own research in the spelling domain was cross-sectional in nature (Faber, 1991, 1992a,b, 1994), the present study, therefore, aimed at reducing this research gap. Consequently, the longitudinal relations between the students' spelling-specific self-concept and their spelling achievement were analyzed. According to relevant developmental assumptions, it was hypothesized that the elementary fourth-graders' prior spelling achievement should more strongly affect their subsequent spelling-specific self-concept. The other away around, the impact of prior spelling-specific self-concept on subsequent spelling achievement was hypothesized to turn out comparatively lesser in magnitude. Hence, the results were expected to empirically support a skill development perspective.

Methodologically, this study used the structural equation modeling approach for clarifying the causal predominance among constructs and across measurement times. The structural model consisted of latent achievement and self-concept variables at both measurement times. As manifest indicator variables for the self-concept construct, the sum scores of subscales measuring students' perceived learning and performance problems, coping with classroom dictations, and negative affective evaluations were included. As manifest indicator variables for the achievement construct in the "spelling test model", two parcels with test items and in the "spelling grade model" single teacher ratings and latest dictation marks were included. In particular, two separate analyses were conducted based on either teacher ratings and marks or on spelling test outcomes.

RESULTS

Based on the zero-order correlations among relevant achievement and self-concept variables (Table 6), the structural equation analyses could clearly demonstrate the causal predominance of the prior spelling achievement variable on the subsequent self-concept variable.

As could be theoretically assumed, in both structural models the latent self-concept variable appeared to explain the students' negative affective evaluations to a lesser degree than their perceived learning and performance problems and coping with classroom dictations. However, in both analyses the measurement model for constituting the latent self-concept variable turned out to be statistically appropriate (Figure 16, 17).

Furthermore, in both structural models the autoregressive path coefficients were evidently higher for the latent achievement variables than for the self-concept variables – thus indicating the achievement construct being more stable over time. In both structural models the cross-lagged path coefficients between prior achievement and subsequent self-concept were statistically significant. Subsequent self-concept could be substantially explained by prior achievement.

Table 6. Correlations among manifest achievement and self-concept variables (retest coefficients underlined) at measurement time 1 and 2

Spelling Achievement (Manifest Variables)

	TSR 1	DICT 1	spTST 2	TSR 2	DICT 2
spTST 1	.73	.67	.83	.73	.67
TSR 1		.87	.71	.88	.80
DICT 1			.65	.83	.79
spTST 2				.62	.64
TSR 2					.62

Spelling-Specific Self-Concept (Manifest Variables)

	copDIC 1	negAFF 1	LPprob 2	copDIC 2	negAFF 2
LPprob 1	-.63	.48	.76	-.54	.31
copDIC 1		-.40	-.55	.72	-.22
negAFF 1			.34	-.32	.59
LPprob 2				-.65	.41
copDIC 2					-.38

LPprob = Perceived Learning and Performance Problems, copDIC = Perceived Coping with Classroom Dictations, negAFF = Negative Affective Evaluations
spTST = Spelling Test Performance, TSR = Teacher Rating of Spelling Performance, DICT = Latest Dictation Mark

Compared with this, in both models the cross-lagged path coefficients between prior self-concept and subsequent achievement were negligibly small and statistically nonsignificant. Overall, both the "spelling test model" and the "spelling grade model" could acceptably fit the data. With regard to the relevant fit indices, the "spelling grade model", however, could represent the relations among constructs to a somewhat better degree (Figure 16, 17).

DISCUSSION

The structural equation results of both the "spelling test model" and the "spelling grade model" could strongly support the skill development perspective on construct relations. This finding was completely in line with longitudinal research on elementary graders' subject-specific self-concepts (Chapman & Tunmer, 1997; Helmke, 1992, Helmke & van Aken, 1995, Pekrun, 1987; Skaalvik & Valås, 1999). Moreover, as the present study could use a conceptually valid and psychometrically sound instrument for measuring students' self-concept, these findings might contribute to refine and extend previous research in the spelling domain (Faber, 1991, 1992a,b).

With regard to the use of standardized test outcomes or teacher ratings as achievement measures, these findings could not support essentially different relations among constructs (Van Aken, Helmke & Schneider, 1997). However, a methodological weakness of the present study was the use of only two measurement times. Therefore, this issue still deserves attention and should be further analyzed by the means of longitudinal studies encompassing more measurement times and longer time intervals.

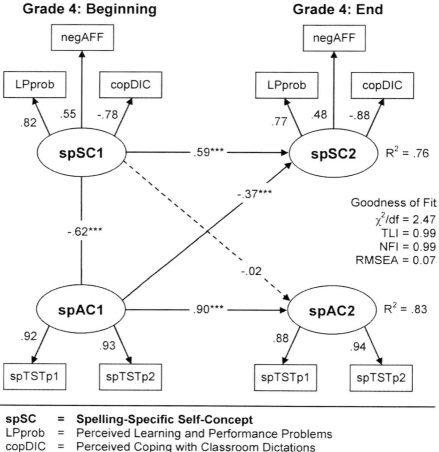

Figure 16. Causal ordering of longitudinal relations between spelling test performance and spelling-specific self-concept: results of structural equation modeling.

Furthermore, the comparatively lower stability coefficients of the self-concept variable might be explained in terms of cognitive-motivational development. In the course of elementary grades, students' self-perceptions will gradually change from more optimistic to more realistic perspectives (Helmke, 1999; Langfeldt, 2009). As academic demands in a certain domain or subject will increase, the students' self-beliefs will vary or fluctuate to some extent – even without individually emerging changes in their academic standing. Therefore, this dynamic moment will still exist during the fourth grade and thus might have contributed to less consistent self-concept scores. However, further research should also clarify this issue with respect to relevant classroom factors and social comparison effects, respectively (Köller, Zeinz & Trautwein, 2008; Marsh, 1987; Marsh & Seaton, 2009; Tiedemann & Billmann-Mahecha, 2004, 2006; Treutlein & Schöler, 2009).

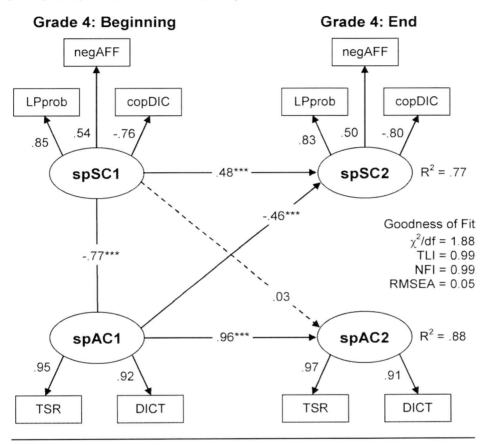

Figure 17. Causal ordering of longitudinal relations between spelling grades and spelling-specific self-concept: results of structural equation modeling.

Chapter 6

DIFFERENTIATING THE CONSTRUCT: ERROR-RELATED SELF-ESTIMATES

SCALE DEVELOPMENT AND RESEARCH OBJECTIVES

Previous research on academic self-concept could not only evidence its multidimensionality and substantiate its differentiation into various subject-specific components. It also could demonstrate these subcomponents to be further differentiated into relevant subcomponents or facets – e.g. concerning empirically separable subcomponents of competence beliefs in reading or in foreign language learning (Chapman & Tunmer, 1995; Holder, 2005; Lau, Yeung, Jin & Low, 1999; Rider & Colmar, 2005). The formation of empirically distinguishable subcomponents could be found already in elementary grade samples.

In the field of research on spelling-specific self-beliefs, this issue had been widely neglected – except for the few previous own studies (Faber, 1991, 2007). These studies revealed a multidimensional structure of elementary graders' spelling-specific self-concept which, likewise, led to the formation of three separate subscales. Though empirically overlapping, their sum scores could represent distinct components of spelling-specific self-perceptions which appeared to most strongly correlate with spelling achievement measures. Similarly, the studies of Rankin and colleagues (Rankin, Bruning & Timme, 1994; Rankin, Bruning, Timme & Katkanant, 1993) reported an interesting approach for measuring the students' spelling-specific self-efficacy. For that purpose, they asked the students to estimate the subjective probability to successfully complete several spelling tasks tapping relevant spelling situations – e.g., correctly spelling words in a letter or spelling words that are not spelled the way they sound. Especially this latter item pointed out an important aspect of spelling-specific self-perceptions as it focused on the coping with relevant word characteristics or orthographic difficulties, respectively. Conceptually, these items referred to a more aggregated understanding of spelling tasks and thus indicated an intermediate level of self-efficacy (Phan & Walker, 2000). As their wording anticipated future success rather than concerned previous success experiences, they were completely in line with Bandura's self-efficacy theory (Bandura, 1986; Bong & Skaalvik, 2003).Due to their aggregated task features, however, these items might inevitably evoke past achievement ex-periences and thus reflect a kind of structural interface between both the self-concept and self-efficacy construct. In terms of the self-concept structure, this interface could be assumed to claim a structural position beneath particular subject-specific subcomponents and above task-specific self-efficacy expectancies (Figure 18). Subject-specific self-perceptions of this type would refer not only to concrete task characteristics of the subject matter but also to prior mastering experiences. From that perspective, subject-specific self-concepts might be further differentiated into more task-related facets. For instance, students' competence beliefs in mathematics might indicate individually different outcome experiences in calculating, fractions, or word problem solving.

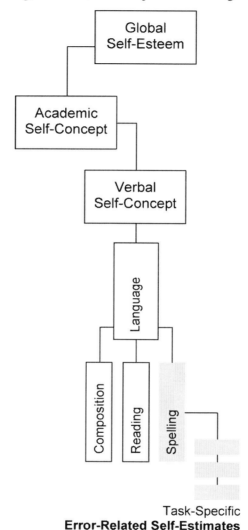

Figure 18. Error-related self-estimates as task-specific self-concept facet.

With regard to the spelling domain, as a more task-related approach to operationalize students' competence beliefs, their error-related self-estimates were analyzed (Faber, 1989b, 1992b). They referred to the individually experienced frequencies of spelling errors or misspellings being typically encountered in elementary classrooms. As these error categories should explicitly not be affected by the students' prior spelling knowledge, they were worded in the most phenomenological manner. Based on a descriptive classification of elementary students' spelling errors (Zingeler-Gundlach, Langheinrich & Kemmler, 1973), seven error types were used. In particular, the students were asked to rate the individually experienced frequency of the following errors: wrong writing of letters or graphs, omitting letters, adding letters, inverting the sequential order of letters, confusing similarly sounding or looking letters, capitalization errors concerning false lower-case characters, and capitalization errors concerning false upper-case characters at the onset of a word. All error categories were extensively introduced to students by means of descriptive sample items.

As the explorative findings of previous studies could demonstrate, the students' error-related self-estimates were unidimensional in nature, and thus their total sum score was analyzed. This sum score could incrementally explain empirical variance in students' spelling outcomes beyond the spelling-specific self-concept variable. Structurally, the error-related self-estimates could be located below the level of subject-specific self-concept and most closely to the achievement variables (Faber, 1989b, 1992b).

Against the background of previous results, the objectives of the present study were to test again the structural feature of the construct, to build an appropriate scale, and to analyze its psychometric properties at both measurement times. Moreover, comprehensive validation analyses should clarify the error-related self-estimates' relations with relevant self-belief and achievement variables. In particular, their relative position within the self-concept construct should be analyzed using the structural equation modeling method.

With regard to the conceptual assumptions (Figure 18), it was hypothesized that the error-related self-estimates should be most strongly related to the achievement variable and thus should be more strongly predicted by the achievement variable than the self-concept variable. Furthermore, it was hypothesized that the error-related self-estimates should be less strongly related to the general academic self-concept and least strongly related to the global self-esteem variable. Methodologically, a structural model of construct relations was tested which included the latent achievement, error estimation, and self-concept variables at measurement time 1 and the latent general self-concept and global self-esteem variables at measurement time 2. As manifest indicator variables for the error-related self-estimates single items were used – each referring to a certain error type. As manifest indicator variables for the remaining latent constructs item parcels were used.

RESULTS

Dimensional Analyses and Scale Formation

At both measurement times, principal components analyses lent clear support to a unidimensional structure of the construct. At measurement time 1 53.4% and at measurement time 2 49.0% of the total item variance could be explained. The factor loadings as well as the corrected item-test correlations appeared to be reasonably high for all items (Table 7). Therefore, the final scale forms included them all. At both measurement times, these scales appeared to be sufficiently reliable (Table 1).

The retest correlations of their sum scores amounted to $r = .73$ ($p < .001$). These results could also demonstrate that the students' estimations of each error category were substantially interrelated – and that the sum scores were more likely to mirror their overall spelling achievement than an intraindividually existing error profile. Hence, the sum scores could reflect the students' self-perceptions on a more task-specific construct level.

Table 7. Principal components analysis of items for measuring error-related self-estimates (at measurement time 1 and 2)

Item	Grade 4 Beginning a	h^2	r_{it}	Grade 4 End a	h^2	r_{it}
errSE-WL	.755	.570	.640	.649	.421	.516
errSE-OL	.724	.524	.609	.690	.476	.557
errSE-AL	.760	.577	.650	.731	.534	.602
errSE-SL	.709	.503	.592	.623	.388	.488
errSE-CL	.748	.560	.637	.729	.531	.601
errSE-CEL	.728	.530	.619	.719	.517	.592
errSE-CEU	.686	.470	.568	.749	.561	.627

a = Factor Loading, h^2 = Communality, r_{it} = Corrected Item-Test Correlation
WL = Wrong Writing of Letters, OL = Omitting Letters, AL = Adding Letters, SL = Inverting the Sequential Order of Letters, CL = Confusing Letters, CEL = Capitalization Error Lower-Case Character, CEU = Capitalization Error Upper Case Character

Validation Results

In order to clarify the relations of error-related self-estimates with relevant self-belief and achievement variables, multiple regression analyses were calculated. At both measurement times, error-related self-estimates appeared to most strongly correlate with the students' perceived learning and performance problems in spelling and, to a lesser degree, also with their spelling-specific test anxiety. Students who perceived high individual error frequencies displayed a more negative self-concept and were more test-anxious. Thus, their error-related self-estimates were more closely associated with spelling-specific than with general self-belief variables (Table 8). Similarly, the error-related self-estimates appeared to most strongly correlate with the students' spelling performance – in particular with the teacher ratings. Their spelling test performance could contribute only a little to explain the error estimations (Table 8). Interestingly, those students who had participated in remedial spelling instructions for a longer time interval estimated their spelling errors being more severely. However, possibly their participation in remedial interventions had been due to initially extreme error rates. Apart from that, all other achievement variables did not significantly contribute to explain the students' error estimations. And finally, at both measurement times no substantial gender differences could be found (r = -.09 at measurement time 1 and r = -.10 at measurement time 2, p > .05).

For further clarification, the structural equation modeling method was used to test a more complex model of longitudinal relations among latent constructs. The structural model included the spelling achievement as exogenous variable, the error-related self-estimates and the spelling-specific self-concept as well as the general academic self-concept and the global self-esteem as sequentially ordered endogenous variables. Except for the error estimates, for all other latent constructs item parcels were used as manifest indicator variables. In the case of error estimates, each particular item served as manifest indicator variable. Furthermore, due to their high overlap (r = .70, p < .001) the two items referring to capitalization errors were summed up and analyzed by means of a composite score. However, one particular item referring to the inversion of letter sequences had been deleted. As more than half of the students reported at both measurement times not to do such misspellings, this item appeared to be expendable. In order to get a most distinctive modeling approach for measuring the achievement construct as manifest indicator variables, both teacher ratings and test outcomes were included.

Table 8. Correlations of error-related self-estimates (errSE) with self-belief and achievement variables (at measurement time 1 and 2)

Self-Belief Variables	errSE 1	errSE 2
Spelling-Specific Self-Concept		
Perceived Learning and Performance Problems	.451***	.615***
Perceived Coping with Classroom Dictations	-.161*	-.145*
Negative Affective Evaluations	-.126**	-.016
Spelling-Specific Test Anxiety	.075	-.074
General Academic Self-Concept	-.267***	-.185**
Global Self-Esteem	.021	.105
R	.767	.732
Adjusted R^2	.578	.524
Achievement Variables	errSE 1	errSE 2
Spelling Test Performance	-.047	-.162*
Teacher Rating of Spelling Performance	-.297**	-.442***
Participation in Remedial Spelling Instruction	.167**	
Teacher Rating German Language	-.036	.086
Teacher Rating Mathematics	-.123	-.145
Teacher Rating General Studies	-.079	.015
R	.635	.574
Adjusted R^2	.387	.315

Standardized Beta-Weights at Measurement Time 1 and 2
Significance ***p ≤ .001, **p ≤ .01, *p ≤ .05

The results of the structural equation analysis could show the error-related self-estimates to be most closely related to the spelling achievement variable. They were, in turn, most closely related to the spelling-specific self-concept. Compared with this, they could only moderately contribute to the general academic self-concept and global self-esteem. The seemingly paradoxical negative regression weight between the achievement and the self-esteem variable must be seen as the result of a statistical suppression effect. As an additionally computed analyses of variance with the spelling achievement and the general academic self-concept as factor variables demonstrated, interindividually existing differences in global self-esteem could be significantly explained by the students' scores in general academic self-concept (F = 22.211, df = 1,235, p = .000, Eta^2 = .088). Thus, also the group of high achieving spellers with a strong negative academic self-concept appeared to display a lowered level of global self-esteem. The global self-esteem variable could be best predicted by the general academic self-concept. Overall, this model had a reasonable fit and thus could adequately reflect the empirical relations among constructs (Figure 19).

As theoretically assumed, the error-related self-estimates were posited most closely to the students' spelling achievement and could, furthermore, evidently mediate the effects of spelling achievement on the spelling-specific self-concept. However, the direct effect of spelling-specific self-concept on global self-esteem appeared to be astonishingly strong in magnitude and thus was not in line with theoretical predictions.

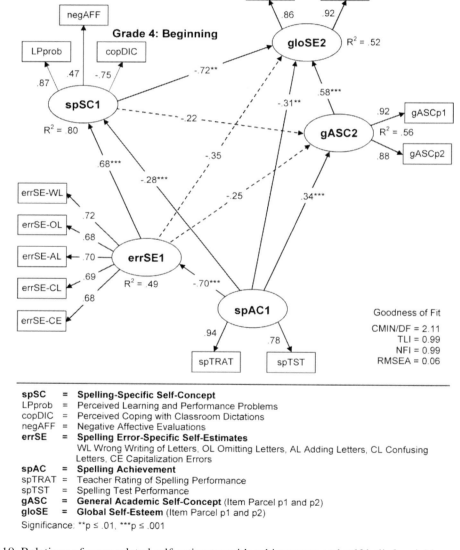

Figure 19. Relations of error-related self-estimates with achievement and self-belief variables: results of structural equation modeling.

DISCUSSION

To summarize, the findings of this study could replicate and extend the previous results. First of all, dimensional analyses led again to a unidimensional scale for measuring students' error-specific self-estimates. Its relations to relevant self-belief and achievement constructs could support the idea of a more task-specific self-concept facet within the spelling domain which was able to incrementally reflect empirical variance of students' spelling achievement. Moreover, it could mediate the effects of the spelling achievement on the spelling-specific self-concept variable. As such, the spelling-specific self-concept variable could be further differentiated.

Theoretically, this finding not only confirmed the structural perspectives concerning the multifaceted feature of subject-specific competence beliefs; it could also demonstrate that it might be conceptually worthwhile to refer construct operationalizations to more task-specific characteristics. Though evidently indicating a task-specific self-concept facet rather than self-efficacy expectancies (Pajares, 2003; Rankin, Bruning & Timme, 1994; Wigfield, Guthrie, Tonks & Perencevich, 2004), the role of students' error-related self-estimates within the nomological network of self-belief constructs still needs further clarification. In particular, the relations between error estimations and the spelling-specific self-concept should be investigated with respect to their cognitive-motivational processing and causal ordering over time. Beyond the present study which could demonstrate the error-related self-estimates strongly affecting the self-concept variable and mediating relevant achievement effects, subsequent studies should also analyze whether the error-related self-estimates will be affected by the spelling-specific self-concept – and therefore will either mirror or differentiate the students' achievement experiences on a task-specific level. Another interesting research issue concerns the question to what extent both the error-related self-estimates and the spelling-specific self-concept might potentially operate as determinants of spelling-specific self-efficacy expectancies (Ferla, Valcke & Cai, 2009). However, even within a certain academic domain the complexity of these bottom-up and top-down processes has yet to be unraveled (Marsh & Yeung, 1998).

Another remarkable result referred to the extremely strong relationship between the spelling-specific self-concept and the global self-esteem variable. Students who display more negative competence beliefs reported strongly lowered feelings of self-worth. Contrary to theoretical assumptions, this direct effect appeared to be stronger than the relative contribution of the general academic self-concept. For the most part, this effect might be due to the meaning of the subscale for measuring students' perceived learning and performance problems – which to a considerable extent tapped their feelings of subject-specific uncontrollability and helplessness. This particular finding demonstrated the impact of negative competence beliefs in the spelling domain beyond academic concerns – and thus indicated the psycho-emotional significance or centrality of elementary fourth-graders' spelling attainment. Hence, this finding might elaborate the research on the importance of self-concept facets and direct it to a more subject-specific perspective (Marsh, 1986c, 1993). More generally, the spelling-specific self-concept seemingly plays a most crucial role as risk or protective factor for further personal development. From a developmental perspective, this effect might be primarily expected to emerge in elementary school grades (Alves-Martins, Peixoto, Gouveia-Pereira,

Amaral & Pedro, 2002). However, the present study could not clarify whether this effect must be considered subject-specific or spelling-specific in nature. Consequently, further research should not only seek to replicate this finding using other self-concept and achievement measures – but also investigate its generalizability with regard to other academic domains or subjects.

Chapter 7

LONGITUDINAL RELATIONS BETWEEN TEST-ANXIETY, SELF-CONCEPT, AND SELF-ESTEEM

RESEARCH CONTEXT AND OBJECTIVES

For the development of individual state and trait test anxiety, the students' academic competence beliefs play cognitive-motivationally a crucial role – insofar as the extent of individual threat expectancies in evaluative settings appears to be determined essentially by their academic self-perceptions (Schwarzer & Jerusalem, 1992). Previous empirical research could consistently demonstrate that high-anxious students displayed strongly lowered competence and control expectancies and thus reported more negative self-concepts (Abu-Hilal, 2000; Britner & Pajares, 2006; Helmke, 1999; Krampen, 1991; Meece, Wigfield & Eccles, 1990; Newbegin & Owens, 1996; Putwain, Woods & Symes, 2010). Moreover, an individually heightened level of test anxiety was also negatively correlated with their general self-esteem or self-worth – indicating the impairing effect of test anxiety beyond academic concerns (Many & Many, 1975; Pekrun, 1983; Skaalvik, 1997b). In the long-term, students' general self-esteem or self-worth must be considered as an important risk or protective factor for further development (Harter, 1990; Wigfield & Karpathian, 1991). As various longitudinal studies could demonstrate, students with lowered self-esteem scores were significantly more prone to later social and emotional problems (Donnellan, Trzesniewski, Robins, Moffitt & Caspi, 2005; Heinonen, Räikkönen & Kelikangas-Järvinen, 2005; Kahle, Kukla & Klingel, 1980; Trzesniewski, Donnellan, Moffitt, Robins, Poulton & Caspi, 2006). Hence, over time the individual emergence of academic anxieties will impede overall self-evaluations which in turn will impair their coping with various academic, social, and emotional demands across domains and settings. The achievement debilitating effects of heightened test anxiety levels will potentially generalize and, thus, will not only directly but also indirectly contribute to level off individually existing learning and performance problems via self-esteem impairment. Unfortunately, most of the relevant research had used rather general than domain- or subject-specific anxiety measures. Therefore, little is known about the association between test anxiety and self-esteem with regard to certain academic subjects.

More than ever this applies to the spelling domain. Except for previous own studies, comparable investigations were missing altogether. The findings of own relevant research could substantiate a spelling-specific construct of elementary students' test anxiety (Faber, 1993,

1995a, 2000, 2006b). In particular, a short scale for measuring spelling-specific worry and emotionality reactions had been developed and evaluated. Despite theoretical assumptions, principal components analyses consistently failed to separate both the worry and the emotionality component. Likewise, an overall scale format was used. Their sum scores could be demonstrated to most strongly correlate with spelling-specific self-belief and achievement variables (Faber, 1993b, 1995a,b). Furthermore, they appeared to be strongly associated with the general self-esteem variable. Students with lower anxiety scores displayed more positive self-evaluations – and vice versa. Heightened test anxiety in the spelling domain significantly contributed to general feelings of lowered self-confidence, self-acceptance, and less positive affective states. By comparison, the relation between spelling achievement and general self-esteem was marginally small in magnitude (Faber, 2002b).

However, these findings were based upon cross-sectional data. In order to investigate the relations between test anxiety and self-esteem with respect to their causal ordering, the present study analyzed longitudinal data. According to the basic model of academic self-beliefs in the spelling domain (Figure 13), these relations should be also considered within the complex network of relevant achievement and self-concept variables. It was hypothesized that the students' global self-esteem should be directly predicted by their spelling-specific self-concept – which in turn should be directly affected by their spelling achievement. The relation between achievement and self-esteem, therefore, was expected to be substantially mediated by self-concept – thus indicating the cognitive-motivational key role of self-concept for determining generalizing effects of academic achievement. Additionally, change over time in the test anxiety and self-esteem variable, each dependent on students' spelling achievement and gender, should be analyzed.

RESULTS

Relations among Constructs

For testing this partial model of construct relations, again the structural equation modeling approach was used. Due to the high overlap among self-beliefs variables, two subsequent steps of statistical analysis were conducted. In order to reduce foreseeable multicollinearity effects and to avoid an inflated size of degrees of freedom (Kline, 2011), in a first step the cross-lagged relations among the latent achievement, test anxiety, and self-esteem variable were considered. Both latent self-beliefs variables were indicated by manifest item parcels, the latent achievement variable was indicated by two single items. As the results of this initial analysis could show, aside from autoregressive path coefficients only two cross-lagged path coefficients were statistically significant: substantial relations could be found between prior test anxiety and subsequent self-esteem as well as between prior achievement and subsequent test anxiety. In terms of causal ordering, this result indicated the self-esteem variable being directly affected by the anxiety variable, and the anxiety variable being directly affected by the achievement variable. Overall, this initial model could fit the data in a statistically acceptable manner (Figure 20).

Based on these initial results, in a second step the final structural model was generated. It included the latent achievement variable only at measurement time 1 and the latent test anxiety and self-esteem variable only at measurement time 2. Furthermore, the latent self-concept variable with three manifest item parcels was added.

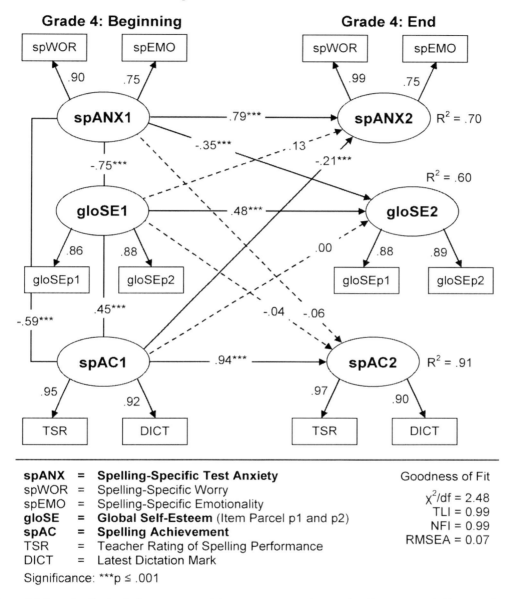

Figure 20. Longitudinal relations among achievement, test anxiety and self-esteem variables: results of structural equation modeling.

As the results of structural equation analysis could demonstrate the latent self-esteem variable appeared to be most strongly affected by the latent test anxiety variable – which in turn appeared to be most strongly affected by the latent self-concept variable. The impact of the latent achievement variable on both the test anxiety and the self-esteem variable was primarily mediated by the self-concept variable (Figure 21). According to this, students who displayed relatively negative competence beliefs in the spelling domain reported higher levels of test anxiety and markedly lowered feelings of self-worth. However, a closer look on the structural equation results revealed a significant negative path coefficient from the achievement to the self-esteem variable. This somewhat unexpected finding might reflect the fact that among those students performing equally in spelling the high-anxious and low-anxious subgroup considerably differed in their self-esteem scores (Figure 22). Overall, this final model could fit the data well.

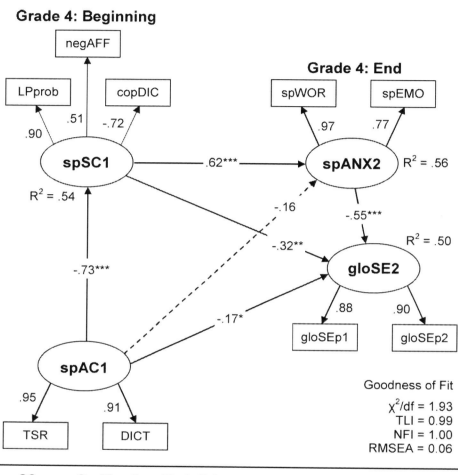

Figure 21. Relations among achievement, self-concept, test anxiety and self-esteem: results of structural equation modeling.

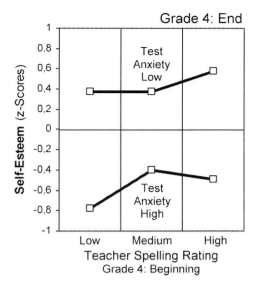

Figure 22. Mean differences in students' self-esteem depending on achievement and test anxiety scores.

Change Over Time

With regard to possible changes across both measurement times, the sum scores of the test anxiety and self-esteem scores were compared by means of analyses of variance with repeated-measure design. In order to get the most differentiated results, the students' spelling performance as assessed by individual teacher ratings and their gender were additionally used as independent factor variables. Thus, for each self-concept variable a 2 (measurement time) x 3 (teacher spelling ratings) x 2 (gender) way analysis was calculated. In particular, the results concerning the test anxiety variable could demonstrate a significant interaction effect depending on achievement differences over time (Table 9).

Apparently, female as well as male students with moderate spelling outcomes showed a somewhat decreased level of spelling-specific test anxiety at measurement time 2 (Figure 23). As an additional analysis of variance with repeated-measure design could show, this difference did not result from an increase in spelling achievement ($F = 1.691$, $df = 1,176$, $p = .195$). All other differences were statistically insignificant. The results concerning the self-esteem variable did not reveal any significant main or interactions effect (Table 9). Across all performance groups, both female and male students did not substantially change in their overall self-evaluation. In sum, the students' self-esteem remained considerably stable over time. Furthermore, interindividually existing differences in students' test anxiety and self-esteem scores could be best explained by differences in spelling performance between subjects.

DISCUSSION

The results of structural equation analyses of longitudinal data could replicate and refine the relevant findings of previous studies (Faber, 1993b, 1994, 1995a, 2002b). According to the theoretical assumptions concerning the relations among constructs, the global self-esteem variable appeared to be strongly affected by the spelling-specific test anxiety variable – which in turn was substantially affected by the spelling-specific self-concept variable. Hence, negative competence beliefs and heightened threat expectancies in the spelling domain also influence students' self-perceptions on a more general level. Obviously, individually consistent failure and anxiety experiences in a certain academic subject will contribute to impair the students' psycho-emotional well-being in a far-reaching way. This generalizing effect was completely in line with the predictions of bottom-up effects within the cognitive-motivational self-system (Marsh & Yeung, 1998; Trautwein, Lüdtke, Köller & Baumert, 2006; Wagner & Valtin, 2004). In the process it will be strongly reinforced and perpetuated by anxious students' increased self-focused attention (Wine, 1982; Zeidner, 1998). Therefore, further research should analyze whether this close connection between test anxiety and self-esteem might be primarily determined by the students' subjective certainty of failure expectancies or by their consistent perceptions of worry and emotionality symptoms – both failure expectancies as well as perceptions of anxious feelings might be subjectively interpreted as indicators of personal weakness and worthlessness.

Table 9. Change over time in test anxiety and self-esteem depending on achievement differences and gender

Spelling-Specific Test Anxiety					
Within Subjects	Wilks λ	F	df	p	Eta^2
MT	0.999	0.289	1,217	.591	.001
MT × TSR	0.971	3.239	2,217	.041	.029
MT × Gender	0.996	0.827	1,217	.364	.004
MT × TSR × Gender	0.998	0.182	2,217	.834	.002
Between Subjects					
TSR		52.876	2,217	.000	.328
Global Self-Esteem					
Within Subjects	Wilks λ	F	df	p	Eta^2
MT	0.996	0.958	1,217	.329	.004
MT × TSR	0.995	0.604	2,217	.547	.005
MT × Gender	0.993	1.504	1,217	.221	.007
MT × TSR × Gender	0.981	2.182	2,217	.115	.019
Between Subjects					
TSR		23.285	2,217	.000	.172

MT = Measurement Time, TSR = Teacher Rating of Spelling Performance

This finding might again reflect the subjective significance or centrality of elementary fourth-graders' spelling attainment. Consequently, it stresses one more time the need for further research which should more strongly focus on developmental determinants as well as on domain- or subject-specific differences in the perceived importance of academic demands and settings (Marsh, 1986c, 1993). According to similar research findings reported elsewhere (Peixoto & Almeida, 2010), students' test anxiety strikingly depressed their global self-esteem – hence, they could not have individually devalued the importance of spelling outcomes to maintain their overall sense of self-worth. Further analyses should, therefore, clarify the generalizability of the present finding across different grade levels and domains.

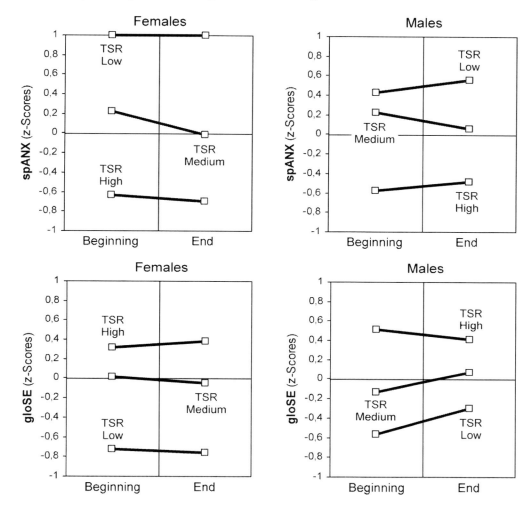

Figure 23. Change over time in test anxiety (spANX) and self-esteem (gloSE) depending on spelling achievement (TSR) and gender.

In any case, however, the individually consistent experience of failure outcomes and test anxiety in the spelling domain evidently appeared to impair elementary students' feelings of overall self-worth, and thus its negative impact beyond academic concerns could be substantiated. From a developmental perspective, individually existing difficulties in the spelling domain might be a potential risk for further development (Harter, 1990; Kahle, Kulka & Klingel, 1980; Martin & Marsh, 2006; Morrison & Cosden, 1997).

According to relevant empirical results in the field for both the test anxiety and the self-esteem variable, a relatively high degree of stability over time could be found (Cassady, 2001; Hill & Sarason, 1966; March, Sullivan & Parker, 1999; Rubin, 1978; Trautwein, 2003; Wagner & Valtin, 2004). Only in the subgroup of students with moderate spelling achievement a significant decrease of spelling-specific test anxiety scores occurred. This particular finding is hard to explain without any further information – possibly these students had developed more realistic achievement standards and thus reduced their failure expectancies. Contrary to relevant studies in the field, there were no substantial gender differences in spelling-specific test anxiety and global self-esteem (Cassady & Johnson, 2002; Hembree, 1988; Kling, Hyde, Showers & Buswell, 1999; Rouxel, 2000; Skaalvik, 1983). In the present study, mean gender differences in both constructs had been statistically controlled for students' achievement level – thus allowing for a less confounded view on gender effects.

Taken altogether, the present findings could confirm the particular predictions made in the basic model of academic self-beliefs (Figure 9). They eventually stress the need for more elaborated research efforts which will be able to integrate subject-specific and general self-belief constructs as well as incorporate relevant behavioral correlates over time and across domains (Green, Martin & Marsh, 2007; Marsh & Craven, 2006; Trautwein, 2003; Trautwein, Lüdtke, Köller & Baumert, 2006). Especially in the elementary grades, and not least most urgent in the spelling domain, investigations of this type are considered to reduce a wide range of theoretical shortcomings and empirical gaps.

Chapter 8

LONGITUDINAL RELATIONS BETWEEN SELF-CONCEPT, TEST ANXIETY, SELF-ESTEEM AND SCHOOL ATTITUDES

RESEARCH CONTEXT AND OBJECTIVES

In the long term, the students' academic self-beliefs in a certain domain or subject will also affect their general self-perceptions of schooling. Due to individually consistent success or failure experiences, students will have developed more mastery- or failure-oriented competence beliefs which might contribute to positively or negatively affect their overall school attitudes. From a reciprocal and transactional perspective on construct relations, these attitudes will in turn influence the students' academic beliefs and behaviors. Accordingly, the experience of mostly negative achievement outcomes, of more pessimistic and self-focused competency and control beliefs as well as of heightened threat expectancies will not only promote lowered academic engagement and inappropriate learning strategies but, likewise, over time lead to a strengthened level of disliking or even discounting school. Principally, these relations might be moderated by students' intraindividually existing achievement differences and dimensional comparison processes as well as by environmental determinants and developmental trends.

However, the construct of school attitudes appears to subsume a widespread range of students' perceptions and evaluations – in particular, existing operationalizations refer to the students' overall liking of school, their sense of belonging and school involvement or their perceptions of teacher relations (Libbey, 2004). Moreover, various instruments for measuring school attitudes were seriously confounded with other construct perspectives such as self-related expectancies or task value (Dolan, 1983; Holfe-Sabel & Gustafsson, 2005; Marjoribanks, 1992; Suldo, Shaffer & Shaunessy, 2008; Voelkl, 1996). Empirical findings are, therefore, contradictory and vary considerably across methods and sample characteristics. With this reservation, relevant studies could at best demonstrate approximative trends in construct relations. There was some evidence for positive associations between school attitudes, academic achievement, and academic or general self-beliefs. Similarly, positive correlations between students' subject-specific and general test anxiety were reported (Alban-Metcalfe, 1981; Alves-Martin, Peixoto, Gouveia-Pereira, Amaral & Pedro, 2002; Chapman & Boersma, 1979; Connolly, Hatchette & McMaster, 1998; Heaven, Mak, Barry & Ciarrochi, 2002; Meier

& McDaniel, 1974; Valeski & Stipek, 2001). For the most part, these correlations were statistically significant but small to moderate in magnitude. They apparently differed with regard to grade level. Especially in elementary grades, somewhat stronger relations between the students' school attitudes and global self-esteem could be found – thus indicating their overall feelings of self-worth to be more closely linked with their school involvement (Fend, Knörzer, Nagl, Specht & Väth-Szusdziara, 1976). Furthermore, as a particularly important component of school attitudes perceived teacher support could be demonstrated in a sample of secondary graders. Across various grade levels, it significantly contributed to predict the students' achievement outcomes in the verbal domain (Goodenow, 1993). Unfortunately, these studies mostly did not regard the multidimensional and multifaceted nature of academic self-beliefs and had used general measures. Therefore, their results might have masked potentially existing differences across domains or subjects. Only few studies had analyzed the relations among subject-specific self-concept and school attitudes. However, their findings could not substantiate any differences in construct relations. In a sample at the upper secondary level, both the mathematics and verbal self-concept were equally correlated with the students' liking for school (Ireson & Hallam, 2005). Conceptually, this particular finding certainly cannot suspend the need for more relevant research with regard to various academic domains or subjects. Rather, it stresses the need for more relevant research to comprehensively investigate the relations among self-beliefs and attitudinal constructs across most diverse subject matters, student characteristics, and grade levels.

Accordingly, with regard to the spelling domain only few studies exist. Despite the commonly held assumptions concerning the negative consequences of consistently experienced failure in the spelling or literacy domain, appropriate empirical investigations are still missing – although several studies could outline the particularly critical role of spelling demands in students' perceptions (Downing, DeStefano, Rich & Bell, 1984; Freedman-Doan, Wigfield, Eccles, Blumenfeld, Arbreton & Harold, 2000; Varnhagen, 2000). Empirical results dealing with the associations between spelling-specific self-beliefs and overall school attitudes solely issue from own previous research activities. In particular, statistically significant correlations had been found between elementary fourth-graders' spelling-specific test anxiety and negative school attitudes. Students who reported a higher level of test anxiety also reported more negative school attitudes (Faber, 1995a, 2002b).

Taking up these preliminary analyses of cross-sectional data, the present study aimed at an investigation of longitudinal construct relations. In particular, a structural model including students' spelling achievement, spelling-specific self-concept and test anxiety as well as their global self-esteem and school attitudes should be tested. The variable of school attitudes was conceptualized in the most general sense as disliking school in various aspects – referring to the students' negative perceptions of schooling, school climate and teacher behavior in the classroom. According to the basic model of academic self-beliefs in the spelling domain (Figure 13), this recursive structural model predicted the relations among constructs in a sequentially conceptualized order: the latent self-concept variable should be strongly affected by the latent spelling achievement variable. All other relations concerning the achievement variable were predicted to be less strong in magnitude. The latent test anxiety variable at measurement time 2 should be directly affected by the latent self-concept variable and, in turn, should directly and most strongly affect the latent self-esteem variable at measurement time 2. The latent school attitudes variable at measurement time 2 was hypothesized to be directly affected by the latent self-esteem variable. Taken altogether, this structural model predicted a pattern of longitudinal construct relations in a sequentially outlined order with the spelling-specific test anxiety variable mediating the spelling-specific self-concept and achievement effects to the general variables. As theoretically assumed, both general constructs should differ in cognitive-motivational functioning: whereas the global self-esteem will operate more internalizing, school attitudes will operate more externalizing. Consequently, the direct effect from the test anxiety variable on the self-esteem variable should be stronger in magnitude than on the school attitudes variable.

RESULTS

Relations among Constructs

Here again, this model of longitudinal construct relations was tested by means of the structural equation modeling procedure. Due to the high overlap among self-belief variables (Table 10), two subsequent steps of statistical analysis were conducted. In order to reduce multicollinearity effects and to avoid an inflated size of degrees of freedom (Kline, 2011), in a first step the cross-lagged relations among the latent test anxiety, self-esteem, and school attitudes variables were considered. All latent constructs were indicated by manifest item parcels. As the results of this initial analysis could demonstrate, aside from the autoregressive path coefficients only the cross-lagged path from prior test anxiety to subsequent self-esteem was statistically significant. Neither prior test anxiety scores nor prior self-esteem scores had any substantial impact on subsequent attitude scores. Similarly, prior school attitudes did not have any substantial impact on subsequent test anxiety or self-esteem scores (Figure 24). Particularly this finding indicated the mediating key role of test anxiety within construct relations and thus could contribute to specify the structural model for further testing. Overall, this initial model could fit the data in a statistically just acceptable manner (Figure 24).

Table 10. Correlations among achievement, self-concept, test anxiety, and school attitudes at measurement time 1 and 2

	DICT 1	LPprob 1	copDIC 1	negAFF 1	spANX 2	gloSE 2	ngATT 2
TSR 1	.87	-.63	.59	-.23	-.54	.36	-.18
DICT 1		-.61	.59	-.23	-.52	.37	-.15
LPprob 1			-.63	.48	.65	-.54	.27
copDIC 1				-.40	-.44	.33	-.17
negAFF 1					.31	-.31	.44
spANX 2						-.62	.32
gloSE 2							-.30

Significance: All Coefficients $p < .01$

TSR = Teacher Rating of Spelling Performance, DICT = Latest Dictation Mark, LPprob = Perceived Learning and Performance Problems, copDIC = Coping with Classroom Dictations, negAFF = Negative Affective Evaluations, spANX = Spelling-Specific Test Anxiety, gloSE = Global Self-Esteem, ngATT = Negative School Attitudes

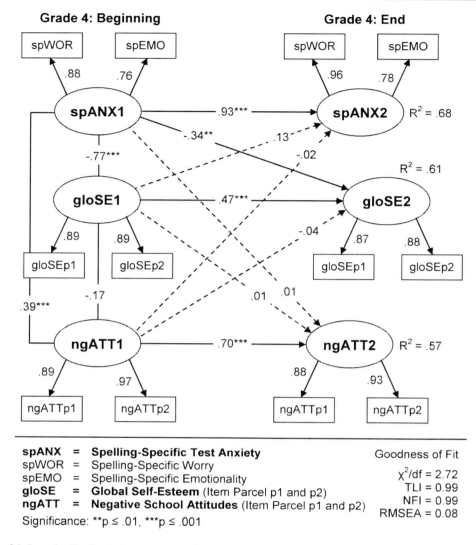

Figure 24. Longitudinal relations among school attitudes, self-esteem and test anxiety: results of structural equation modeling.

Accordingly, in a second step the final structural model was analyzed. It included the latent self-concept variable only at measurement time 1 and the latent test anxiety as well as the latent self-esteem and attitude variable only at measurement time 2. Additionally, the latent achievement variable was entered at measurement time 1. It was indicated by two single manifest items. As the results of structural equation analysis could demonstrate, the latent self-esteem variable at measurement time 2 could be best predicted by the latent test anxiety variable at measurement time 2 which, in turn, was most strongly affected by the latent self-concept variable at measurement time 1. The latent achievement variable at measurement time 1 could substantially predict the latent self-concept variable. With regard to all other constructs, their relations were statistically insignificant. However, the latent attitude variable at measurement time 2 could not be explained by any of the model variables (Figure 25). Though this model appeared to fit the data in a statistically just acceptable manner, it could not confirm the predictive role of self-belief variables with regard to general school attitudes. Instead, the attitude construct was demonstrated to take a completely independent position within the structural framework under consideration.

This result could have been conceptually and methodologically determined. As the zero-order correlations among manifest variables could indicate, the school attitudes were differently related to both facets of the spelling-specific self-concept. The attitude variable appeared to be more strongly related to the subscale measuring the students' negative affective evaluations than with the subscale measuring their perceived learning and performance problems (Table 10).

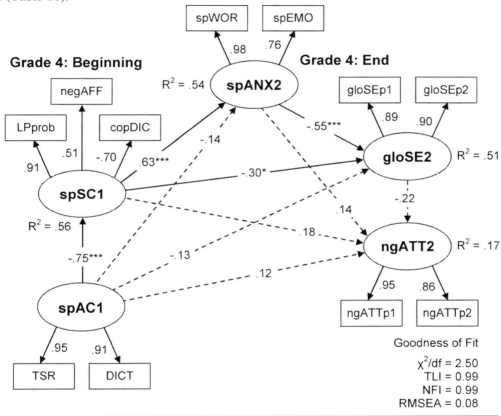

spSC = Spelling-Specific Self-Concept
LPprob = Perceived Learning and Performance Problems
copDIC = Perceived Coping with Classroom Dictations
negAFF = Negative Affective Evaluations
spAC = Spelling Achievement
TSR = Teacher Rating of Spelling Performance
DICT = Latest Dictation Mark
spANX = Spelling-Specific Test Anxiety
spWOR = Spelling-Specific Worry
spEMO = Spelling-Specific Emotionality
gloSE = Global Self-Esteem (Item Parcel p1 and p2)
ngATT = Negative School Attitudes (Item Parcel p1 and p2)
Significance: *p ≤ .05, ***p ≤ .001

Figure 25. Relations among achievement, self-concept, test anxiety, self-esteem and school attitudes: result of structural equation modeling.

Thus, the use of a highly aggregated latent self-concept variable including both self-concept facets as manifest indicators could have masked these differentiating aspects of construct relations. Therefore, a revised and trimmed model version was tested additionally. It included both self-concept facets as separate but correlated latent variables which were indicated by manifest item parcels. Furthermore, the latent achievement variable was deleted as it could not explain any substantial variance in the dependent self-esteem and attitude variable. The results of this structural equation analysis could draw a more differentiated picture of construct relations. According to the second analysis, here again, the latent self-esteem variable at measurement time 2 could be best predicted by the test anxiety variable at measurement time 2 – which in turn appeared to be strongly affected by the perceived learning and performance problems at measurement time 1. The negative affective evaluations of spelling exerted a strong direct effect upon the negative school attitudes at measurement time 2. Furthermore, negative school attitudes were – moderately but statistically significant – predicted by the spelling-specific test anxiety variable. Overall, this revised model could claim to fit the data well (Figure 26).

Table 11. Relations among spelling-specific and general academic self-concept, test anxiety and school attitudes: results of structural equation modeling

	LPprob 1	negAFF 1	spANX 2	gASC 2	gloSE 2
spANX 2	.790***	-.069			
gASC 2	-.252*	.052	-.523***		
gloSE 2	-.096	-.062	-.420***	.257***	
ngATT 2	-.349*	.538***	.172	-.293*	-.060

Goodness of Fit
$\chi^2/df = 1.19$, TLI = 0.99, NFI = 0.99, RMSEA = 0.03
LPprob = Perceived Learning and Performance Problems, negAFF = Negative Affective Evaluations, spANX = Spelling-Specific Test Anxiety, gASC = General Academic Self-Concept, ngATT = Negative School Attitudes

For further differentiation, this revised model was extended. In order to explore the generalizing effects of spelling-specific self-beliefs in the most differentiated way, the general academic self-concept at measurement time 2 was additionally included. Though achieving an improved model fit, the structural equation result could not yield any substantial improvement. In this extended model version, the effects of test anxiety on global self-esteem appeared to be partially mediated by the academic self-concept variable (Table 11).

However, the negative path between prior perceptions of learning and performance problems to subsequent school attitudes was somewhat unexpected and paradoxical in nature. Due to possible collinearities among self-belief constructs, a certain moderator effect could be assumed. Despite the significant positive relation of students' perceived learning and performance problems with their negative school attitudes (r = .27, p < .01) in the two path diagrams, it appeared to be associated with lowered negative attitudes. An additionally calculated analysis of variance with the attitude variable as dependent and both self-concept facets as factor variables could unravel this issue. Interindividually existing differences in students' negative school attitudes could be explained by their negative affective evaluations of spelling (F = 13.797, df = 2,244, p = 000, Eta^2 = .105). The main effect of perceived learning and performance problems was statistically insignificant (F = 0.658, df = 2,244, p = .519). In particular, students with high negative evaluations of spelling displayed the highest level of negative school attitudes across all levels of perceived learning and performance problems (Figure 27).

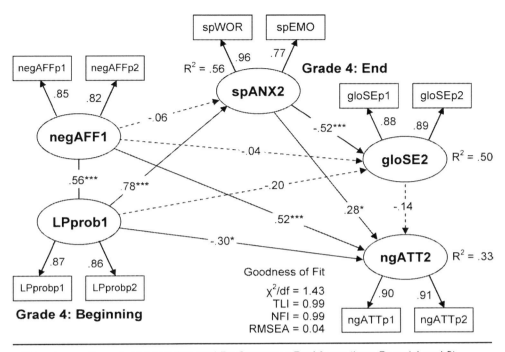

Figure 26. Relations of negative affective evaluations and perceived learning and performance problems in spelling with test anxiety, self-esteem and school attitudes: results of structural equation modeling.

Therefore, within the subgroup of students with strongly perceived learning and performance problems in spelling high and moderate as well as low levels of negative affective evaluations occurred. Once statistically controlled for negative affective evaluations, the perceived learning and performance problems will force a misleading regression result.

Change Over Time

With regard to their possible change across both measurement times, the school attitudes scores were compared by means of an analysis of variance with repeated-measure design. Here again, in order to get most differentiated results the students' spelling performance as assessed by individual teacher ratings and their gender were additionally used as independent factor variables. Thus a 2 (measurement time) x 3 (teacher spelling ratings) x 2 (gender) way analysis was calculated. In sum, the results could not demonstrate any significant main or interaction effect depending on achievement and gender differences over time. Moreover, interindividually existing differences in negative school attitudes could be moderately but significantly explained by the students' spelling achievement (Table 12).

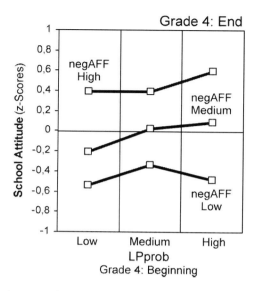

Figure 27. Mean differences in general school attitudes depending on negative affective evaluations (negAFF) and perceived learning and performance problems (LPprob) in spelling.

Table 12. Change over time in school attitudes depending on achievement differences and gender

Negative School Attitudes Within Subjects	Wilks λ	F	df	p	Eta²
MT	0.999	0.126	1,230	.723	.001
MT × TSR	0.998	0.274	2,230	.761	.002
MT × Gender	0.998	0.405	1,230	.525	.002
MT × TSR × Gender	0.988	1.406	2,230	.247	.012
Between Subjects TSR		5.608	2,230	.038	.028

MT = Measurement Time, TSR = Teacher Rating of Spelling Performance

DISCUSSION

To summarize, the structural equation analyses of longitudinal data could replicate and refine the relevant findings of previous studies (Faber, 1995a, 2002b). According to the theoretical assumptions concerning the relations among constructs the global self-esteem variable appeared to be strongly dependent on the spelling-specific test anxiety variable – which in turn was substantially affected by the spelling-specific self-concept variable.

With regard to the negative school attitudes, the findings appeared to be more complicated. Within the theoretically hypothesized framework of construct relations, they constituted a unique factor being completely independent from self-belief and achievement constructs. Only when entering the facets of the latent self-concept construct as separated variables into a revised structural equaling modeling approach the results became more differentiated. They then could demonstrate the negative school attitudes at measurement time 2 to be strongly affected by the negative affective evaluations of spelling at measurement time 1. Furthermore, though theoretically hypothesized as mediated by the self-esteem variable, spelling-specific test anxiety had rather a direct impact on the attitude variables. Therefore, the students' negative perceptions of schooling and teacher behavior always will reflect their individually impairing threat experiences. Nevertheless, the relations between negative school attitudes and the other constructs were still statistically insignificant.

Most importantly, the structural equation results of the revised model versions could outline the problem of latent construct conceptualization. If the latent variable being analyzed in a certain framework will subsume manifest indicator variables which refer to empirically overlapping but conceptually and processually yet distinguishable components or facets, the statistically achieved confirmation of construct relations might yield exaggerated complexities – consequently, highly aggregated modeling variables might lead to less meaningful and valid solutions which are principally prone to mask relevant structural relations. In particular, complications of this type will primarily threaten multivariate analyses of complex cognitive-motivational constructs which comprise structurally more homogeneous but functionally more heterogeneous components or facets (Pekrun, 1988).

Apart from this, an additionally conducted analysis of variance could not demonstrate any differences in negative school attitudes across measurement times. Hence, they appeared to be quite stable. Also there were no significant gender or achievement effects over time. Again, this particular finding might refine relevant results in the field as the impact of students' gender had been controlled for spelling achievement (Goodenow, 1993; Ireson & Hallam, 2005; Valeski & Stipek, 2001; Whaley-Klahn, Loney, Weissenburger & Prinz, 1976). From a developmental perspective, these findings indicate the students' negative attitudes to be less dynamic over time. As they will emerge on the background of individually accumulated and most diverse experiences they will, therefore, inadequately reflect changes in students' academic or school-relevant perspectives.

With regard to the spelling domain, the results of the present study could contribute not only to refine previous findings but also to revise relevant theoretical assumptions. Most notably, negative affective evaluations of educational spelling demands evidently contributed to heightened negative school attitudes. Therefore, spelling-specific self-beliefs do have a generalizing effect beyond subject matter. This effect can be both direct and indirect in nature as concerning the mediational role of test anxiety. In line with conceptual assumptions, the direct relation between self-concept in the spelling domain and general school attitudes appears to be somewhat stronger in magnitude as commonly reported among general constructs only (Connolly, Hatchette & McMaster, 1998; Goodenow, 1993; Meier & McDaniel, 1974). However, this finding also concerns the validity of construct operationalizations. In particular, it raises the question whether the negative affective evaluations of spelling are likely to constitute an affective subcomponent of the self-concept construct or a subject-specific subcomponent of the attitudinal construct. Further research should clarify this issue within a broadened framework of self-concept and attitude constructs.

Also the present study failed to confirm the conceptually predicted relation between the students' global self-esteem and their school attitudes. As the self-esteem variable was significantly related to spelling-specific test anxiety, this finding, altogether, lends support to the assumption that self-esteem and school attitudes will play rather distinctive roles in cognitive-motivational processing.

Further research should clarify this issue not only with regard to the spelling domain in elementary grades. It would be worthwhile to analyze the longitudinal relations among relevant constructs from a conceptually extended perspective and to consider differences as well as similarities across grade levels and domains or subjects. In order to further differentiate those potentially generalizing effects of subject-specific self-beliefs, it should be also worthwhile to decompose the attitudinal construct using empirically separable operationalizations for assessing particular dimensions or components – e.g., concerning the overall school involvement, perceived teacher support, classroom climate, and peer relations (Dart, Burnett, Boulton-Lewis, Campbell, Smith & McCrindle, 1999; Fraser, 1994; Libbey, 2004; Marshall & Weinstein, 1984).

Chapter 9

CAUSAL ATTRIBUTIONS OF SUCCESS AND FAILURE IN SPELLING

SCALE DEVELOPMENT AND RESEARCH OBJECTIVES

Over time, students develop individually definitive competence and control beliefs which are most prevailingly represented in their academic self-concept and causal attributions. The construct of self-attributions refer to their subjective explanations of own success and failure in an academic domain or subject. In particular, these explanations inevitably reflect a certain cause being internal or external as well as being stable or variable – and thus being always more or less controllable. Following Weiner's (2010) prominent classification scheme, students will generally attribute positive or negative outcomes to their own ability and effort, to the difficulty of a task or to luck. In the meantime, however, numerous research findings could extend this conceptualization and consistently demonstrate that students generally were able to use various causal ascriptions beyond these original four factors – e.g. emotional mood, task familiarity, use of learning strategies, support and quality of classroom instruction or teacher support. With increasing age their causal attributions appeared to become more refined and differentiated though the attributional core factors ability and effort did not lessen in importance (Connell, 1985; Frieze & Snyder, 1980; Mok, Kennedy & Moore, 2011; Pekrun, 1983; Raviv, Bar-Tal, Raviv & Bar-Tal, 1980).

From a cognitive-motivational perspective, the type of an individually inferred cause largely depends on a student's processing of socially, temporally, and contextually available information (Kelley & Michela, 1980). Likewise, this information processing will be more strongly affected by his or her academic self-concept than by achievement outcome only. Accordingly, relevant studies could demonstrate the students' self-perceptions to be more strongly related to outcome attributions than related achievement measures (Faber, 1990; Frieze, 1980). Furthermore, with regard to the multidimensional and multifaceted nature of academic self-beliefs, causal attributions are assumed to be domain- or subject-specific. However, previous empirical analyses could yield only mixed results. Most consistently, the subject-specific structure of internal ability and effort attributions could be demonstrated – whereas the subject-specific structure of external attributions appeared to be less clear (Marsh, 1984b; Marsh, Cairns, Relich, Barnes & Debus, 1984; Moreano, 2004; Vispoel & Austin, 1995). Nevertheless, in all relevant studies the students' internal attributions were evidently more closely associated with their subject-specific self-concept than with their academic performance. Hence, in a given domain or subject the students' self-concept obviously played an important mediating role in the formation of internal attributions at least (Butkowsky & Willows, 1980; Marsh, 1986b; Moreano, 2004; Nicholls, 1979; Watkins & Gutierrez, 1989). Due to individually existing competence experiences and beliefs, in the long term, typically habitualized attribution tendencies will emerge and gradually lead to the formation of attributional patterns which in turn will influence the students' academic engagement and learning behaviors (Heckhausen, 1987). Across most diverse research designs and sample characteristics, particular attributional patterns could be consistently found. Especially poor achieving students with lowered competence beliefs were more likely to attribute their failure to a lack of own ability and their success to external support or luck. Thus, they suffered from stronger feelings of uncontrollability, resignation, and helplessness (Abramson, Garber & Seligman, 1980). Contrarily, normally or high achieving students with moderate or heightened competence beliefs were more likely to attribute their success to own ability or effort and failure, if at all, to a lack of own effort or external constraints (Bell, McCallum, Bryles, McDonald, Park & Williams, 1994; Butkowsky & Willows, 1980; Faber 1990; Nicholls, 1979; Pekrun, 1983). In particular, internal ability attributions of failure and external attributions of success will lead to seriously reduced or even suspended agency expectancies and must, therefore, be considered as a cognitive-motivational risk factor which will impede the students' perspectives to alter maladaptive learning behaviors and to actively reach for improved learning outcomes (Skinner, Zimmer-Gembeck & Connell, 1998).

Taken altogether, students' attributional patterns to explain own academic outcomes will claim a crucial role in supporting or hindering their further academic development – e.g. with regard to self-regulated learning approaches. Accordingly, educational settings should know this issue and systematically foster their students' appropriate control beliefs (Schunk, 2008; Zimmerman, 2000).

With regard to the spelling domain, only few studies had investigated the structure and role of causal attributions. Unfortunately, most of them had used general control belief or attribution measures for analyzing their relation with spelling achievement or individually existing spelling disabilities, respectively. Consequently, their results were less consistent and could, at best, demonstrate rough trends (Dodds, 1994; Frederickson & Jacobs, 2001; Humphrey & Mullins, 2002; Petkovic, 1980). Against this, only the studies of Bruning and colleagues (Rankin, Bruning & Timme, 1994; Shell, Colvin & Bruning, 1995) explicitly had analyzed students' attributions of spelling outcomes. Across various grade levels, significant relations of spelling outcome attributions with self-efficacy expectancies, but not with spelling performance, could be found.

Furthermore, as a part of own previous research activities, elementary fourth-graders´ spelling-related attributions were analyzed. Using Weiner's classic causal factors (Weiner, 2010), the students were asked to rate the importance of ability, effort, task difficulty, and luck for explaining spelling success and failure. As the results from two independent studies could show, only the ability attributions for success and failure as well as the luck attributions for success could be considered subject-specific. Students with poor spelling achievement and a low spelling-specific self-concept were more likely to attribute success to good luck and failure to a lack of own ability. However, one particular finding was theoretically unexpected. Especially students with lowered self-concept scores explained failure not only with a lack of own ability but also with a lack of own effort. Though inferring inferior spelling abilities, they blamed themselves for less appropriate practicing (Faber, 1996, 2002a). Against the background of learning helplessness theory, this finding appeared, at first glance, contradictory – however, it could also indicate the students' compensatory understanding of own ability and effort expenditure (Heckhausen, 1987). In sum, these previous results could partially support the subject-specificity of causal attribution measures – but also could point out their limitations. Therefore, a conceptually and methodologically extended approach should use more differentiated causal factors. In this respect, the effort factor in particular was still held much too general. Its operationalization depended on one single item and was semantically rather complex in nature. Thus, this item could have been interpreted very differently by each individual student.

For this reason, in the present study an item pool had been devised including 14 relevant causal factors, for the most part following the general attribution scale Pekrun (1983) had presented. In detail, these items referred to a series of internal and external causes which in turn also tapped the stability dimension – and as such, indicated various levels of personal controllability. The effort factor was related to the students' practicing at home and during classroom instruction. As further internal causes, the students' spelling competence or ability, their interest in spelling and their enjoyment in completing spelling tasks were included. As external causes, the difficulty of spelling tasks, the quality of teacher instruction, the perceived teacher relation, the feeling of being disturbed during classroom dictation, and luck were included. Altogether, two separate scales for assessing success and failure attributions with regard to a dictation outcome were administered. Each scale consisted of 6 items with internal causes and 8 items with external causes. The students were asked to rate the importance of each causal factor for explaining success and failure. As this instrument was newly developed no psychometric or validation information was available.

Therefore, it was the main objective of the present study to clarify the scales' underlying dimensionality and thus to determine an appropriate framework for final scale construction. This first step concerned the structural feature of the attribution construct – namely, whether it could distinctively represent the locus of control and the stability aspects as operationalized in the manifest attribution items (Weiner, 2010).

The final scale versions should then be tested with respect to their psychometric properties. With this proviso, the relations of their sum scores with relevant achievement and self-belief variables should be analyzed. According to the multifaceted nature of academic self-beliefs, these analyses should clarify to what extent the attribution scales could be considered spelling-specific and, hence, were most closely associated with spelling-related achievement and self-belief variables.

For further validation, students' attributional patterns depending on achievement level and self-concept should be explored. Against the background of relevant consistency theories (Bradley, 1978; Chapman & Lawes, 1984; Ickes & Layden, 1978), it was hypothesized that especially poor achieving students with lowered competence beliefs should display an attributional pattern that explained failure more internally and success more externally. In contrast, normally and best achieving students with moderate to heightened competence beliefs should display an attributional pattern that explained success more internally and failure more externally. In detail, in should be also investigated which attributional pattern referred to more stable or variable causes, respectively. And finally, possible changes across both measurement times in the scales' sum scores should be analyzed.

RESULTS

Dimensional Analyses and Scale Formation

For each measurement time, separate principal components analyses were devised for success and failure attributions. Due to the initially obtained eigenvalues (Cattell, 1966), two-factorial solutions were extracted and rotated by means of the varimax procedure.

At measurement time 1, the first five eigenvalues for the items assessing success attributions amounted to $e_1 = 24.7$, $e_2 = 16.0$, $e_3 = 9.5$, $e_4 = 8.1$, $e_5 = 6.9$, and for the items assessing failure attributions $e_1 = 28.5$, $e_2 = 12.0$, $e_3 = 8.8$, $e_4 = 7.6$, $e_5 = 6.6$. At measurement time 2, the eigenvalues for the items assessing success attributions amounted to $e_1 = 25.8$, $e_2 = 16.9$, $e_3 = 10.6$, $e_4 = 7.0$, $e_5 = 6.2$, and for the items assessing failure attributions $e_1 = 31.6$, $e_2 = 12.0$, $e_3 = 10.1$, $e_4 = 7.4$, $e_5 = 6.4$. These results led to a two-factorial solution at both measurement times which presents itself as quite succinct and consistent in each case (Table 13). For success attributions, the two factors could explain 40.7% of the total variance at measurement time 1, and 42.7% of the total variance at measurement time 2. For failure attributions, they could explain 41.5% of the total variance at measurement time 1, and 42.7% of the total variance at measurement time 2. All items could be used as factorial marker variables (Fürntratt, 1969) at both measurement times, insofar as their factor loadings turned out sufficiently high ($a \geq .40$) and contributed in a substantial degree to the respective communalities ($a^2/h^2 \geq .50$).

Among the success attributions, those items were loading high on factor 1 at both measurement times which referred to external causes. Aside from the good luck item, these items were articulating various aspects of the classroom and home learning setting – among others, remarkably and somewhat unexpected, both effort items as well. This external success factor could explain 22.4% of the rotated variance at measurement time 1, and 23.6% of the rotated variance at measurement time 2. On factor 2, those items were loading high at both measurement times which referred to internal causes. Aside from the items for ability, interest, and fun, both teacher relation items showed remarkably strong loadings. This internal success factor could explain 18.3% of the rotated variance at measurement time 1, and 19.1% of the rotated variance at measurement time 2.

Among the failure attributions, quite similar results could be found: with only slight differences, those items which referred to the practicing at home and during classroom instruction were also loading high on factor 1 at both times of measurement – likewise including both effort items. This external failure factor could explain 23.2% of the rotated variance at measurement time 1, and 22.1% of the rotated variance at measurement time 2 (Table 13). On factor 2, those items were again loading high at both measurement times which referred to internal causes – including both teacher relation items here as well. This internal failure factor could explain 18.3% of the rotated variance at measurement point 1, and 21.5% of the rotated variance at measurement time 2.

As the success items suc04 (attentiveness in class) and suc07 (well-being) did not allow for a distinct and consistent factorial interpretation across both measurement times, they were excluded from further analyses and not taken into consideration in the formation of respective subscales. The same applied to the failure items fail02 (bad luck) and fail07 (lack of well-being).

On the basis of these dimensional analyses, overall 24 items could eventually be used for the formation of final subscales:

Table 13. Principal components analyses of causal attribution items at measurement time 1 and 2 (a = factor loadings, h² = communalities)

Item	Measurement Time 1 a_1	a_2	h^2	Measurement Time 2 a_1	a_2	h^2
Success Attributions						
suc 01	-.240	**.644**	.499	-.339	**.621**	.771
suc 04	.328	.353	.232	.353	.427	.308
suc 06	-.021	**.832**	.694	-.088	**.826**	.691
suc 09	-.023	**.777**	.605	-.069	**.753**	.571
suc 12	.194	**.477**	.265	.252	**.478**	.292
suc 14	.251	**.513**	.326	.230	**.496**	.299
suc 02	**.506**	-.136	.275	**.553**	-.197	.345
suc 03	**.549**	.111	.314	**.557**	.029	.311
suc 05	**.576**	-.041	.333	**.552**	.135	.322
suc 07	.482	.299	.322	.353	.439	.318
suc 08	**.795**	.127	.513	**.719**	.092	.525
suc 10	**.632**	-.008	.400	**.671**	.082	.456
suc 11	**.690**	.057	.479	**.756**	.031	.572
suc 13	**.614**	.251	.440	**.599**	.326	.465
Failure Attributions						
fail 01	.152	**.708**	.524	.199	**.594**	.392
fail 06	.188	**.768**	.625	.088	**.668**	.455
fail 09	.221	**.739**	.596	.177	**.709**	.534
fail 12	.031	**.605**	.368	.073	**.721**	.525
fail 14	.125	**.575**	.346	.047	**.758**	.578
fail 02	.377	.149	.164	.169	.288	.111
fail 03	**.503**	.135	.271	**.628**	.077	.400
fail 04	**.538**	.149	.311	**.652**	.047	.428
fail 05	**.656**	.066	.434	**.550**	.167	.330
fail 07	.491	.221	.290	.378	.492	.385
fail 08	**.655**	.143	.451	**.655**	.217	.476
fail 10	**.663**	.297	.529	**.592**	.411	.519
fail 11	**.742**	.035	.552	**.758**	.145	.595
fail 13	**.594**	-.004	.353	**.604**	.123	.380

Item List: Appendix B

- The scale "Internal Success Attributions" (INsuc) consists of 5 items. It measured the perceived relevance of success causes dependent upon the person. Students with high total scores explain good dictation outcomes with their own ability, with interest and fun in spelling, with their sympathy for the teacher, as well as the teacher's suspected sympathy for the student.

- The scale "External Success Attributions" (EXsuc) consisted of 7 items. It measured the perceived relevance of success causes depending upon good luck and the environment, in particular classroom and home influences. Students with high total scores explained positive dictation outcomes with good luck, sufficient practice and exercise efforts at home, a low level of task difficulty, and favorable classroom learning conditions.
- The scale "Internal Failure Attributions" (INfail) consisted of 5 items. It measured the perceived relevance of failure causes depending upon personal characteristics. Students with high total scores explained negative dictation outcomes with a lack of ability, with a lack of interest and enjoyment in spelling, with their lack of sympathy for the teacher, as well as an inferred lack of the teacher's sympathy for them.
- The scale "External Failure Attributions" (EXfail) consisted of 7 items. It measured the perceived relevance of home and classroom causes for failure in dictations. Students with high total scores explained negative dictation outcomes with insufficient practice and exercise at home, with a high level of task difficulty, as well as with unfavorable classroom learning conditions.

All subscales turned out to be reasonably reliable (Table 1). With regard of their intercorrelations, they could be empirically well separated. However, it was particularly striking that the external success and failure attributions were positively correlated to a moderate but significant degree. Hence, those students who ex-plained success to be externally determined also blamed external causes with regard to failure. The retest correlations for all subscales appeared to be moderate to low (Table 14).

Table 14. Intercorrelations and retest coefficients (underlined) of the attribution scales at measurement time 1 and 2

Causal Attributions		INsuc	EXsuc	INfail	EXfail
INsuc	1		.13*	-.33***	-.08
	2	.49***	.09	-.37***	-.07
EXsuc	1			.18**	.38***
	2		.44***	.24***	.49***
INfail	1				.38***
	2			.57***	.41***
EXfail	1				
	2				.36***

Significance: *$p \leq .05$, **$p \leq .01$, ***$p \leq .001$
INsuc = Internal Success Attributions, EXsuc = External Success Attributions
INfail = Internal Failure Attributions, EXfail = External Failure Attributions

Validation Results

Concerning their relations with relevant achievement variables only for the internal attribution scales, subject-specific correlations could be demonstrated. At both measurement times, internal success as well as internal failure attributions were more strongly related to the spelling than to the mathematics outcome measures (Table 15).

Table 15. Correlations of attribution subscales with students' achievement, self-beliefs, and gender (at measurement time 1 and 2)

Validation Variables		INsuc	EXsuc	INfail	EXfail
Spelling Test	1	.23***	-.16**	-.34***	-.12*
	2	.18**	-.18**	-.37***	-.20**
Spelling Rating	1	.26***	-.12	-.48***	-.16**
	2	.24***	-.22***	-.50***	-.20**
Math Rating	1	-.07	.17**	-.29***	.13*
	2	.08	-.13*	-.27***	-.15*
LPprob	1	-.37***	.22***	.56***	.34***
	2	-.26***	.29***	.61***	.33***
copDIC	1	.47***	-.08	-.41***	-.19**
	2	.41***	-.21***	-.50***	-.17**
negAFF	1	-.58***	-.04	.50***	.13*
	2	-.48***	.15*	.55***	.17**
Test Anxiety	1	-.24***	.22***	.48***	.32***
	2	-.22***	.29***	.56***	.33***
Academic Self	1	.41***	-.08	-.43***	-.14*
	2	.38***	-.19**	-.50***	-.15*
Self-Esteem	1	.15*	-.04	-.42***	-.22***
	2	.18*	-.15*	-.48***	-.20**
Gender	1	-.10	-.01	-.16**	-.02
	2	.01	-.08	-.13*	.03

Significance: *$p \leq .05$, **$p \leq .01$, ***$p \leq .001$
INsuc = Internal Success Attributions, EXsuc = External Success Attributions, INfail = Internal Failure Attributions, EXfail = External Failure Attributions, LPprob = Perceived Learning and Performance Problems, copDIC = Perceived Coping with Classroom Dictations, negAFF = Negative Affective Evaluations

In contrast, external success as well as external failure attributions showed similar correlations across subjects at both measurement times. Concerning their relations with relevant self-belief variables at both measurement times, all attribution subscales appeared to be more closely related to the spelling-specific self-concept than to the general academic self-concept variable. In particular, the relations among attributions and perceived learning and performance problems in spelling were most strongly in magnitude. Also, all attribution subscales were significantly related to the spelling-specific test anxiety variable. Those students who attributed spelling success more internally reported a lesser degree of test anxiety whereas those students who attributed spelling success more externally reported a higher degree of test anxiety. This also applied to those students who attributed spelling success and failure more externally. Thus, explaining spelling outcomes with uncontrollable causes evidently led to increasing threat expectancies. Accordingly, the relations between internal as well as external failure attributions with the global self-esteem variable were significantly negative – thus indicating an impairing effect of perceived uncontrollability beyond academic concerns. Significant gender differences could be only found in internal failure attributions. To a lower but significant degree, girls attributed spelling failure more internally than boys.

Table 16. Relations between causal attributions and concurrent achievement and self-belief measures: Results of multiple regression analyses (at measurement time 1 and 2)

Predictor Variables	Causal Attributions			
	INsuc	EXsuc	INfail	EXfail
Achievement Measures				
Spelling Rating 1	.321***	.016	-.454***	-.103
Math Rating 1	-.122	-.183*	-.026	-.069
Adjusted R^2	.065	.023	.214	.016
Spelling Rating 2	.292***	-.215**	-.509***	-.174*
Math Rating 2	-.084	-.003	.021	.047
Adjusted R^2	.056	.039	.241	.034
Self-Belief Measures				
LPprob 1	.046	.440***	.275***	.382***
copDIC 1	.225**	.044	.036	-.035
negAFF 1	-.492***	-.197**	.304***	-.044
Academic Self 1	.154*	.012	-.131	.115
Self-Esteem 1	-.096	.159*	-.138*	-.042
Adjusted R^2	.416	.076	.393	.107
LPprob 2	.185*	.274**	.264**	.366***
copDIC 2	.218**	-.014	-.070	.040
negAFF 2	-.419***	.040	.344***	.055
Academic Self 2	.235**	-.017	-.098	.081
Self-Esteem 2	-.031	.040	-.157*	-.023
Adjusted R^2	.313	.066	.498	.096

Significance: *$p \leq .05$, **$p \leq .01$, ***$p \leq .001$

INsuc = Internal Success Attributions, EXsuc = External Success Attributions, INfail = Internal Failure Attributions, EXfail = External Failure Attributions, LPprob = Perceived Learning and Performance Problems, copDIC = Perceived Coping with Classroom Dictations, negAFF = Negative Affective Evaluations

In order to control for construct interrelations, multiple regression analyses were conducted additionally. Altogether, their results could elaborate and confirm the correlational findings for both measurement times (Table 16). For the most part, attributions of dictation outcomes could be best predicted by spelling achievement measures. However, the external success subscale could be significantly predicted by the students' mathematics performance. With regard to the self-belief constructs, internal success and failure attributions appeared to be most strongly correlated with the students negative affective evaluations of spelling –

whereas the external success and failure attributions appeared to be most strongly correlated with the students' perceived learning and performance problems. Hence, attributing spelling failure more internally was associated with more aversive feelings against relevant demands. Attributing spelling success or failure more externally was associated with stronger perceptions of incompetence and helplessness. Controlling for interrelations between constructs, the role of global self-esteem was neglectibly small or even insignificant. Hence, it would have been mostly mediated by the students' spelling-specific self-concept. In sum, these findings could demonstrate a nomologically interesting pattern of re-lations. Students with positive spelling-specific self-concepts were more likely to attribute success internally and failure externally. Students with negative spelling-specific self-concepts were more likely to attribute success externally and failure internally as well as externally. According to conceptual assumptions, the self-belief variables could explain more empirical variance in students' attributions than the achievement variables.

Table 17. Causal attributions of success (at measurement time 1 and 2) depending on differences in spelling achievement and self-concept

Internal Success Attributions Factor Variables	F	df	p	Eta^2
Measurement Time 1				
LPprob	13.583	1,256	.000	.050
TSR	1.830	2,256	.163	.014
LPprob × TSR	1.408	2,256	.246	.011
Measurement Time 2				
LPprob	1.910	1,235	.168	.008
TSR	1.756	2,235	.175	.015
LPprob × TSR	0.169	2,235	.845	.001
External Success Attributions Factor Variables	F	df	p	Eta^2
Measurement Time 1				
LPprob	2.140	1,256	.145	.008
TSR	2.098	2,256	.125	.016
LPprob × TSR	2.389	2,256	.094	.019
Measurement Time 2				
LPprob	5.750	1,235	.017	.024
TSR	5.828	2,235	.003	.048
LPprob × TSR	0.480	2,235	.586	.005

LPprob = Perceived Learning and Performance Problems
TSR = Teacher Rating of Spelling Performance

Attributional Patterns

In order to further clarify the correlational results, relevant differences in students' attributions depending on their achievement and self-concept level were investigated. For that purpose several one-way analyses of variance were calculated with the teacher spelling ratings and the perceived problems subscale of students' spelling-specific self-concept as factor variables. Using the terciles in the raw score distribution of teacher ratings and the median in the raw score sums of the relevant self-concept measure, the student sample was split into three performance and two self-concept subgroups. In order to avoid unnecessary redundancy effects, only data from the LPrpb-subscale (perceived learning and performance problems) were considered.

Table 18. Causal attributions of failure (at measurement time 1 and 2) depending on differences in spelling achievement and self-concept

Internal Failure Attributions				
Factor Variables	F	df	p	Eta^2
Measurement Time 1				
LPprob	25.171	1,256	.000	.091
TSR	10.687	2,256	.000	.078
LPprob × TSR	0.290	2,256	.748	.002
Measurement Time 2				
LPprob	22.493	1,235	.000	.089
TSR	10.878	2,235	.000	.086
LPprob × TSR	0.024	2,235	.976	.009
External Failure Attributions				
Factor Variables	F	df	p	Eta^2
Measurement Time 1				
LPprob	9.865	1,256	.002	.038
TSR	0.375	2,256	.687	.003
LPprob × TSR	0.499	2,256	.608	.004
Measurement Time 2				
LPprob	12.715	1,235	.000	.052
TSR	1.673	2,235	.190	.014
LPprob × TSR	1.507	2,235	.224	.013

LPprob = Perceived Learning and Performance Problems
TSR = Teacher Rating of Spelling Performance

With respect to the internal success attributions at measurement time 1, a significant main effect of the self-concept factor could be found (Table 17). Students with more strongly perceived learning and performance problems attribute spelling success to a significantly lesser degree to internal causes. However, this effect did not appear at measurement time 2. Furthermore, only at measurement time 2 significant main effects of the performance and the self-concept factor could explain interindividually existing differences in external success attributions. In particular, those poor and average achieving students who perceived more strongly learning and performance problems in spelling attributed success to a higher degree to external causes. All other main or interaction effects did not reach statistical significance. With respect to the internal failure attributions at both measurement times, significant main effects of the self-concept and achievement factor occurred (Table 18). Especially those students with a more negative self-concept and poorer performance scores assigned internal causes as being more relevant. Similarly, with respect to the external failure attributions, a significant main effect of the self-concept factor could be found at both measurement times. Across all performance levels, those students attributed spelling failure to a stronger degree on external causes who reported a more negative self-concept.

According to theoretical assumptions and empirical findings in the field, the self-concept variable could evidently more strongly contribute to explain the students' attributional patterns than the achievement variable. Interindividually existing differences in the students' spelling specific self-concept appeared to more properly determine success and failure attributions even across various performance levels – and thus could indicate their mediating role in cognitive-motivational functioning. Therefore, in order to further enlighten this issue, several analyses of variance with only the self-concept as factor variable were conducted. As the results could demonstrate at both measurement times, highly significant main effects occurred for all attribution subscales (Table 19).

Table 19. Causal attributions (at measurement time 1 and 2) depending on differences in spelling-specific self-concept

Factor Variable	F	df	p	Eta^2
Internal Success Attributions Measurement Time 1				
LPprob	30.464	1,272	.000	.101
External Success Attributions Measurement Time 1				
LPprob	13.640	1,272	.000	.050
Internal Failure Attributions Measurement Time 1				
LPprob	58.410	1,272	.000	.216
External Failure Attributions Measurement Time 1				
LPprob	20.888	1,272	.000	.078
Internal Success Attributions Measurement Time 2				
LPprob	9.011	1,256	.003	.036
External Success Attributions Measurement Time 2				
LPprob	19.547	1,256	.000	.077
Internal Failure Attributions Measurement Time 2				
LPprob	53.952	1,256	.000	.213
External Failure Attributions Measurement Time 2				
LPprob	22.751	1,256	.000	.090

LPprob = Perceived Learning and Performance Problems

In particular, those students who more strongly perceived learning and performance problems in spelling attributed success less internally and more externally. Moreover, they attributed failure more internally and somewhat lesser externally – but even more strongly than their classmates who displayed a positive self-concept (Figure 28). Hence, students with lowered self-concepts were blaming both internal and external causes for failure and thus performed a lesser degree of explanative distinctiveness as well as a higher degree of explanative intensity.

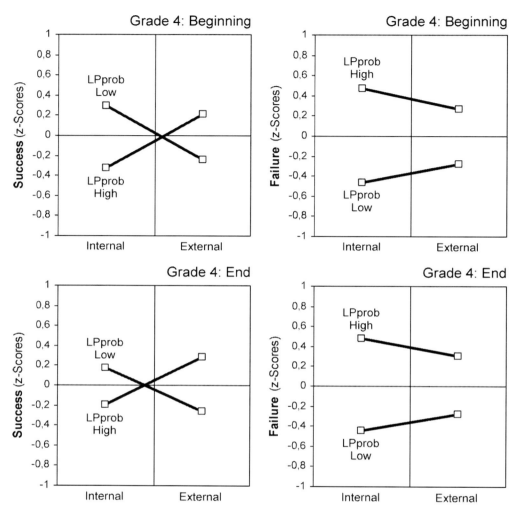

Figure 28. Mean differences in causal attributions of dictation outcomes depending on perceived learning and performance problems (LPprob) in spelling.

Change Over Time

With regard to their possible change across both measurement times, the mean scores of all attribution scales were compared by means of an analysis of variance with repeated-measure design. Here again, in order to get most differentiated results, the students' spelling-specific self-concept and their gender were additionally used as independent factor variables. Thus several 2 (measurement time) x 3 (teacher spelling ratings) x 2 (gender) way analyses were calculated. In sum, the results could not demonstrate any significant main or interaction effect depending on self-concept and gender differences over time. Moreover, interindividually existing differences in all success and failure attributions could be significantly explained by the students' perceived learning and performance problems (Table 20).

Table 20. Change over time in success and failure attributions depending on differences in spelling-specific self-concept and gender

Internal Success Attributions Within Subjects	Wilks λ	F	df	p	Eta²
MT	1.000	0.081	1,240	.776	.000
MT × LPprob	0.989	2.563	1,240	.111	.011
MT × Gender	0.999	0.216	1,240	.642	.001
MT × LPprob × Gender	0.998	0.545	1,240	.461	.002
Between Subjects					
LPprob		21.017	1,240	.000	.081
External Success Attributions Within Subjects	Wilks λ	F	df	p	Eta²
MT	0.999	0.349	1,240	.555	.001
MT × LPprob	0.996	1.014	1,240	.315	.004
MT × Gender	0.993	1.757	1,240	.186	.007
MT × LPprob × Gender	0.997	0.735	1,240	.392	.003
Between Subjects					
LPprob		24.152	1,240	.000	.091
Internal Failure Attributions Within Subjects	Wilks λ	F	df	p	Eta²
MT	1.000	0.002	1,240	.961	.000
MT × LPprob	0.988	2.991	1,240	.085	.012
MT × Gender	0.995	1.137	1,240	.287	.005
MT × LPprob × Gender	0.999	0.226	1,240	.635	.001
Between Subjects					
LPprob		70.764	1,240	.000	.228
External Failure Attributions Within Subjects	Wilks λ	F	df	p	Eta²
MT	1.000	0.029	1,240	.864	.000
MT × LPprob	1.000	0.028	1,240	.868	.000
MT × Gender	1.000	0.002	1,240	.960	.000
MT × LPprob × Gender	0.998	0.502	1,240	.479	.002
Between Subjects					
LPprob		27.400	1,240	.000	.102

MT = Measurement Time
LPprob = Perceived Learning and Performance Problems

DISCUSSION

The findings of the present study could, first of all, extend previous research results and led to the formation of separate subscales for measuring the students' causal attributions in the spelling domain which were based on a broader set of explanative causes (Faber, 1996, 2002a). Though these final scale versions could distinctly reflect the locus of control dimension of causes, they could not reflect their underlying stability dimension. Moreover, as principal components analyses indicated, the dimensional feature of spelling attributions appeared to be more complicated than theoretically predicted. In particular, the students interpreted the effort causes as a component part of the educational setting – quasi as a requirement to be mastered reactively. They perceived the matter of practicing at home or during classroom instruction as causal influences being not controllable – and thus they were not responsible for them. This most defensive explanation of success and failure in spelling might possibly reflect a kind of protective self-worth management (Covington, 1992). It is this perspective which possibly might explain the positive correlations between external success and failure attributions. In this regard, the findings of previous own studies appear, in retrospect, in a somewhat different light (Faber, 1996, 2002a). This particular finding has, of course, to be replicated in other students samples before sufficiently explicable. However, conceptually and methodologically it also suggests the need for using more differentiated effort attributions – e.g. concerning the students' study skills and learning strategies in the spelling domain (Connell, 1985; Mok, Kennedy & Moore, 2011). Accordingly, further analyses should clarify whether this external interpretation of effort attributions might be a spelling-specific phenomenon in students' causal inferences – and whether it might be dependent on developmental trends or grade level differences, respectively.

With this proviso, the results of the present study could also provide partial support for the subject-specificity of students' spelling attributions – at least with regard to the internal attribution scales. Though this finding was completely in line with relevant research from other domains or subjects, it deserves further attention (Marsh, 1984b, 1986b; Moreano, 2004; Vispoel & Austin, 1995; Watkins & Gutierrez, 1989). Due to the commonly strong relationships between competence beliefs and ability attributions, it underlines the determining role of subject-specific self-concepts with regard to related ability attributions. But this relationship cannot profoundly explain existing differences in external attributions of subject-specific outcomes. As there is consistent evidence for external attributions to generalize across domains or subjects (Vispoel & Austin, 1995) the use of external causes to attribute subject-specific outcomes should be affected by other cognitive-motivational mechanisms. Especially this issue has to be further analyzed with regard to most diverse academic domains and student characteristics.

Apart from this, the findings of the present study could also produce clear evidence for interindividually existing attribution patterns. They became most distinctive when relating to differences in students' spelling-specific self-concepts. Altogether, these findings could lend support for relevant self-consistency perspectives (Heckhausen, 1987; Marsh, 1986b) as they indicated elementary students with more positive self-perceptions to use more competence-based, and elementary students with more negative self-perceptions to use more helpless, attributions for success and failure in spelling. Especially the latter group's attribution pattern must be considered in terms of reduced controllability expectancies and suspended agency perspectives which in the long term might provoke a state of personal helplessness (Abramson, Garber & Seligman, 1980; Shell, Colvin & Bruning, 1995).

Chapter 10

SUMMARY AND CONCLUSION

STUDY RESULTS

The present study had analyzed the spelling-specific self-beliefs of elementary fourth-graders across two measurement times. In sum, its results could extend and elaborate empirical knowledge about this issue in various aspects:

- The analysis of a somewhat revised questionnaire for measuring the spelling-specific self-concept led at both measurement times to three distinct but correlated subscales concerning the students' perceived learning and performance problems, coping with classroom dictations, and negative affective evaluations. All three subscales could display sufficient psychometric properties. With relevant achievement and self-belief constructs they were correlated in a subject-specific manner – and thus they could claim construct validity.

- With respect to their causal ordering, the analysis of longitudinal achievement and self-concept data could strongly support the skill development perspective on construct relations. In particular, structural equation results using both spelling test and spelling grade variables as achievement measures revealed equally fitting models.

- In order to further differentiate the spelling-specific self-concept construct, a unidimensional scale for measuring the students' error-related self-estimates was analyzed. Its relations with relevant achievement and self-belief variables could support the idea of a more task-specific self-concept facet within the spelling domain. In particular, the sum score of error estimations was able to incrementally explain empirical variance in students' spelling achievement. Moreover, it could mediate the effects of spelling achievement on the self-concept variable.

- According to theoretical assumptions, the global self-esteem variable appeared to be strongly affected by the spelling-specific test anxiety variable which in turn was substantially affected by the self-concept variable. Hence, negative competence beliefs and heightened threat expectancies in the spelling domain could influence the students' self-beliefs beyond academic concerns.

- An analysis of relations between spelling-specific constructs and the students' general school attitudes revealed more complicated findings. Only when using particular subscales instead of the whole latent self-concept construct, a strong correlation between the students' negative affective evaluations and their negative school attitudes could be demonstrated.

- A newly developed instrument for measuring the students' causal attributions of dictation outcomes was analyzed. The scale construction was based on a broader set of explanative causes tapping internal and external as well as more stable and more variable factors. At both measurement times, principal components analyses led to four separable subscales assessing internal and external attributions of success and failure. Though these subscales could distinctly reflect the locus of control dimension, they could not reflect the stability dimension of attributions. Moreover, correlational analyses at both measurement times could demonstrate only the internal subscales to correlate with relevant achievement and self-belief constructs in a subject-specific manner.

- Further analyses of these attributional subscales could also substantiate different attributional patterns for student subgroups. Whereas students with more positive self-perceptions were more likely to use competence-based attributions, students with more negative self-perceptions were more likely to use helpless attributions for success and failure in spelling.

- Analyses of changes over time could indicate all variables under consideration being relatively stable across both measurement times.

- And finally, in all analyses the role of students' gender appeared to be mostly low or marginal, respectively.

Taken altogether, these results could contribute to further clarify the issue of spelling-specific self-beliefs at the elementary grade level and thus, not least, reduce some conceptual and methodological shortcomings of previous studies in the field (Frederickson & Jacobs, 2001; Humphrey, 2002a,b; Riddick, 2010; Ridsdale, 2004). However, they also indicated the need for further analyzing several aspects of construct operationalizations and construct relations.

CONCEPTUAL IMPLICATIONS

With regard to the theoretical framework of construct relations which has been represented in the basic model of academic self-beliefs (Figure 9), the crucial role of the spelling-specific self-concept variable appears to be largely confirmed and refined. In terms of causal ordering, the spelling-specific self-concept is directly affected by prior achievement and in turn directly affects subsequent test anxiety. Hence, the self-concept variable mediates interindividually existing differences in spelling achievement to the students' threat expectancies which directly have a negative impact on their global self-esteem (Figure 29). These direct and mediated effects among constructs are completely in line with theoretical assumptions (Marsh & Craven, 2006; Zeidner, 1998) and demonstrate, in particular, the generalizing influences of spelling-specific self-beliefs beyond the students' academic concerns. Altogether, the relations among self-concept, test anxiety and causal attributions evidently play a crucial role in determining the students' cognitive-motivational orientations (Martin, 2002). However, they refer to longitudinal data from the beginning to the end of one school year and cannot completely clarify the reciprocal relations and transactional processes in the long term. For a more comprehensive perspective on construct relations, their contextual determinants must be considered. Further investigations should include relevant variables for conceptually embedding the relations among individual variables – e.g., concerning the role of potentially existing big-fish-little pond effects of classroom achievement levels, the role of perceived classroom climate, the impact of teacher behavior and teacher expectancies on spelling-specific and general self-beliefs (Fraser, 1994; Meece, Glienke & Askew, 2009; Marsh & Hau, 2003; Pekrun, 1985; Rubie-Davies, 2010; Treutlein & Schöler, 2009).

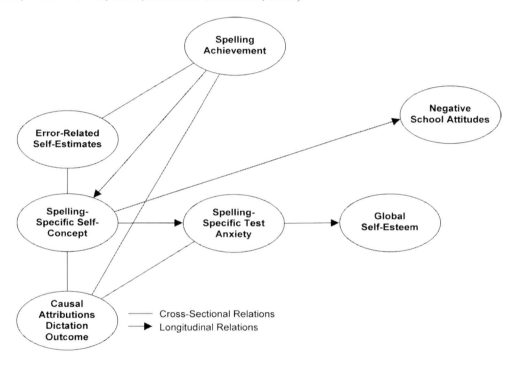

Figure 29. Relations among achievement and self-belief constructs: empirical findings of the present study.

Furthermore, the present findings have demonstrated again the spelling-specific self-concept to represent not only cognitive but also affective facets. According to empirical results reported elsewhere (Arens, Yeung, Craven & Hasselhorn, 2011; Marsh, Craven & Debus, 1999), a subscale for measuring the students' negative affective evaluations of spelling can be separated. Both cognitive and affective facets appear to empirically overlap but conceptually represent distinguishable information. However, as particular findings of the present study also can show, the students' negative affective evaluations of spelling correlate most strongly with the students' negative school attitudes. Thus, this particular subscales' construct validity has to be further clarified. Possibly, various self-beliefs and attitude constructs might more strongly be associated on a subject-specific than on a general level of conceptualization.

Analyzing the role of error-related self-estimates, the present findings have also addressed the issue of further construct differentiation. Theoretically, these findings not only confirm the structural perspectives concerning the multifaceted feature of subject-specific competence beliefs; they can also demonstrate that it might be conceptually worthwhile to refer construct operationalizations to more task-specific characteristics.

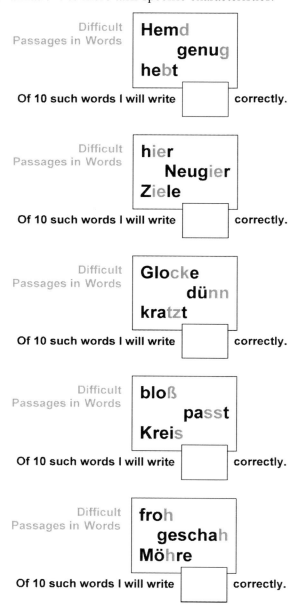

Figure 30. Measuring error-related self-estimates: an alternate scale format.

However, this first step in differentiating the spelling-specific self-concept deserves further attention. The most descriptive error categories used in the present study might be one possible operationalization of error estimations. Their generalizability across different grade levels will be strongly limited as the students' conceptions of spelling-errors will change with increasing grade level and spelling demands. Thus, it can be assumed that appropriate operationalizations of error estimations must gradually reflect relevant characteristics of changing word materials and spelling tasks – e.g., with respect to various types of orthographic spelling rules. For that purpose, an alternate scale format has been developed and analyzed meanwhile. It consists of visually represented types of orthographic errors (Figure 30).

The students are asked to rate the number of words they expect to spell correctly. Though referring to a highly aggregated level of task characteristics, its response format appears to be more closely reflecting a self-efficacy perspective (Phan & Walker, 2000; Rankin, Bruning & Timme, 1994). As the results of a small pilot study with N = 54 preadolescent students with spelling difficulties could show, this scale had psychometrically sufficient consistency coefficients (Cronbach's alpha α = .87 at measurement time 1 and α = .82 at measurement time 2). Furthermore, its sum scores could be demonstrated to substantially correlate with self-concept measures in spelling (r = .41, p < .01) but not in mathematics (r = 09, p > .05). Thus, this scale can be considered subject-specific. Further research should clarify the role of these error-estimates within the framework of relevant constructs and in particular analyze their association with self-concept and achievement variables (Ferla, Valcke & Cai, 2009; Marsh & Yeung, 1998).

Another conceptually striking problem refers to the construct of causal attributions. The findings of the present study have failed to separate the stability dimension of causal attributions (Weiner, 2010). Moreover, the attribution items focusing on the students' efforts in practicing appear to be interpreted as external causes of success and failure. This particular finding addresses the need for alternate operationalizations of the effort cause. Within the framework of construct relations, however, both the internal and external attributions are associated with the students' achievement and self-beliefs as theoretically predicted. However, subject-specific correlation patterns only occur in the case of internal attributions – thus confirming the results of previous research (Marsh, 1984b, 1986b; Moreano, 2004; Vispoel & Austin, 1995; Watkins & Gutierrez, 1989). With regard to the conceptual framework of spelling-specific self-beliefs, this issue remains yet unresolved and should be further analyzed. Evidently the development of external attributions will be determined by other than subject-specific factors. Further analyses should therefore seek to directly explore the students' perceptions and interpretations of external causes.

The findings of the present study have also demonstrated the students' gender to contribute only marginally to interindividually existing differences in spelling-specific as well as in general self-beliefs. As this particular result only refers to a sample of elementary fourth-graders, further analyses should address this aspect in order to follow up emerging gender differences across grade levels (Bornholt, Goodnow & Cooney, 1994; Hergovich, Sirch & Felinger, 2004; Wilgenbusch & Merrell, 1999).

And finally, a conceptually and educationally most import variable of academic self-belief and achievement relations has been absolutely neglected in the present study – namely, the analysis of the students' learning behavior (Figure 9). As the present study has primarily aimed at an investigation of self-belief constructs, this constraint has been thought to be defensible. With respect to a broader research perspective, properly designed analyses of relations among self-beliefs, achievement and learning behavior within the spelling domain will essentially depend on appropriate knowledge about self-belief constructs and evaluated self-belief instruments as well. However, the relations between self-belief and achievement variables are assumed to be substantially mediated by relevant behavioral variables. In particular, the students' study skills, learning strategies, and classroom behaviors will claim an important role in mediating spelling-specific self-beliefs to spelling outcomes (Chapman, Tunmer & Prochnow, 2004; Määttä, Stattin & Nurmi, 2002; Mantzipcopoulos, 1990; Phan, 2010; Skinner, Wellborn & Connell, 1990). In this regard, a wide field of research efforts is foreseeable in the future. Relevant analyses should clarify the reciprocal relations between spelling-specific self-beliefs and learning behaviors in the spelling domain most differentiated – e.g. concerning the causal links between the students' self-concept, causal attributions, self-regulating strategies and achievement outcomes (Pintrich & Zusho, 2002; Zimmerman, 2000).

METHODOLOGICAL IMPLICATIONS

With regard to research methodology, the findings of the present study may indicate a twofold perspective.

With regard to construct operationalizations, the instrument for measuring students' causal attributions does not sufficiently represent the explanations for success and failure in the spelling domain. Instead, the results point out the need for further extending the range of possible explanations (Connell, 1985; Mok, Kennedy & Moore, 2011; Normandeau & Gobeil, 1998) – especially to further refine the assessment of effort-related causes. Therefore, a revised version of spelling-specific attribution scales should also include items concerning the use of learning strategies, the role of perceived teacher support, and the relevance of task-specific characteristics beyond difficulty perceptions. Similarly, the use of an unidimensional scale for measuring the students' general school attitudes might have masked relevant relations among constructs. Further research should, therefore, seek to decompose this construct into its relevant facets and design an instrument which allows for assessing separable aspects of school attitudes (Dart, Burnett, Boulton-Lewis, Campbell, Smith & McCrindle, 1999; Rowe, Kim, Baker, Kamphaus & Horne, 2010).

With regard to the research design, the present study appears to be limited in several ways. As it refers to longitudinal data from elementary fourth grade only, its causal ordering results are less generalizable. Moreover, the present study has included two measurement times only. Consequently, further analyses should use a broader time interval as well as a student sample across various grade levels. In that way, longitudinal results should more strongly allow for robust causal and developmental interpretations. Additionally, with regard to relevant contextual determinants of spelling-specific self-beliefs, further research should also use multilevel modeling methods (Heck & Thomas, 2009) to identify existing differences in students' cognitive-motivational orientations across various classrooms (Köller, Zeinz & Trautwein, 2008; Tiedemann & Billmann-Mahecha, 2004, 2006; Treutlein & Schöler, 2009).

EDUCATIONAL IMPLICATIONS

With the reservation of research perspectives, the findings of the present study also may offer several implications for educational settings, especially for classroom instruction in spelling and remedial spelling training. First of all, the students' competence, control, and threat expectancies substantially represent their cognitive-motivational orientations in the spelling domain. Hence, the measurement of relevant self-beliefs should be subject-specific. The use of assessment procedures which refer to more general construct operationalizations must come, therefore, as a misconception. In order to explore the cognitive-motivational orientations of students with spelling difficulties, it should be reasonably argued for spelling-specific measures of the core constructs – in particular, to get educationally useful information about the students' individually existing self-concept, test anxiety, and causal attributions. This does not necessarily rule out the assessment of more general self-beliefs – if explicitly aiming at the psychoemotional consequences of spelling-specific self-beliefs. Furthermore, as cognitive-motivational characteristics cannot adequately be inferred from overt student behavior, informal teacher observations are prone to biased judgments. Instead, educational measurements should be absolutely based on psychometrically well-proven self-belief instruments (Argulewicz & Miller, 1985; Faber, 2001, 2006b; Medway, 1979).

Furthermore, the findings of the present study have lent support for the causal predominance of spelling achievement over the spelling-specific self-concept – thus supporting a skill development perspective on causal ordering. This particular result, however, must be understood against the background of the research design and does not allow for a one tailored view of construct relations. Rather, the students' achievement and self-concept will be reciprocally related over time. Therefore, educational interventions should not focus on either fostering the students' spelling skills or supporting their self-perceptions (Marsh, 2006). Instead, they should, in any case, consider both aspects. Most importantly, they should refer to subject-specific perspectives (O'Mara, Marsh, Craven & Debus, 2006). Spelling instructions or remedial spelling interventions which succeed in positively influencing both the students' spelling skills and their spelling-specific self-beliefs will reflect the process of subject-specific learning at best.

Therefore, appropriate educational settings will need an institutionally well-established and empirically well-evaluated system of most diverse strategies and methods to remedy or prevent students' spelling difficulties. These strategies and methods should contribute to scaffold the students' learning process and to facilitate most relevant experiences of controllability and agency (Englert & Marriage, 2003; Hogan & Pressley, 1997). As Hay (2005) convincingly argues, for that purpose it might be considered an essential prerequisite to strengthen the students' elementary cognitive skills and self-related abilities – e.g. concerning their competencies to adequately verbalize own experiences, feelings and expectancies and to think more reflectively about their learning.

Remedial treatments in the spelling domain should always integrate the students' self-beliefs and thus should principally warrant most transparent and self-relevant learning situations. In particular, the students should receive individually tailored and differentiated feedback concerning their strengths and problems in spelling as well as documenting their competence development (Faber, 1989a; Hattie & Timperley, 2007; van Oudenhoven, Siero, Veen & Siero, 1982). Accordingly, feedback procedures should be used to initiate and foster mastery-oriented attributions of own success and failure – thus especially stressing the relevance of learning strategies as causal factors (Robertson, 2000; Schunk, 2008). Most transparent learning requirements and individual feedback procedures should also contribute to reduce the students' threat expectancies and test anxiety, respectively (Suppon, 2004). Furthermore, the use of task-specific information should enable the students to develop more realistic self-efficacy beliefs which might, in the long term, substantially support their acquisition of spelling skills and learning strategies (Cleary, 2009; Klassen, 2007). For instance, the students' error-related self-estimates might be used to assess and modify their task-specific self-perceptions – e.g. by means of intervention modules which will enhance the students' participation in remedial assessment, planning, and evaluation.

In order to establish a most transparent, differentiated, and self-relevant remedial setting, the systematic use of visualizing and verbalizing methods (Faber, 2006a) might be a fruitful approach: it seeks to scaffold the students' acquisition of spelling skills and strategies by means of algorithmic and self-instructional task formats. In particular, these task formats are designed to support the students' strategic competencies and control experiences. As several evaluation studies could demonstrate, this approach led to significantly increased spelling outcomes. Furthermore, it could significantly contribute to reduce the students' spelling-specific test anxiety (Faber, 2010). Accordingly, further intervention studies should also analyze the effects of remedial spelling training on the students' self-concept and causal attributions.

REFERENCES

Abramson, L.Y., Garber, J. & Seligman, M.E.P. (1980). Learned helplessness in humans: An attributional analysis. In J. Garber & M.E.P. Seligman (Eds.), *Human helplessness. Theory and applications* (pp. 3-34). New York: Academic Press.

Abu-Hilal, M.B. (2000). A structural model for predicting mathematics achievement: Its relation with anxiety and self-concept in mathematics. *Psychological Reports, 86,* 835-847.

Alban Metcalfe, B.M. (1981). Self-concept and attitude to school. *British Journal of Educational Psychology, 51,* 66-76.

Alexander-Passe, N. (2006). How dyslexic teenagers cope: an investigation of self-esteem, coping and depression. *Dyslexia, 12,* 256-275.

Alsaker, F.D. (1989). School achievement, perceived academic competence and global self-esteem. *School Psychology International, 10,* 147-158.

Alves-Martins, M., Peixoto, F., Gouveia-Pereira, M., Amaral, V. & Pedro, I. (2002). Self-esteem and academic achievement among adolescents. *Educational Psychology, 22,* 51-62.

Antunes, C. & Fontaine, A.M. (2007). Gender differences in the causal relation between adolescents' math self-concept and scholastic performance. *Psychologica Belgica, 47,* 71-94.

Arbuckle, J.L. & Wothke, W. (1999). *Amos 4.0 user's guide.* Chicago: SmallWaters Corporation.

Arens, A.K., Yeung, A.S., Craven, R.G. & Hasselhorn, M. (2011). The twofold multidimensionality of academic self-concept: Domain specificity and separation between competence and affect components. *Journal of Educational Psychology, 103,* 970-981.

Argulewicz, E.N. & Miller, D.C. (1985). Self-reported and teachers' rankings of anxiety among first-grade children. *School Psychology Review, 14,* 75-78.

Arnold, E.M., Goldston, D.B., Walsh, A.K., Reboussin, B.A., Daniel, S.S., Hickman, E. & Wood, F.B. (2005). Severity of emotional and behavioral problems among poor and typical readers. *Journal of Abnormal Child Psychology, 33,* 205-217.

Ashcraft, M.H. & Kirk, E.P. (2001). The relationship among working memory, math anxiety, and performance. *Journal of Experimental Psychology: General, 130,* 224-237.

Aunola, K., Leskinen, E., Onatsu-Arvilommi, T. & Nurmi, J.-E. (2002). Three models for studying developmental change: A case of reading skills and self-concept. *British Journal of Educational Psychology, 72,* 343-364.

Bäcker, A. & Neuhäuser, G. (2003). Internalisierende und externalisierende Syndrome bei Lese- und Rechtschreibstörungen. *Praxis der Kinderpsychologie und Kinderpsychiatrie, 52,* 329-337.

Baker, L. & Wigfield, A. (1999). Dimensions of children's motivation for reading and their relation to reading activity and reading achievement. *Reading Research Quarterly, 34,* 452-477.

Bandalos, D.L. (2002). The effects of item parceling on goodness-of-fit and parameter estimate bias in structural equation modeling. *Structural Equation Modeling, 9,* 78-102.

Bandalos, D.L., Yates, K. & Thorndike-Christ, T. (1995). Effects of math self-concept, perceived self-efficacy, and attributions for failure and success on test anxiety. *Journal of Educational Psychology, 87,* 611-623.

Bandura, A. (1986). *Social foundations of thought and action. A social cognitive theory.* Englewood Cliffs: Prentice-Hall.

Bandura, A. (2001). Social cognitive theory: An agentic perspective. *Annual Review of Psychology, 52,* 1-26.

Barker, K.L., Dowson, M. & McInerney, D.M. (2005). *Effects between motivational goals, academic self-concept and academic achievement: What is the causal ordering?* Paper presented at the annual Australian Association for Research in Education (AARE) Conference, Parramatta, Nov. 27 - Dec. 1, 2005.

Bar-Tal, D. & Darom, E. (1979). Pupils' attributions of success and failure. *Child Development, 50,* 264-267.

Bauer, C.F. (2005). Beyond "student attitudes": Chemistry self-concept inventory for assessment of the affective component of student learning. *Journal of Chemical Education, 82,* 1864-1870.

Becker, P., Schneider, J. & Schumann, C. (1975). Über die Bereichsspezifität der Angstneigung. Ein Beitrag zur situationsbezogenen Eigenschaftsmessung. *Psychologische Beiträge, 17,* 112-132.

Bell, S.M., McCallum, R.S., Bryles, J., McDonald, J., Park, S.H. & Williams, A. (1994). Attributions for academic success and failure: An individual difference investigation of academic achievement and gender. *Journal of Psychoeducational Assessment, 12,* 4-13.

Bender, W.N. & Wall, M.E. (1994). Social-emotional development of students with learning disabilities. *Learning Disability Quarterly, 17,* 323-341.

Bhanot, R. & Jovanovic, J. (2005). Do parents' academic gender stereotypes influence whether they intrude on their children's homework? *Sex Roles, 52,* 597-607.

Biermann, H. (1992). *Chancengerechtigkeit in der Grundschule – Anspruch und Wirklichkeit.* Frankfurt/Main: Lang.

Blackwell, L.S., Trzesniewski, K.H. & Dweck, C.S. (2007). Implicit theories of intelligence predict achievement across an adolescent transition: A longitudinal study and an intervention. *Child Development, 78,* 246-263.

Bleeker, M.M. & Jacobs, J.E. (2004). Achievement in math and science: Do mothers' beliefs matter 12 years later? *Journal of Educational Psychology, 96,* 97-109.

Boekaerts, M. (1996). Personality and the psychology of learning. *European Journal of Personality, 10,* 377-404.

Boersma, F.J., Chapman, J.W. & Maguire, T.O. (1979). The Student's Perception of Ability Scale: An instrument for measuring academic self-concept in elementary school children. *Educational and Psychological Measurement, 39,* 1035-1041.

Boggiano, A.K., Main, D.S., Flink, C., Barrett, M., Silvern, L. & Katz, P. (1989). A model of achievement in children: The role of controlling strategies in helplessness and affect. In R. Schwarzer, H.M. van der Ploeg & C.D. Spielberger (Eds.), *Advances in test anxiety re-*

search. Volume 6 (pp. 13-26). Lisse: Swets and Zeitlinger.

Bong, M. & Skaalvik, E.M. (2003). Academic self-concept and self-efficacy: How different are they really? *Educational Psychology Review, 15,* 1-40.

Bornholt, L.J., Goodnow, J.J. & Cooney, G.H. (1994). Influences of gender stereotypes on adolescents' perceptions of their own achievement. *American Educational Research Journal, 31,* 675-692.

Bossong, B. (1994). Scholastic stressors and achievement-related anxiety. In J. Kuhl & J. Beckmann (Eds.), *Volition and personality. Action versus state orientation* (pp. 397-406). Seattle: Hogrefe and Huber Publishers.

Bottomley, D.M., Henk, W.A. & Melnick, S.A. (1997). Assessing children's views about themselves as writers using the Writing Self-Perception Scale. *The Reading Teacher, 51,* 286-296.

Bradley, G.W. (1978). Self-serving biases in the attributional process: A reexamination of the fact or fiction question. *Journal of Personality and Social Psychology, 36,* 56-71.

Britner, S.L. (2010). Science anxiety, Relationship to achievement, self-efficacy, and pedagogical factors. In J.C. Cassady (Ed.), *Anxiety in schools. The causes, consequences, and solutions for academic anxieties* (pp. 79-94). New York: Lang.

Britner, S.L. & Pajares, F. (2006). Sources of science self-efficacy beliefs of middle school students. *Journal of Research in Science Teaching, 43,* 485-499.

Brookover, W.B., Thomas, S. & Paterson, A. (1964). Self-concept of ability and school achievement. *Sociology of Education, 37,* 271-278.

Brophy, J. (1985). Interaction of male and female students with male and female teachers. In L.C. Wilkinson & C.B. Marrett (Eds.), *Gender influences in classroom interaction* (pp. 115-166). Orlando: Academic Press.

Brozo, W.G., Schmelzer, R.V. & Spires, H.A. (1983). The Reading Anxiety Scale: A better predictor of college reading achievement. *Journal of Learning Skills, 2*(4), 22-33.

Brunner, M., Keller, U., Dierendonck, C., Reichert, M., Ugen, S., Fischbach, A. & Martin, R. (2010). The structure of academic self-concept revisited: The nested Marsh/Shavelson model. *Journal of Educational Psychology, 102,* 964-981.

Brunner, M., Keller, U., Hornung, C., Reichert, M. & Martin, R. (2009). The cross-cultural generalizability of a new structural model of academic self-concept. *Learning and Individual Differences, 19,* 387-403.

Bryan, T., Burstein, K. & Ergul, C. (2004). The social-emotional side of learning disabilities: A science-based presentation of the state of the art. *Learning Disability Quarterly, 27,* 45-51.

Bryant, F.B. & Yarnold, P.R. (1995). Principal-components analysis and exploratory and confirmatory analysis. In L.G. Grimm & P.R. Yarnold (Eds.), *Reading and understanding multivariate statistics* (pp. 99-136). Washington: American Psychological Association.

Buehl, M.M. & Alexander, P.A. (2009). Beliefs about learning in academic domains. In K.R. Wentzel & A. Wigfield (Eds.), *Handbook of motivation at school* (pp. 479-501). New York: Routledge.

Burden, R. (2005). *Dyslexia and self-concept. Seeking a dyslexic identity.* London: Whurr.

Burden, R. (2008). Is dyslexia necessarily associated with negative feelings of self-worth? A review and implications of future research. *Dyslexia, 14,* 188-196.

Burden, R. & Burdett, J. (2005). Factors associated with successful learning in pupils with dyslexia: a motivational analysis. *British Journal of Special Education, 32,* 100-104.

Butkowsky, I.S. & Willows, D.M. (1980). Cognitive-motivational characteristics of children varying in reading ability: Evidence for learned helplessness in poor readers. *Journal of Educational Psychology, 72,* 408-422.

Butler, R. (1998). Age trends in the use of social and temporal comparison for self-evaluation: Examination of a novel developmental hypothesis. *Child Development, 69,* 1054-1073.

Byrne, B.M. (1986). Self-concept/academic achievement relations: An investigation of dimensionality, stability, and causality. *Canadian Journal of Behavioral Science, 18,* 173-186.

Byrne, B.M. (1996). Academic self-concept: Its structure, measurement, and relation to academic achievement. In B.A. Bracken (Ed.), *Handbook of self-concept. Developmental, social, and clinical considerations* (pp. 287-316). New York: Wiley.

Byrne, B. M. (2010). *Structural equation modeling with AMOS: Basic concepts, applications, and programming* (2nd ed.). New York: Routledge.

Byrne, B.M. & Shavelson, R.J. (1987). Adolescent self-concept: Testing the assumption of equivalent structure across gender. *American Educational Research Journal, 24,* 365-385.

Calsyn, R. & Kenny, D. (1977). Self-concept of ability and perceived evaluations by others: Cause or effect of academic achievement? *Journal of Educational Psychology, 69,* 136-145.

Campbell, M.A., Rapee, R.M. & Spence, S.H. (2001). The nature of feared outcome representations in anxious and non-anxious children. *Australian Journal of Guidance and Counselling, 11,* 85-99.

Carroll, J.M. & Iles, J.E. (2006). An assessment of anxiety levels in dyslexic students in higher education. *British Journal of Educational Psychology, 76,* 651-662.

Carroll, J.M., Maughan, B., Goodman, R. & Meltzer, H. (2005). Literacy difficulties and psychiatric disorders: evidence for comorbidity. *Journal of Child Psychology and Psychiatry, 46,* 524-532.

Cassady, J.C. (2001). The stability of undergraduate students' cognitive test anxiety levels. *Practical Assessment, Research and Evaluation, 7*(20).

Cassady, J.C. & Johnson, R.E. (2002). Cognitive test anxiety and academic performance. *Contemporary Educational Psychology, 27,* 270-295.

Cattell, R.B. (1966). The scree test for the number of factors. *Multivariate Behavioral Research, 1,* 245-276.

Chan, K.-W. (2000). Conceptualizing the role of beliefs in self-concept research. In R.G. Craven & H.W. Marsh (Eds.), *Self-concept theory, research and practice: Advances for the new millenium* (pp. 172-179). Collected papers of the inaugural Self-concept Enhancement and Learning Facilitation (SELF) Research Centre international conference, Sydney, Australia, October 5-6, 2000. University of Western Sydney: Self-concept Enhancement and Learning Facilitation (SELF) Centre.

Chanal, J.P., Marsh, H.W., Sarrazin, P.G. & Bois, J.E. (2005). Big-fish-little-pond effects on gymnastics self-concept: Social comparison processes in a physical setting. *Journal of Sport and Exercise Psychology, 27,* 53-70.

Chanal, J.P. & Sarrazin, P.G. (2007). Big-fish-little-pond effect versus positive effect of upward comparisons in the classroom: How does one reconcile contradictory results? *Revue Internationale de Psychologie Sociale, 20,* 69-86.

Chanal, J.P., Sarrazin, P.G., Guay, F. & Boiché, J. (2009). Verbal, mathematics, and physical education self-concepts and achievements: An extension and test of the internal/external frame of reference model. *Psychology of Sport and Exercise, 10,* 61-66.

Chapman, J.W. (1988). Learning disabled children's self-concepts. *Review of Educational Research, 58,* 347-371.

Chapman, J.W. & Boersma, F.J. (1979). Academic self-concept in elementary learning disabled children: A study with the Student's Perception of Ability Scale. *Psychology in the Schools, 16,* 201-206.

Chapman, J.W. & Lawes, M.M. (1984). Consistency of causal attributions for expected and actual examination outcome: A study of the expectancy confirmation and egotism models. *British Journal of Educational Psychology, 54,* 177-188.

Chapman, J.W. & Tunmer, W.E. (1995). Development of young children's reading self-concepts: An examination of emerging subcomponents and their relationship with reading achievement. *Journal of Educational Psychology, 87,* 154-167.

Chapman, J.W. & Tunmer, W.E. (1997). A longitudinal study of beginning reading achievement and reading self-concept. *British Journal of Educatinonal Psychology, 67,* 279-291.

Chapman, J.W. & Tunmer, W.E. (1999). Reading Self-Concept Scale. In R. Burden (Ed.), *Children's self-perceptions* (pp. 29-34). Windsor: NFER-Nelson.

Chapman, J.W., Tunmer, W.E. & Prochnow, J.E. (2004). Repressed resilience? A longitudinal study of reading, self-perceptions, and teacher behavior ratings of poor and average readers in New Zealand. *Thalamus, 22,* 9-15

Cheng, Y.-S. (2004). A measure of second language writing anxiety. Scale development and preliminary validation. *Journal of Second Language Writing, 13,* 313-335.

Cheng, Y.-S., Horwitz, E.K. & Schallert, D. (1999). Language anxiety: Differentiating writing and speaking components. *Language Learning, 49,* 417-446.

Chiu, M.-S. (2008). Achievements and self-concepts in a comparison of math and science: exploring the internal/external frame of reference model across 28 countries. *Educational Research and Evaluation, 14,* 235-254.

Chouinard, R., Karsenti, T. & Roy, N. (2007). Relations among competence beliefs, utility value, achievement goals, and effort in mathematics. *British Journal of Educational Psychology, 77,* 501-517.

Cialdini, R.B. & Richardson, K.D. (1980). Two indirect tactics of image management: Basking and blasting. *Journal of Personality and Social Psychology, 39,* 406-415.

Cleary, T.J. (2009). Monitoring trends and accuracy of self-efficacy beliefs during interventions: Advantages and potential applications to school-based settings. *Psychology in the Schools, 46,* 154-171.

Cloer, T. & Ross, S.Y. (1997). The relationship of standardized reading scores to children's self-perceptions as readers. In K. Camperel, B.L. Hayes & R. Telfer (Eds.), *American Reading Forum online yearbook. Volume XVII. Promises, progress, and possibilities: Perspectives on literacy education* (pp. 93-104). Newark: American Reading Forum.

Cole, D.A., Martin, J.M., Peeke, L.A., Seroczynski, A.D. & Fier, J. (1999). Children's over- and underestimation of academic competence: A longitudinal study of gender differences, depression, and anxiety. *Child Development, 70,* 459-473.

Connell, J.P. (1985). A new multidimensional measure of children's perception of control. *Child Development, 56,* 1018-1041.

Connolly, J.A., Hatchette, V. & McMaster, L.E. (1998). *School achievement of Canadian boys and girls in early adolescence: Links with personal attitudes and parental and teacher support for school.* Quebec: Human Resources Development Canada, Applied Research Branch.

Corbière, M., Fraccarolli, F., Mbekou, V. & Perron, J. (2006). Academic self-concept and academic interest measurement: A multi-sample European study. *European Journal of Psychology of Education, 21,* 3-15.

Cortina, J.M. (1993). What is coefficient alpha? An examination of theory and applications. *Journal of Applied Psychology, 78,* 98-104.

Covington, M.V. (1984). The self-worth theory of achievement motivation: Findings and implications. *Elementary School Journal, 85,* 5-20.

Covington, M.V. (1985). Strategic thinking and the fear of failure. In J.W. Segal, S.F. Chipman & R. Glaser (Eds.), *Thinking and learning skills. Volume 1: Relating instruction to research* (pp. 389-416). Hillsdale: Erlbaum.

Covington, M.V. (1986). Anatomy of failure-induced anxiety: The role of cognitive mediators. In R. Schwarzer (Ed.), *Self-related cognitions in anxiety and motivaton* (pp. 247-263). Hillsdale: Erlbaum.

Covington, M.V. (1992). *Making the grade. A self-worth perspective on motivation and school reform.* New York: Cambridge University Press.

Covington, M.V. & Omelich, C.L. (1987). "I knew it cold before the exam": A test of the anxiety-blockage hypothesis. *Journal of Educational Psychology, 79,* 393-400.

Craven, R.G. & Marsh, H.W. (2008). The centrality of the self-concept construct for psychological wellbeing and unlocking human potential: Implications for child and educational psychologists. *Educational and Child Psychology, 25,* 104-118.

Cretchley, P.C. (2008). Advancing research into affective factors in mathematics learning: Clarifying key factors, terminology, and measurement. In M. Goos, R. Brown & K. Makar (Eds.), *Proceedings of the 31st Annual Conference of the Mathematics Education Research Group of Australasia.* Volume 1 (pp. 147-153). Adelaide: MERGA.

Croizet, J.-C., Désert, M., Dutrévis, M. & Leyens, J.-P. (2001). Stereotype threat, social class, gender, and academic under-achievement: when our reputation catches up to us and takes over. *Social Psychology of Education, 4,* 295-310.

Cvencek, D., Meltzoff, A.N. & Greenwald, A.G. (2011). Math-gender stereotypes in elementary school children. *Child Development, 82,* 766-779.

Dai, D.Y. (2002). Incorporating parent perceptions: A replication and extension study of the internal-external frame of reference model of self-concept development. *Journal of Adolescent Research, 17,* 617-645.

Daniels, Z. (2008). *Entwicklung schulischer Interessen im Jugendalter.* Münster: Waxmann.

Dart, B., Burnett, P., Boulton-Lewis, G., Campbell, J., Smith, D. & McCrindle, A. (1999). Classroom learning environments and students' approaches to learning. *Learning Environments Research, 2,* 137-156.

deCharms, R. (1977). Students need not to be pawns. *Theory into Practice, 16,* 296-301.

Deffenbacher, J.L. (1980). Worry and emotionality in test anxiety. In I.G. Sarason (Ed.), *Test anxiety: Theory, research and applications* (pp. 111-128). Hillsdale: Erlbaum.

De Fraine, B., Van Damme, J. & Onghena, P. (2007). A longitudinal analysis of gender differences in academic self-concept and language achievement: A multivariate multilevel latent growth approach. *Contemporary Educational Psychology, 32,* 132-150.

Dew, K.M.H., Galassi, J.P. & Galassi, M.D. (1984). Math anxiety: Relation with situational test anxiety, performance, physiological arousal, and math avoidance behavior. *Journal of Counseling Psychology, 31*, 580-583.

Dickhäuser, O. (2005a). A fresh look: testing the internal/external frame of reference model with frame-specific academic self-concepts. *Educational Research, 47*, 279-290.

Dickhäuser, O. (2005b). Teachers' inferences about students' self-concepts – the role of dimensional comparison. *Learning and Instruction, 15*, 225-235.

Dickhäuser, O. & Galfe, E. (2004). Besser als... schlechter als... Leistungsbezogene Vergleichsprozesse in der Grundschule. *Zeitschrift für Entwicklungspsychologie und Pädagogische Psychologie, 36*, 1-9.

Dickhäuser, O. & Meyer, W.-U. (2006). Gender differences in young children's math ability attributions. *Psychology Science, 48*, 3-16.

Dickhäuser, O., Reuter, M. & Hilling, C. (2005). Coursework selection: A frame of reference approach using structural equation modeling. *British Journal of Educational Psychology, 75*, 673-688.

Dickhäuser, O., Seidler, A. & Kölzer, M. (2005). Kein Mensch kann alles? Effekte dimensionaler Vergleiche auf das Fähigkeitsselbstkonzept. *Zeitschrift für Pädagogische Psychologie, 19*, 97-106.

Dickhäuser, O. & Stiensmeier-Pelster, J. (2003). Wahrgenommene Lehrereinschätzungen und das Fähigkeitsselbstkonzept von Jungen und Mädchen in der Grundschule. *Psychologie in Erziehung und Unterricht, 50*, 182-190.

Diener, C.I. & Dweck, C.S. (1978). An analysis of learned helplessness: Continuous changes in performance, strategy, and achievement cognitions following failure. *Journal of Personality and Social Psychology, 36*, 451-462.

Diener, C.I. & Dweck, C.S. (1980). An analysis of learned helplessness: II. The processing of success. *Journal of Personality and Social Psychology, 39*, 940-952.

Dijkstra, P., Kuyper, H., van der Werf, G., Buunk, A.P. & van der Zee, Y.G. (2008). Social comparison in the classroom: A review. *Review of Educational Research, 78*, 828-879.

Dinnel, D.L., Brittain, T., Johnson, K., King, M., Pust, K. & Thompson, T. (2002). A structural model of self-worth protection and achievement: Goals, evaluative anxiety, attributions, self-esteem, and uncertainty. In R.G. Craven, H.W. Marsh & K.B. Simpson (Eds.), *Self-concept research: Driving international research agendas*. Collected papers of the Second Biennial Self-concept Enhancement and Learning Facilitation (SELF) Research Centre International Conference. University of Western Sydney: SELF Research Centre.

DiPerna, J.C., Volpe, R.J. & Elliott, S.N. (2001). A model of academic enablers and elementary reading/language arts achievement. *School Psychology Review, 31*, 298-312.

Dodds, J. (1994). Spelling skills and causal attributions in children. *Educational Psychology in Practice, 10*, 111-119.

Dörnyei, Z. & Clément, R. (2001). Motivational characteristics of learning different target languages: Results of a nationwide survey. In Z. Dörnyei & R. Schmidt (Eds.), *Motivation and second langu-age acquisition*. Technical Report #23 (pp. 399-432). Honululu, University of Hawai'i: Second Language Teaching and Curriculum Center.

Dolan, L.J. (1983). Validity analysis for the School Attitude Measures at three grade levels. *Educational and Psychological Measurement, 43*, 295-303.

Donnellan, M.B., Trzesniewski, K.H., Robins, R.W., Moffitt, T.E. & Caspi, A. (2005). Low self-esteem is related to aggression, antisocial behavior, and delinquency. *Psychological Science, 16*, 328-335.

Downing, J., DeStefano, J., Rich, G. & Bell, A. (1984). Children's views of spelling. *Elementary School Journal, 85,* 185-198.

Dusek, J.B. (1980). The development of test anxiety in children. In I.G. Sarason (Ed.), *Test anxiety: Theory, research, and applications* (pp. 87-110). Hillsdale: Erlbaum.

Dweck, C.S. & Legett, E.L. (1988). A social-cognitive approach to motivation and personality. *Psychological Review, 95,* 256-273.

Dweck, C.S. & Wortman, C.B. (1982). Learned helplessness, anxiety, and achievement motivation. Neglected parallels in cognitive, affective, and coping responses. In H.W. Krohne (Ed.), *Achievement, stress, and anxiety* (pp. 93-125). Washington: Hemisphere.

Eccles, J.S. & Wigfield, A. (2002). Motivational beliefs, values, and goals. *Annual Review of Psychology, 53,* 109-132.

Eccles, J.S., Wigfield, A. & Schiefele, U. (1998). Motivation to succeed. In N. Eisenberg (Ed.), *Handbook of child psychology. Volume 3: Social, emotional, and personality development* (5th ed., pp. 1017-1095). New York: Wiley.

Ehm, J.-H., Duzy, D. & Hasselhorn, M. (2011). Das akademische Selbstkonzept bei Schulanfängern. Spielen Geschlecht und Migrationshintergrund eine Rolle? *Frühe Bildung, 0,* 37-45.

Elbaum, B. & Vaughn, S. (2001). School-based interventions to enhance the self-concept of students with learning disabilities: A meta-analysis. *Elementary School Journal, 101,* 303-329.

Enders, C.K. & Bandalos, D.L. (2001). The relative performance of full information maximum likelihood estimation for missing data in structural equation models. *Structural Equation Modeling, 8,* 430-457.

Englert, C.S. & Mariage, T. (2003). The sociocultural model in special education interventions: Apprenticing students in higher-order thinking. In H.L. Swanson, K.R. Harris & S. Graham (Eds.), *Handbook of learning disabilities* (pp. 450-467). New York: Guilford Press.

Epstein, S. (1980). The self-concept: A review and the proposal of an integrated theory of personality. In E. Staub (Ed.), *Personality. Basic aspects and current research* (pp. 81-132). Englewood Cliffs: Prentice-Hall.

Everson, H.T., Tobias, S., Hartman, H. & Gourgey, A. (1993). Test anxiety and the curriculum: The subject matters. *Anxiety, Stress, and Coping, 6,* 1-8.

Faber, G. (1988). Schülerselbstkonzepte und lehrerperzipierte Verhaltensauffälligkeiten – eine Erkundungsstudie in dritten Grundschulklassen. *Heilpädagogische Forschung, 14,* 44-51.

Faber, G. (1989a). Kurzzeiteffekte schülerorientierender Leistungsrückmeldungen im Rechtschreiben. *Empirische Pädagogik, 3,* 161-176.

Faber, G. (1989b). Fehlerartspezifische Selbsteinschätzungen im Kontext von Schülerselbstkonzepten, Rechtschreibleistungen und Lehrerurteilen. *Zeitschrift für Pädagogische Psychologie, 3,* 181-191.

Faber, G. (1989c). Wahrnehmung eigener Rechtschreibleistungen. Zur Urteilsgüte fehlerartspezifischer Selbsteinschätzungen bei Grundschülern. *Pädagogische Welt, 43,* 468-471, 476.

Faber, G. (1990). Allgemein leistungsthematische Kausalattributionen in Abhängigkeit von Schulleistungen und Schülerselbstkonzepten. Eine Querschnittuntersuchung gegen Ende der Grundschulzeit. *Empirische Pädagogik, 4,* 329-352.

Faber, G. (1991). Entwicklung und Erprobung eines Fragebogens zum rechtschreibbezogenen Selbstkonzept von Grundschülern. *Empirische Pädagogik, 5,* 317-347.

Faber, G. (1992a). Bereichsspezifische Beziehungen zwischen leistungsthematischen Schülerselbstkonzepten und Schulleistungen. *Zeitschrift für Entwicklungspsychologie und Pädagogische Psychologie, 24,* 66-82.

Faber, G. (1992b). Rechtschreibbezogene Selbsteinschätzungen im Zusammenhang von Schülerselbstkonzept und Schulleistung: Eine Untersuchung im vierten Grundschuljahr. *Zeitschrift für Pädagogische Psychologie, 6,* 185-196.

Faber, G. (1993a). *Bereichsspezifische Erfassung von Selbstkonzept und Leistungsangst bei Grundschülern: Empirische Ergebnisse und Folgerungen für die Forschung.* Unveröffentlichtes Typoskript zu einem Referat auf der 2. Tagung „Grundschulforschung" am Institut für Pädagogik der Universität Regensburg, 18.-19. Juni 1993.

Faber, G. (1993b). Eine Kurzskala zur Erfassung von Leistungsangst vor schulischen Rechtschreibsituationen: LARs. *Empirische Pädagogik, 7,* 253-284.

Faber, G. (1994). Das schulfachspezifische Erleben von Hilflosigkeit, Zuversicht und Leistungsangst – Eine vergleichende Untersuchung zu den selbstbezogenen Überzeugungen und zum lehrerperzipierten Verhalten rechtschreibschwacher Grundschüler. *Sonderpädagogik, 24,* 188-201.

Faber, G. (1995a). Die Diagnose von Leistungsangst vor schulischen Rechtschreibsituationen: Neue Ergebnisse zu den psychometrischen Eigenschaften und zur Validität einer entsprechenden Kurzskala. *Praxis der Kinderpsychologie und Kinderpsychiatrie, 44,* 110-119.

Faber, G. (1995b). Schulfachbezogen erfragte Leistungsängste bei Grundschulkindern: Eine Analyse ihrer differentiellen Beziehungen zu ausgewählten Selbstkonzept- und Leistungsmaßen. *Psychologie in Erziehung und Unterricht, 42,* 278-284.

Faber, G. (1996). Leistungs- und selbstkonzeptabhängige Unterschiede in den Ausprägungen schulfachspezifisch vorgenommener Kausalattributionen. Weitere Ergebnisse einer vergleichenden Untersuchung zu den selbstbezogenen Überzeugungen rechtschreibschwacher Grundschüler. *Sonderpädagogik, 26,* 16-32.

Faber, G. (2000). Rechtschreibängstliche Besorgtheits- und Aufgeregtheitskognitionen: Empirische Untersuchungsergebnisse zum subjektiven Kompetenz- und Bedrohungserleben rechtschreibschwacher Grundschulkinder. *Sonderpädagogik, 30,* 191-201.

Faber, G. (2001). Das Verhalten rechtschreibängstlicher Grundschulkinder im Lehrerurteil: Empirische Untersuchungsergebnisse zur Problematik informeller Alltagsdiagnosen. *Heilpädagogische Forschung, 27,* 58-65.

Faber, G. (2002a). Diktatbezogene Erfolgs- und Misserfolgsattributionen: Empirische Untersuchungsergebnisse zum subjektiven Kompetenz- und Kontrollerleben rechtschreibschwacher Grundschulkinder. *Heilpädagogische Forschung, 28,* 2-10.

Faber, G. (2002b). Rechtschreibängstliche Besorgtheits- und Aufgeregtheitskognitionen: Empirische Untersuchungsergebnisse zu ihrer Bedeutung für das Selbstwertgefühl und die Schulunlust rechtschreibschwacher Grundschulkinder. *Sonderpädagogik, 32,* 3-12.

Faber, G. (2003). Analyse geschlechtsabhängiger Ausprägungen im rechtschreibspezifischen Selbstkonzept von Grundschulkindern. *Zeitschrift für Entwicklungspsychologie und Pädagogische Psychologie, 35,* 208-211.

Faber, G. (2006a). The systematic use of visualizing and verbalizing methods in remedial spelling training: Conceptual issues, practical applications, and empirical findings. In C. B. Hayes (Ed.), *Dyslexia in children: New research* (pp. 1-45). New York: Nova Science

Publishers.

Faber, G. (2006b). Die Erfassung rechtschreibängstlicher Besorgtheit und Aufgeregtheit. Zur Bedeutung ausgewählter Forschungsergebnisse für lerntherapeutische Diagnose- und Interventionskonzepte. *Sprachrohr Lerntherapie,* Ausgabe 2, 5-14.

Faber, G. (2007). Academic self-beliefs in the spelling domain: Empirical research findings on elementary school students' subject-specific self-concept, causal attributions, and test anxiety. In E.M. Vargios (Ed.), *Educational psychology research focus* (pp. 65-120). New York: Nova Science Publishers.

Faber, G. (2009). Die Erfassung kognitiv-motivationaler Lernermerkmale gegen Ende der gymnasialen Sekundarstufe I. Ergebnisse aus einem interdisziplinären Forschungsprojekt zur mündlichen Erzählkompetenz in Englisch. *Zeitschrift für Fremdsprachenforschung, 20,* 179-212.

Faber, G. (2010). Enhancing orthographic competencies and reducing domain-specific test anxiety: The systematic use of algorithmic and self-instructional task formats in remedial spelling training. *International Journal of Special Education, 25*(2), 78-88.

Faber, G. & Billmann-Mahecha, E. (2012). Schulfachliche Leistungen und Selbsteinschätzungen in Abhängigkeit von Familiensprache und Geschlecht: Befunde aus einer Studie in dritten und vierten Grundschulklassen. In F. Hellmich, S. Förster & F. Hoya (Hrsg.), *Bedingungen des Lehrens und Lernens in der Grundschule. Bilanz und Perspektiven. Jahrbuch Grundschulforschung Band 16* (S. 271-274). Wiesbaden: Verlag für Sozialwissenschaften.

Faber, G., Tiedemann, J. & Billmann-Mahecha, E. (2011). Selbstkonzept und Lernfreude in der Grundschulmathematik: Die Bedeutung von Migration und Geschlecht. Längsschnittliche Ergebnisse aus der Hannoverschen Grundschulstudie. *Heilpädagogische Forschung, 37,* 127-143.

Fend, H., Knörzer, W., Nagl, W., Specht, W. & Väth-Szuszdziara, R. (1976). *Sozialisationseffekte der Schule. Soziologie der Schule II.* Weinheim: Beltz.

Ferla, J., Valcke, M. & Cai, Y. (2009). Academic self-efficacy and academic self-concept: Reconsidering structural relationships. *Learning and Individual Differences, 19,* 499-505.

Field, A. (2009). *Discovering statistics using SPSS* (3rd ed.). Los Angeles: Sage Publications.

Fincham, F.D., Diener, C.I. & Hokoda, A. (1987). Attributional style and learned helplessness: Relationship to the use of causal schemata and depressive symptoms in children. *British Journal of Social Psychology, 26,* 1-7.

Fincham, F.D., Hokoda, A. & Sanders, R. (1989). Learned helplessness, test anxiety, and academic achievement: A longitudinal analysis. *Child Development, 60,* 138-145.

Finkbeiner, G. & Isele, H. (1974). *Rechtschreibversager. Vergleichende Untersuchung zur Persönlichkeit und Leistung in Lehrer-, Eltern- und Schülereinschätzung.* Villingen-Schwenningen: Neckar-Verlag.

Flammer, A. & Schmid, D. (2003). Attribution of conditions for school performance. *European Journal of Psychology of Education, 18,* 337-355.

Franklin-Guy, S. (2006). *The interrelationships among written language ability, self-concept, and epistemological beliefs.* Wichita State University, College of Health Professions and Faculty of the Graduate School: doctoral dissertation.

Fraser, B.J. (1994). Research on classroom and school climate. In D.L. Gabel (Ed.), *Handbook of research on science teaching and learning* (pp. 493-541). New York: MacMillan.

Frederickson, N. & Jacobs, S. (2001). Controllability attributions for academic performance and the perceived scholastic competence, global self-worth and achievement of children with dyslexia. *School Psychology International, 22,* 401-416.

Freedman-Doan, C., Wigfield, A., Eccles, J.S., Blumenfeld, P., Arbreton, A. & Harold, R.D. (2000). What am I best at? Grade and gender differences in children's beliefs about ability improvement. *Journal of Applied Developmental Psychology, 21,* 379-402.

Frenzel, A., Pekrun, R. & Goetz, T. (2007). Girls and mathematics – A "hopeless" issue? A control-value approach to gender differences in emotions toward mathematics. *European Journal of Psychology of Education, 22,* 497-514.

Frieze, I.H. (1980). Beliefs about success and failure in the classroom. In J.H. McMillan (Ed), *The social psychology of school learning* (pp. 39-78). New York: Academic Press.

Frieze, I.H. & Snyder, H.N. (1980). Children's beliefs about the causes of success and failure in school settings. *Journal of Educational Psychology, 72,* 186-196.

Frome, P.M. & Eccles, J.S. (1998). Parents' influences on children's achievement-related perceptions. *Journal of Personality and Social Psychology, 74,* 435-452.

Frühauf, S. (2008). *Bereichsspezifische Selbstkonzepte bei Grundschulkindern. Operationalisierung und Validierung eines hypothetischen Konstrukts.* Hamburg: Kovač.

Fürntratt, E. (1969). Zur Bestimmung der Anzahl interpretierbarer gemeinsamer Faktoren in Faktorenanalysen psychologischer Daten. *Diagnostica, 15,* 62-75.

Gadeyne, E., Ghesquière, P. & Onghena, P. (2004). Psychosocial functioning of young children with learning problems. *Journal of Child Psychology and Psychiatry, 45,* 510-521.

Gambell, T.J. & Hunter, D.M. (1999). Rethinking gender differences in literacy. *Canadian Journal of Education, 24,* 1-16.

Garden, R.A. & Smith, T.A. (2000). TIMSS test development. In M.O. Martin, K.D. Gregory & S.E. Stemler (Eds.), *TIMSS 1999 technical report: IEA's repeat of the Third Mathematics and Science Study at eighth grade* (pp. 49-67). Chestnut Hill: International Study Center, Boston College.

Georgiou, S.N., Christou, C., Stavrinides, P. & Panaosura, G. (2002). Teacher attributions of student failure and teacher behavior towards the failing student. *Psychology in the Schools, 39,* 583-595.

Gipps, C. & Tunstall, P. (1998). Effort, ability and the teacher: young children's explanations for success and failure. *Oxford Review of Education, 24,* 149-165.

Gjesme, T. (1981). The factor structure of test anxiety among children with different characteristics. *Scandinavian Journal of Educational Research, 25,* 63-98.

Glogauer, W. (1980). *Rechtschreibtests zur Fehlerdiagnose und objektiven Leistungsmessung und -beurteilung für die 3./4. Jahrgangsstufe mit 15 Testbogen zum Kopieren, Lösungen und Prozentrangtabellen.* München: Ehrenwirth.

Goetz, T., Cronjaeger, H., Frenzel, A.C., Lüdtke, O. & Hall, N.C. (2010). Academic self-concept and emotion relations: Domain specificity and age effects. *Contemporary Educational Psychology, 35,* 44-58.

Goetz, T., Frenzel, A.C., Hall, N.C. & Pekrun, R. (2008). Antecedents of academic emotions: Testing the internal/external frame of reference model for academic enjoyment. *Contemporary Educational Psychology, 33,* 9-33.

Goodenow, C. (1993). Classroom belonging among early adolescent students: Relationships to motivation and achievement. *Journal of Early Adolescence, 13,* 21-43.

Gottfried, A.E. (1982). Relationships between academic intrinsic motivation and anxiety in children and young adolescents. *Journal of School Psychology, 20,* 205-215.

Green, J., Martin, A.J. & Marsh, H.W. (2007). Motivation and engagement in English, mathematics and science high school subjects: Towards an understanding of multidimensional domain specificity. *Learning and Individual Differences, 17,* 269-279.

Green, J., Nelson, G., Martin, A.J. & Marsh, H. (2006). The causal ordering of self-concept and academic achievement and its effect on academic achievement. *International Education Journal, 7,* 534-546.

Guay, F., Marsh, H.W. & Boivin, M. (2003). Academic self-concept and academic achievement: Developmental perspectives on their causal ordering. *Journal of Educational Psychology, 95,* 124-136.

Hackett, G. (1985). Role of mathematics self-efficacy in the choice of math-related majors of college women and men: A path analysis. *Journal of Counseling Psychology, 32,* 47-56.

Hadwin, J.A., Brogan, J. & Stevenson, J. (2005). State anxiety and working memory in children: A test of processing efficiency theory. *Educational Psychology, 25,* 379-393.

Haferkamp, W. & Rost, D.H. (1980). Angst geht zur Grundschule. *Die Deutsche Schule, 72,* 119-134.

Hagtvet, K.A. (1976). Worry and emotionality components of test anxiety in different sex and age groups of elementary school children. *Psychological Reports, 39,* 1327-1334.

Hannula, M.S., Maijala, H. & Pehkonen, E. (2004). Development of understanding and self-confidence in mathematics; grades 5-8. In M. Høines & A.-B. Fuglestad (Eds.), *Proceedings of the 28th Conference of the International Group for the Psychology of Mathematics Education* (Volume 3, pp. 17-24). Bergen: University College.

Hargreaves, M., Homer, M. & Swinnerton, B. (2008). A comparison of performance and attitudes in mathematics among the 'gifted'. Are boys better at mathematics or do they just think they are? *Assessment in Education: Principles, Policy and Practice, 15*(1), 19-38.

Harter, S. (1990). Causes, correlates, and the functional role of global self-worth: A life-span perspective. In R.J. Sternberg & J. Kolligian (Eds.), *Competence considered* (pp. 67-97). New Haven: Yale University Press.

Harter, S. & Connell, J.B. (1984). A model of children's achievement and related self-perceptions of competence, control, and motivational orientation. In J.G. Nicholls (Ed.), *Advances in motivation and achievement. Volume 3: The development of achievement motivation* (pp. 219-250). Greenwich: JAI Press.

Hattie, J. (1992). *Self-concept.* Hillsdale: Erlbaum.

Hattie, J. & Marsh, H.W. (1996). Future directions in self-concept research. In B.A. Bracken (Ed.), *Handbook of self-concept. Developmental, social, and clinical considerations* (pp. 421-462). New York: Wiley.

Hattie, J. & Timperley, H. (2007). The power of feedback. *Review of Educational Research, 77,* 81-112.

Hau, K.-T. & Salili, F. (1993). Measurement of achievement attribution: A review of instigation methods, question contents, and measurement formats. *Educational Psychology Review, 5,* 377-422.

Hay, I. (2005). Facilitating children's self-concept: A rationale and evaluative study. *Australian Journal of Guidance and Counselling, 15,* 60-67.

Hay, I., Ashman, A. & van Kraayenoord, C.E. (1997). Investigating the influence of achievement on self-concept using intra-class design and a comparison of the PASS and SDQ-1 self-concept tests. *British Journal of Educational Psychology, 67,* 311-321.

Hay, I., Ashman, A.F. & van Kraayenoord, C.E. (1998a). Educational characteristics of students with high or low self-concept. *Psychology in the Schools, 35,* 391-400.

Hay, I., Ashman, A.F. & van Kraayenoord, C.E. (1998b). The influence of gender, academic achievement and non-school factors upon pre-adolescent self-concept. *Educational Psychology, 18,* 461-470.

Heaven, P.C.L., Mak, A., Barry, J. & Ciarrochi, J. (2002). Personality and family influences on adolescent attitudes to school and self-related academic performance. *Personality and Individual Differences, 32,* 453-462.

Heck, R.H. & Thomas, S.L. (2009). *An introduction to multilevel modeling techniques* (2nd ed.). New York: Routledge.

Heckhausen, H. (1977). Achievement motivation and its constructs: A cognitive model. *Motivation and Emotion, 1,* 283-329.

Heckhausen, H. (1987). Causal attribution patterns for achievement outcomes: Individual differences, possible types and their origins. In F.E. Weinert & R.H. Kluwe (Eds.), *Metacognition, motivation, and understanding* (pp. 143-184). Hillsdale: Erlbaum.

Heiervang, E., Stevenson, J., Lund, A. & Hugdahl, K. (2001). Behaviour problems in children with dyslexia. *Nordic Journal of Psychiatry, 55,* 251-256.

Heinonen, K., Räikkönen, K. & Kelikangas-Järvinen, L. (2005). Self-esteem in early and late adolescence predicts dispositional optimism-pessimism in adulthood: A 21-year longitudinal study. *Personality and Individual Differences, 39,* 511-521.

Heinzmann, S. (2009). "Girls are better at language learning than boys": Do stereotypic beliefs about language learning contribute to girls' higher motivation to learn English in primary school? *Bulletin Suisse de Linguistique Appliquée, 89,* 19-36.

Helmke, A. (1988). The role of classroom context factors for the achievement-impairing effect of test anxiety. *Anxiety Research, 1,* 37-52.

Helmke, A. (1992). *Selbstvertrauen und schulische Leistungen.* Göttingen: Hogrefe.

Helmke, A. (1997). Entwicklung lern- und leistungsbezogener Motive und Einstellungen: Ergebnisse aus dem SCHOLASTIK-Projekt. In F.E. Weinert & A. Helmke (Hrsg.), *Entwicklung im Grundschulalter* (S. 59-76). Weinheim: Beltz.

Helmke, A. (1999). From optimism to realism? Development of children's academic self-concept from kindergarten to grade 6. In F.E. Weinert & W. Schneider (Eds.), *Individual development from 3 to 12. Findings from the Munich Longitudinal Study* (pp. 198-221). New York: Cambridge University Press.

Helmke, A. (2009). *Unterrichtsqualität und Lehrerprofessionalität. Diagnose, Evaluation und Verbesserung des Unterrichts.* Seelze: Kallmeyer/Klett.

Helmke, A., Schrader, F.-W., Wagner, W., Nold, G. & Schröder, K. (2008). Selbstkonzept und Motivation im Fach Englisch. In DESI-Konsortium (Hrsg.), *Unterricht und Kompetenzerwerb in Deutsch und Englisch. Ergebnisse der DESI-Studie* (S. 244-257). Weinheim: Beltz.

Helmke, A. & van Aken, M.A.G. (1995). The causal ordering of academic achievement and self-concept of ability during elementary school: A longitudinal study. *Journal of Educational Psychology, 87,* 624-637.

Hembree, R. (1988). Correlates, causes, effects, and treatment of test anxiety. *Review of Educational Research, 58,* 47-77.

Hembree, R. (1990). The nature, effects, and relief of mathematics anxiety. *Journal for Research in Mathematics Education, 21,* 33-46.

Henk, W.A., Bottomley, D.M. & Melnick, S.A. (1996). Preliminary validation of the Writer

Self-Perception Scale. In E.G. Sturtevant & W.M. Linek (Eds.), *Growing literacy. The eighteenth yearbook of the College Reading Association* (pp. 188-199). Harrisonburg: College Reading Association.

Henk, W.A. & Melnick, S.A. (1995). The Reader Self-Perception Scale (RSPS): A new tool for measuring how children feel about themselves as readers. *The Reading Teacher, 48,* 470-482.

Henry, A. (2009). Gender differences in compulsatory school pupils' L2 self-concepts: A longitudinal study. *System, 37,* 177-193.

Herbert, J. & Stipek, D. (2005). The emergence of gender differences in children's perceptions of their academic performance. *Applied Developmental Psychology, 26,* 276-295.

Hergovich, A., Sirch, U. & Felinger, M. (2004). Gender differences in the self-concept of preadolescent children. *School Psychology International, 25,* 207-222.

Hiebert, E.H., Winograd, P.N. & Danner, F.W. (1984). Children's attributions for failure and success in different aspects of reading. *Journal of Educational Psychology, 76,* 1139-1148.

Hill, K.T. & Sarason, S.B. (1966). The relation of test anxiety and defensiveness to test and school performance over the elementary school years: A further longitudinal study. *Monographs for the Society for Research in Child Development, 31*(2), 1-76.

Hock, M. (1992). Exchange of aversive communicative acts between mother and child as related to perceived child-rearing practices and anxiety of the child. In K.A. Hagtvet & T. B. Johnson (Eds.), *Advances in test anxiety research. Volume 7* (pp. 156-174). Lisse: Swets and Zeitlinger.

Hodapp, V. (1989). Anxiety, fear of failure, and achievement: Two path-analytical models. *Anxiety Research, 1,* 301-312.

Hogan, K. & Pressley, M. (1997). Becoming a scaffolder of students' learning. In K. Hogan & M. Pressley (Eds.), *Scaffolding student learning. Instructional approaches and issues* (pp. 185-191). Cambridge: Brookline Books.

Hoge, D.R., Smit, E.K. & Crist, J.T. (1995). Reciprocal effects of self-concept and academic achievement in sixth and seventh grade. *Journal of Youth and Adolescence, 24,* 295-314.

Holder, M.C. (2005). *Fähigkeitsselbstkonzept und Leistungsmotivation im Fremdsprachenunterricht.* Bern: Lang.

Holfve-Sabel, M.-A. & Gustafsson, J.-E. (2005). Attitudes towards school, teacher, and classmates at classroom and individual levels: An application of two-level confirmatory factor analysis. *Scandinavian Journal of Educational Research, 49,* 187-202.

Hopko, D.R., Ashcraft, M.H., Gute, J., Ruggiero, K.J. & Lewis, C. (1998). Mathematics anxiety and working memory: Support for the existence of a deficient inhibition mechanism. *Journal of Anxiety Disorders, 12,* 343-355.

Horwitz, E.K. (2001). Language anxiety and achievement. *Annual Review of Applied Linguistics, 21,* 112-126.

Huguet, P., Dumas, F., Marsh, H., Régner, I., Wheeler, L., Suls, J., Seaton, M. & Nezlek, J. (2009). Clarifying the role of social comparison in the big-fish-little-pond effect (BFLPE): An integrative study. *Journal of Personality and Social Psychology, 97,* 156-170.

Huguet, P., Dumas, F., Monteil, J.-M., & Genestoux, N. (2001). Social comparison choices in the classroom: Further evidence for students' upward comparison tendency and its beneficial impact on performance. *European Journal of Social Psychology, 31,* 557–578.

Humphrey, N. (2002a). Teacher and pupil ratings of self-esteem in developmental dyslexia. *British Journal of Special Education, 29,* 29-36.

Humphrey, N. (2002b). Self-concept and self-esteem in developmental dyslexia: Implications for theory and practice. In R.G. Craven, H.W. Marsh & K.B. Simpson (Eds.), *Self-concept research: Driving international research agendas.* Collected papers of the Second Biennial Self-concept Enhancement and Learning Facilitation (SELF) Research Centre International Conference. University of Western Sydney: SELF Research Centre.

Humphrey, N. & Mullins, P.M. (2002). Personal constructs and attribution for academic success and failure in dyslexia. *British Journal of Special Education, 29,* 196-203.

Ickes, W. & Layden, M.A. (1978). Attributional styles. In J.H. Harvey, W. Ickes & R.F. Kidd (Eds.), *New directions in attribution research. Volume 2* (pp. 119-152). Hillsdale: Erlbaum.

Ingesson, S.G. (2007). Growing up with dyslexia: Interviews with teenagers and young adults. *School Psychology International, 28,* 574-591.

Ireson, J. & Hallam, S. (2005). Pupils' liking for school: Ability grouping, self-concept and perceptions of teaching. *British Journal of Educational Psychology, 75,* 297-311.

Ireson, J., Hallam, S. & Plewin, I. (2001). Ability grouping in secondary schools: Effects on pupils' self-concepts. *British Journal of Educational Psychology, 71,* 315-326.

Jacobs, B. (1982). *Die Fachspezifität der Prüfungsängstlichkeit.* Universität des Saarlandes: Arbeitsberichte aus der Fachrichtung Allgemeine Erziehungswissenschaft, Nr. 13.

Jacobs, J.E., Lanza, S., Osgood, D., Eccles, J.S. & Wigfield, A. (2002). Changes in children's self-competence and values: Gender and domain differences across grade one through twelve. *Child Development, 73,* 509-527.

Jacobsen, B., Lowery, B. & DuCette, J. (1986). Attributions of learning disabled children. *Journal of Educational Psychology, 78,* 59-64.

Jain, S. & Dowson, M. (2009). Mathematics anxiety as a function of multidimensional self-regulation and self-efficacy. *Contemporary Educational Psychology, 34,* 240-249.

Jen, T.-H. & Chien, C.-L. (2008*). The influence of the academic self-concept on academic achievement: From a perspective of learning motivation.* Paper presented at the 3rd IEA International Research Conference (IRC-2008). Taipei City, September 18-20, 2008.

Jerusalem, M. (1984). Reference group, learning environment and self-evaluations: A dynamic multi-level analysis with latent variables. In R. Schwarzer (Ed.), *The self in anxiety, stress and depression* (pp. 61-73). Amsterdam: Elsevier.

Jerusalem, M. (1993). Personal resources, environmental constraints, and adaptional processes: The predictive power of a theoretical stress model. *Personality and Individual Differences, 14,* 15-24.

Jerusalem, M. & Schwarzer, R. (1989). Anxiety and self-concept as antecedents of stress and coping: A longitudinal study with German and Turkish adolescents. *Personality and Individual Differences, 10,* 785-792.

Joët, G., Usher, E.L. & Bressoux, P. (2011). Sources of self-efficacy: An investigation of elementary school students in France. *Journal of Educational Psychology, 103,* 649-663.

Jopt, U.-J. (1978). *Selbstkonzept und Ursachenerklärung in der Schule. Zur Attribuierung von Schulleistungen.* Bochum: Kamp.

Jovanovic, J. & King, S.S. (1998). Boys and girls in the performance-based science classroom: Who's doing the performing? *American Educational Research Journal, 35,* 477-496.

Jussim, L. (1989). Teacher expectations: Self-fulfilling prophecies, perceptual bias, and accuracy. *Journal of Personality and Social Psychology, 57,* 469-480.

Jussim, L. & Eccles, J. (1992). Teacher expectations II: Construction and reflection of student achievement. *Journal of Personality and Social Psychology, 63,* 947-961.

Kahle, L.R., Kukla, R.A. & Klingel, D.M. (1980). Low adolescent self-esteem leads to multiple interpersonal problems: A test of social-adaptation theory. *Journal of Personality and Social Psychology, 39,* 496-502.

Kammermeyer, G. & Martschinke, S. (2006). Selbstkonzept- und Leistungsentwicklung in der Grundschule – Ergebnisse aus der KILIA-Studie. *Empirische Pädagogik, 20,* 245-259.

Keith, L.K. & Bracken, B.A. (1996). Academic self-concept: Its structure, measurement, and relation to academic achievement. In B.A. Bracken (Ed.), *Handbook of self-concept. Developmental, social, and clinical considerations* (pp. 91-170). New York: Wiley.

Kelley, H.H. & Michela, J.L. (1980). Attribution theory and research. *Annual Review of Psychology, 31,* 457-501.

Kershner, J.R. (1990). Self-concept and IQ as predictors of remedial success in children with learning disabilities. *Journal of Learning Disabilities, 23,* 368-374.

Kiefer, A. & Shih, M. (2006). Gender differences in persistence and attributions in stereotype relevant contexts. *Sex Roles, 54,* 859-868.

Klassen, R. (2002). A question of calibration: A review of the self-efficacy beliefs of students with learning disabilities. *Learning Disability Quarterly, 25,* 88-103.

Klassen, R.M. (2007). Using predictions to learn about the self-efficacy of early adolescents with and without learning disabilities. *Contemporary Educational Psychology, 32,* 173-187.

Kline, R.B. (2011). *Principles and practice of structural equation modeling* (3rd. ed.). New York: Guilford Press.

Kling, K.C., Hyde, J.S., Showers, C.J. & Buswell, B.N. (1999). Gender differences in self-esteem: A meta-analysis. *Psychological Bulletin, 125,* 470-500.

Knabe, G. (1973). Multidimensionale experimentelle Analysen des Legasthenie-Syndroms. In R. Valtin (Hrsg.), *Einführung in die Legasthenieforschung* (S.117-139). Weinheim: Beltz.

Köller, O., Zeinz, H. & Trautwein, U. (2008). Class-average achievement, marks, and academic self-concept in German primary schools. In H.W. Marsh, R.G. Craven & D.M. McInerney (Eds.), *Self-processes, learning, and enabling human potential. Dynamic new approaches* (pp. 331-352). Charlotte: Information Age Publishing.

Koumi, I. & Meadows, S. (1997). The multidimensional, hierarchical model of academic self-concept: The case of Greek secondary school pupils. *Evaluation and Research in Education, 11,* 164-173.

Krampen, G. (1988). Toward an action-theoretical model of personality. *European Journal of Personality, 2,* 39-55.

Krampen, G. (1991). Competence and control orientations as predictors of test anxiety in students: Longitudinal results. In R. Schwarzer & R.A. Wicklund (Eds.), *Anxiety and self-focused attention* (pp. 111-123). Chur: Harwood.

Krampen, G. & Zinßer, A. (1981). Wie erklären Sonderschüler das Zustandekommen von Deutschnoten. *Psychologie in Erziehung und Unterricht, 28,* 361-366.

Krohne, H.W. (1992). Developmental conditions of anxiety and coping: A two-process model of child-rearing effects. In K.A. Hagtvet & T.B. Johnson (Eds.), *Advances in test anxiety research. Volume 7* (pp. 143-155). Lisse: Swets and Zeitlinger.

Kurdek, L.A. & Sinclair, R.J. (2001). Predicting reading and mathematics achievement in fourth-grade children from kindergarten readiness scores. *Journal of Educational Psychology, 93,* 451-455.

Kurtz-Costes, B., Rowley, S.J., Harris-Britt, A. & Woods, T.A. (2008). Gender stereotypes about mathematics and science and self-perceptions of ability in late childhood and early adolescence. *Merrill-Palmer Quarterly, 54,* 386-409.

Kurtz-Costes, B.E. & Schneider, W. (1994). Self-concept, attributional beliefs, and school achievement: A longitudinal analysis. *Contemporary Educational Psychology, 19,* 199-216.

Langfeldt, H.-P. (2009). *Academic self-concepts in elementary school – Why children are both optimistic and realisitic.* Paper presented at the 5th International Biennial SELF Research Conference. Enabling human potential: The centrality of self and identity. Dubai, January 13-15, 2009.

Lau, I.C., Yeung, A.S., Jin, P. & Low, R. (1999). Toward a hierarchical, multidimensional English self-concept. *Journal of Educational Psychology, 91,* 747-755.

Lazarus, R.S. & Folkman, S. (1984). *Stress, appraisal, and coping.* New York: Springer.

Lee, F.L.-M. & Yeung, A.S. (2007). *Specificity of components of self-concept.* Paper presented at the AARE International Educational Research Conference, Fremantle, November 2007.

Lee, J. & Shute, V.J. (2009). *The influence of noncognitive domains on academic achievement in K-12.* Research report. Princeton: Educational Testing Service.

Lee, J. & Shute, V.J. (2010). Personal and social-contextual factors in K-12 academic performance: An integrative perspective on student learning. *Educational Psychologist, 45,* 1-19.

Leppin, A., Schwarzer, R., Belz, D., Jerusalem, M. & Quast, H.-H. (1987). Causal attribution patterns of high and low test-anxious students. In R. Schwarzer, H.M. van der Ploeg & C.D. Spielberger (Eds.), *Advances in test anxiety research. Volume 5* (pp. 67-86). Lisse: Swets and Zeitlinger.

Libbey, H.P. (2004). Measuring student relationship to school: Attachment, bonding, connectedness, and engagement. *Journal of School Health, 74,* 274-283.

Licht, B.G. & Kistner, J.A. (1986). Motivational problems of learning-disabled children: Individual differences and their implications for treatment. In J.K. Torgesen & B.Y.L. Wong (Eds.), *Psychological and educational perspectives on learning disabilities* (pp. 225-255). Orlando: Academic Press.

Licht, B.G., Stader, S.R. & Swanson, C.C. (1989). Children's achievement-related beliefs: Effects of academic area, sex, and achievement level. *Journal of Educational Research, 82,* 253-260.

Lindberg, S.M., Hyde, J.S., Petersen, J.L. & Linn, M.C. (2010). New trends in gender and mathematics performance: A meta-analysis. *Psychological Bulletin, 136,* 1123-1135.

Linver, M. & Davis-Kean, P.E. (2005). The slippery slope: What predicts math grades in middle and high school? *New Directions for Child and Adolescent Development, 110,* 49-64.

Little, A.W. (1985). The child's understanding of the causes of academic success and failure: A case study of British schoolchildren. *British Journal of Educational Psychology, 55,*

11-23.

Little, T.D., Cunningham, W.A., Shahar, G. & Widaman, K.F. (2002). To parcel or not to parcel: Exploring the question, weighting the merits. *Structural Equation Modeling, 9,* 151-173.

Lohrmann, K., Götz, T. & Haag, L. (2010). Zusammenhänge von fachspezifischen Leistungen und Fähigkeitsselbstkonzepten im Grundschulalter. In B. Schwarz, P. Nenniger & R. S. Jäger (Hrsg.), *Erziehungswissenschaftliche Forschung – nachhaltige Bildung.* Beiträge zur 5. DGfE-Sektionstagung „Empirische Bildungsforschung"/AEPF-KBBB im Frühjahr 2009 (S. 296-303). Landau: Verlag Empirische Pädagogik.

Lüdtke, O., Köller, O., Marsh, H.W. & Trautwein, U. (2005). Teacher frame of reference and the big-fish-little-pond effect. *Contemporary Educational Psychology, 30,* 263-285.

Lukesch, H. (1982). Fachspezifische Prüfungsängste. Eine deskriptive Analyse der schulsystem- und schulartbezogenen Verbreitung der Ängste von Schülern vor mündlichen und schriftlichen Prüfungen. *Psychologie in Erziehung und Unterricht, 29,* 257-267.

Ma, X. (1999). A meta-analysis of the relationship between anxiety toward mathematics and achievement in mathematics. *Journal for Research in Mathematics Education, 30,* 520-540.

Ma, X. (2010). Gender differences in mathematics achievement. Evidence from regional and international student assessments. In H.J. Forgasz, J.R. Becker, K.-H. Lee & O.B. Steinthorsdottir (Eds.), *International perspectives on gender and mathematics education* (pp. 225-248). Charlotte: Information Age Publishing.

Ma, X. & Xu, J. (2004). The causal ordering of mathematics anxiety and mathematics achievement: A longitudinal panel analysis. *Journal of Adolescence, 27,* 165-179.

MacIntyre, P.D., Dörnyei, Z., Clément, R. & Noels, K.A. (1998). Conceptualizing willingness to communicate in a L2: A situational model of L2 confidence and affiliation. *Modern Language Journal, 82,* 545-562.

MacLeod, C. & Donnellan, A.M. (1993). Individual differences in anxiety and the restriction of working memory capacity. *Personality and Individual Differences, 15,* 163-173.

Määttä, S., Stattin, H. & Nurmi, J.-E. (2002). Achievement strategies at school: types and correlates. *Journal of Adolescence, 25,* 31-46.

Mägi, K., Lerkkanen, M.-K., Poikkeus, A.-M., Rasku-Puttonen, H. & Kikas, E. (2010). Relations between achievement goal orientations and math achievement in primary grades: A follow-up study. *Scandinavian Journal of Educational Research, 54,* 295-312.

Magson, N.R., Craven, R.G., Nelson, G.F. & Yeung, A.S. (2008). *Domain-specific school motivation.* Paper presented at the AARE 2008 International Education Conference, Brisbane, Nov. 30 – Dec. 4.

Manger, T. & Eikeland, O.-J. (1997). The effect of social comparison on mathematics self-concept. *Scandinavian Journal of Psychology, 38,* 237-241.

Manger, T. & Eikeland, O.-J. (1998). The effect of mathematics self-concept on girls' and boys' mathematical achievement. *School Psychology International, 19,* 5-18.

Mantzicopoulos, P. (1990). Coping with school failure: Characteristics of students employing successful and unsuccessful coping strategies. *Psychology in the Schools, 27,* 138-143.

Many, M.A. & Many, W.A. (1975). The relationship between self-esteem and anxiety in grades four through eight. *Educational and Psychological Measurement, 35,* 1017-1021.

March, J.S., Sullivan, K. & Parker, J. (1999). Test-retest reliability of the Multidimensional Scale for Children. *Journal of Anxiety Disorders, 13,* 349-358.

Marjoribanks, K. (1992). The predictive validity of an attitudes-to-school scale in relation to children's academic achievement. *Educational and Psychological Measurement, 52,* 945-949.

Markus, H. (1980). The self in thought and memory. In D.M. Wegner & R.R. Vallacher (Eds.), *The self in social psychology* (pp. 102-130). Oxford: Oxford University Press.

Marsh, H.W. (1984a). Self-concept: The application of a frame of reference model to explain pa-radoxical results. *Australian Journal of Education, 28,* 165-181.

Marsh, H.W. (1984b). Relations among dimensions of self-attribution, dimensions of self-concept and academic achievements. *Journal of Educational Psychology, 76,* 1291-1308.

Marsh, H.W. (1986a). Verbal and math self-concepts: An internal/external frame of reference model. *American Educational Research Journal, 23,* 129-149.

Marsh, H.W. (1986b). Self-serving effect (bias?) in academic attributions: Its relation to academic achievement and self-concept. *Journal of Educational Psychology, 78,* 190-200.

Marsh, H.W. (1986c). Global self-esteem: Its relation to specific facets of self-concept and their importance. *Journal of Personality and Social Psychology, 51,* 1224-1236.

Marsh, H.W. (1987). The big-fish-little-pond effect on academic self-concept. *Journal of Educational Psychology, 79,* 280-295.

Marsh, H.W. (1988a). The content specificity of math and English anxieties: The high school and beyond study. *Anxiety Research, 1,* 137-149.

Marsh, H.W. (1988b). Causal effects of academic self-concept on academic achievement: A reanalysis of Newman (1984). *Journal of Experimental Education, 56,* 100-103.

Marsh, H.W. (1989a). Sex differences in the development of verbal and mathematics constructs: The high school and beyond study. *American Educational Research Journal, 26,* 191-225.

Marsh, H.W. (1989b). Age and sex effects in multiple dimensions of self-concept: Preadolescence to early adulthood. *Journal of Educational Psychology, 81,* 417-430.

Marsh, H.W. (1990a). A multidimensional, hierarchical model of self-concept: Theoretical and empirical justification. *Educational Psychology Review, 2,* 77-172.

Marsh, H.W. (1990b). Causal ordering of academic self-concept and academic achievement: A multiwave, longitudinal panel analysis. *Journal of Educational Psychology, 82,* 646-656.

Marsh, H.W. (1992). Content specificity of relations between academic achievement and academic self-concept. *Journal of Educational Psychology, 84,* 35-42.

Marsh, H.W. (1993). Relations between global and specific domains of self: The importance of individual importance, certainty, and ideals. *Journal of Personality and Social Psychology, 65,* 975-992.

Marsh, H.W. (2002). A multidimensional physical self-concept: A construct validity approach to theory, measurement, and research. *Psychology: The Journal of the Hellenic Psychological Society, 9,* 459-493.

Marsh, H.W. (2006). *Self-concept theory, measurement and research into practice: The role of self-concept in educational psychology.* Leicester: The Education Section of the British Psychological Society.

Marsh, H.W., Balla, J.R. & Hau, K.T. (1996). An evaluation of incremental fit indices: A clarification of mathematical and empirical processes. In G.A. Marcoulides & R.E. Schumacker (Eds.), *Advanced structural equation modeling techniques* (pp. 315-353). Hillsdale: Erlbaum.

Marsh, H.W., Byrne, B.M. & Yeung, A.S. (1999). Causal ordering of academic self-concept and achievement: Reanalysis of a pioneering study and revised recommendations. *Educational Psychologist, 34,* 155-167.

Marsh, H.W., Cairns, L., Relich, J., Barnes, J. & Debus, R.L. (1984). The relationship between dimensions of self-attribution and dimensions of self-concept. *Journal of Educational Psychology, 76,* 3-32.

Marsh, H.W. & Craven, R.G. (2002). The pivotal role of frames of reference in academic self-concept formation: The "big-fish-little-pond" effect. In F. Pajares & T. Urdan (Eds.), *Academic motivation of adolescents* (pp. 83-123). Greenwich: Information Age Publishing.

Marsh, H.W. & Craven, R.G. (2006). Reciprocal effects of self-concept and performance from a multidimensional perspective. Beyond seductive pleasure and unidimensional perspectives. *Perspectives on Psychological Science, 1,* 133-163.

Marsh, H.W., Craven, R. & Debus, R. (1998). Structure, stability, and development of young children's self-concepts: A multi-cohort-multi-occasion-study. *Child Development, 69,* 1030-1053.

Marsh, H.W., Craven, R. & Debus, R. (1999). Separation of competency and affect components of multiple dimensions of academic self-concept: A developmental perspective. *Merrill-Palmer Quarterly, 45,* 567-601.

Marsh, H.W., Gerlach, E., Trautwein, U., Lüdtke, O. & Brettschneider, W.-D. (2007). Longitudinal study of preadolescent sport self-concept and performance: Reciprocal effects and causal ordering. *Child Development, 78,* 1640-1656.

Marsh, H.W. & Hau, K.-T. (2003). Big-fish-little-pond effect on academic self-concept: A cross-cultural (26 country) test of the negative effects of academically selective schools. *American Psychologist, 58,* 364-576.

Marsh, H.W., Hau, K.-T.& Kong, C.-K. (2002). Multilevel causal ordering of academic self-concept and achievement: Influences of language of instruction (English compared with Chinese) for Hong Kong students. *American Educational Research Journal, 39,* 727-763.

Marsh, H.W., Kong, C.K. & Hau, K. (2001). Extension of the internal/external frame of reference model of self-concept formation: Importance of native and nonnative languages for Chinese students. *Journal of Educational Psychology, 93,* 543-553.

Marsh, H.W. & MacDonald Holmes, I.W. (1990). Multidimensional self-concepts: Construct validation of responses by children. *American Educational Research Journal, 27,* 89-117.

Marsh, H.W. & Martin, A.J. (2011). Academic self-concept and academic achievement: Relations and causal ordering. *British Journal of Educational Psychology, 81,* 59-77.

Marsh, H.W. & O'Mara, A.J. (2008a). Self-concept is as multidisciplinary as it is multidimensional. A review of theory, measurement, and practice in self-concept research. In H.W. Marsh, R.G. Craven & D.M. McInerney (Eds.), *Self-processes, learning, and enabling human potential. Dynamic new approaches* (pp. 87-115). Charlotte: Information Age Publishing.

Marsh, H.W. & O'Mara, A. (2008b). Reciprocal effects between academic self-concept, self-esteem, achievement, and attainment over seven adolescent years: Unidimensional and multidimensional perspectives of self-concept. *Personality and Social Psychology Bulletin, 34,* 542-552.

Marsh, H.W., Seaton, M., Kuyper, H., Dumas, F., Huguet, P., Régner, I., Buunk, A.P., Manteil, J.-M. & Gibbons, F.X. (2010). Phantom behavioral assimilation effects: Systematic biases in social comparison choice studies. *Journal of Personality, 78*, 671-709.

Marsh, H.W. & Shavelson, R.J. (1985). Self-concept: Its multifaceted, hierarchical structure. *Educational Psychologist, 20*, 107-123.

Marsh, H.W., Smith, I.D., Barnes, J. & Butler, S. (1983). Self-concept: Reliability, dimensionality, validity, and the measurement of change. *Journal of Educational Psychology, 75*, 772-790.

Marsh, H.W., Trautwein, U., Lüdtke, O., Köller, O. & Baumert, J. (2005). Academic self-concept, interest, grades, and standardized test scores: Reciprocal effects models of causal ordering. *Child Development, 76*, 397-416.

Marsh, H.W., Walker, R. & Debus, R. (1991). Subject-specific components of academic self-concept and self-efficacy. *Contemporary Educational Psychology, 16*, 331-345.

Marsh, H.W. & Yeung, A.S. (1996). The distinctiveness of affects in specific school subjects: An application of confirmatory factor analysis with the national educational longitudinal study of 1988. *American Educational Research Journal, 33*, 665-689.

Marsh, H.W. & Yeung, A.S. (1997). Causal effects of academic self-concept on academic achievement: Structural equation models of longitudinal data. *Journal of Educational Psychology, 89*, 41-54.

Marsh, H.W. & Yeung, A.S. (1998). Top-down, bottom-up, and horizontal models: The direction of causality in multidimensional, hierarchical self-concept models. *Journal of Personality and Social Psychology, 75*, 509-527.

Marshall, H.H. & Weinstein, R.S. (1984). Classroom factors affecting students' self-evaluations: An interactional model. *Review of Educational Research, 54*, 301-325.

Martin, A.J. (2002). The lethal cocktail: Low self-belief, low control, and high fear of failure. *Australian Journal of Guidance and Counselling, 12*, 74-85.

Martin, A.J. (2007). Examining a multidimensional model of student motivation and engagement using a construct validation approach. *British Journal of Educational Psychology, 77*, 413-440.

Martin, A.J. & Marsh, H.W. (2006). Academic resilience and its psychological and educational correlates: A construct validity approach. *Psychology in the Schools, 43*, 267-281.

Martin, A.J., Marsh, H.W., Williamson, A. & Debus, R.L. (2005). Fear of failure in students' academic lives. Exploring the roles of self-handicapping and defensive pessimism from longitudinal, multidimensional, and qualitative perspectives. In H.W. Marsh, R.G. Craven & D.M. McInerney (Eds.), *New frontiers for self research* (pp. 357-385). Greenwich: Information Age Publishing.

Mata, M.L., Monteiro, V. & Peixoto, F. (2009). *Reading self-perceptions and their relations to reading achievement and gender.* Poster presented at the 13th EARLI Biennial Conference: Fostering communities of learning. Amsterdam, The Netherlands, 25-29 August.

Matthews, G., Zeidner, M. & Roberts, R.D. (2006). Models of personality and affect for education: A review and synthesis. In P.A. Alexander & P.H. Winne (Eds.), *Handbook of educational psychology* (2nd ed., pp. 163-186). New York: Erlbaum.

Medway, F.J. (1979). Causal attributions for school-related problems: Teacher perceptions and teacher feedback. *Journal of Educational Psychology, 71*, 809-818.

Meece, J.L., Glienke, B.B. & Askew, K. (2009). Gender and motivation. In K.R. Wentzel & A. Wigfield (Eds.), *Handbook of motivation at school* (pp. 411-431). New York: Routledge.

Meece, J.L., Wigfield, A. & Eccles, J.S. (1990). Predictors of math anxiety and its influence on young adolescents' course enrollment intentions and performance in mathematics. *Journal of Educational Psychology, 82,* 60-70.

Meelissen, M. & Luyten, H. (2008). The Dutch gender gap in mathematics: Small for achievement, substantial for beliefs and attitudes. *Studies in Educational Evaluation, 34,* 82-93.

Meier, R. & McDaniel, E. (1974). A measure of attitude toward school. *Educational and Psychological Measurement, 34,* 997-998.

Melnick, S.A., Henk, W.A. & Marinak, B.A. (2009). *Validation of a Reader Self Perception Scale (RSPS2) for use in grades 7 and above.* Paper presented at the Northeastern Educational Research Association (NERA) Conference 2009.

Meltzer, L., Katzir-Cohen, T., Miller, L. & Roditi, B. (2001). The impact of effort and strategy use on academic performance: Student and teacher perceptions. *Learning Disability Quarterly, 24,* 85-98.

Möller, J. & Köller, O. (2001). Dimensional comparisons: An experimental approach to the internal/external frame of reference model. *Journal of Educational Psychology, 93,* 826-835.

Möller, J., Pohlmann, B., Köller, O. & Marsh, H.W. (2009). A meta-analytic path analysis of the internal/external frame of reference model of academic achievement and academic self-concept. *Review of Educational Research, 79,* 1129-1167.

Möller, J., Retelsdorf, J., Köller, O. & Marsh, H.W. (2011). The reciprocal internal/external frame of reference model: An integration of models of relations between academic achievement and self-concept. *American Educational Research Journal, 48,* 1315-1346.

Möller, J., Streblow, L. & Pohlmann, B. (2006). The belief in a negative interdependence of math and verbal abilities as determinant of academic self-concept. *British Journal of Educational Psychology, 76,* 57-70.

Möller, J., Streblow, L., Pohlmann, B. & Köller, O. (2006). An extension to the internal/external frame of reference model to two verbal and numerical domains. *European Journal of Psychology of Education, 21,* 467-487.

Mösko, E. (2010). *Elterliche Geschlechtsstereotype und deren Einfluss auf das mathematische Selbstkonzept von Grundschulkindern.* Universität Kassel, Fachbereich Humanwissenschaften: Dissertation.

Mok, M.M.C., Kennedy, K.J. & Moore, P.J. (2011). Academic attributions of secondary students: gender, year level and achievement level. *Educational Psychology, 31,* 87-104.

Moreano, G. (2004). The relationship between academic self-concept, causal attribution for success and failure, and academic achievement in pre-adolescents. In H.W. Marsh, J. Baumert, G.E. Richards & U. Trautwein (Eds.), *Self-concept, motivation, and identity. Where to from here? Proceedings of the Third International Biennial SELF Research Conference.* Berlin: Max Planck Institute for Human Development.

Morris, L.W., Davis, M.A. & Hutchings, C.H. (1981). Cognitive and emotional components of anxiety: Literature review and a revised worry-emotionality scale. *Journal of Educational Psychology, 73,* 541-555.

Morris, L.W., Kellaway, D.S. & Smith, D.H. (1978). Mathematics Anxiety Rating Scale: Predicting anxiety experiences and academic performance in two groups of students. *Journal of Educational Psychology, 70,* 589-594.

Morrison, G.M. & Cosden, M.A. (1997). Risk, resilience, and adjustment of individuals with learning disabilities. *Learning Disability Quarterly, 20,* 43-60.

Müller, R. (1983). *Diagnostischer Rechtschreibtest für dritte Klassen DRT 3* (2. Aufl.). Weinheim: Beltz.

Mugnaini, D., Lassi, S., La Malfa, G. & Albertini, G. (2009). Internalizing correlates of dyslexia. *World Journal of Pediatrics, 5,* 255-264.

Mujis, R.D. (1997). Predictors of academic achievement and academic self-concept: a longitudinal perspective. *British Journal of Educational Psychology, 67,* 263-277.

Nagengast, B. & Marsh, H.W. (2011). The negative effect of school-average ability on science self-concept in the UK, the UK countries and the world: the big-fish-little-pond effect for PISA 2006. *Educational Psychology, 31,* 629-656.

Nagy, G., Trautwein, U., Baumert, J., Köller, O. & Garrett, J. (2006). Gender and course selection in upper secondary education: Effects of academic self-concept and intrinsic value. *Educational Research and Evaluation, 12,* 323-345.

Nagy, G., Watt, H.M.G., Eccles, J.S., Trautwein, U., Lüdtke, O. & Baumert, J. (2010). The development of students' mathematics self-concept in relation to gender: Different countries, different trajectories? *Journal of Research on Adolescence, 20,* 482-506.

Newbegin, I. & Owens, A. (1996). Self-esteem and anxiety in secondary school achievement. *Journal of Social Behavior and Personality, 11,* 521-530.

Newman, R.S. (1984). Children's achievement and self-evaluations in mathematics: A longitudinal study. *Journal of Educational Psychology, 76,* 857-873.

Nicholls, J.G. (1979). Development of perception of own attainment and causal attributions for success and failure in reading. *Journal of Educational Psychology, 71,* 94-99.

Nicholls, J.G. & Miller, A.T. (1983). The differentiation of the concepts of difficulty and ability. *Child Development, 54,* 951-959.

Nolen-Hoeksema, S., Girgus, J.S. & Seligman, M.E.P. (1986). Learned helplessness in children: A longitudinal study of depression, achievement, and explanatory style. *Journal of Personality and Social Psychology, 51,* 435-442.

Nolen-Hoeksema, S., Girgus, J.S. & Seligman, M.E.P. (1992). Predictors and consequences of childhood depressive symptoms: A 5-year longitudinal study. *Journal of Abnormal Psychology, 101,* 405-422.

Normandeau, S. & Gobeil, A. (1998). A developmental perspective on children's understanding of causal attributions in achievement-related situations. *International Journal of Behavioral Development, 22,* 611-632.

Nurmi, A., Hannula, M.S., Maijala, H. & Pehkonen, E. (2003). On pupils' self-confidence in mathematics: gender comparisons. In N.A. Pateman, B.J. Dougherty & J. Zilliox (Eds.), *Proceedings of the 27th Conference of the International Group for the Psychology of Mathematics Education* (Volume 3, pp. 453-460). Honolulu: University of Hawaii.

O'Mara, A.J., Marsh, H.W., Craven, R.G. & Debus, R.L. (2006). Do self-concept interventions make a difference? A synergistic blend of construct validation and meta-analysis. *Educational Psychologist, 41,* 181-206.

Pajares, F. (2003). Self-efficacy beliefs, motivation, and achievement in writing: A review of the literature. *Reading and Writing Quarterly, 19,* 139-158.

Pajares, F. & Schunk, D.H. (2001). Self-beliefs and school success: Self-efficacy, self-concept, and school achievement. In R.J. Riding & S.G. Rayner (Eds.), *Self perception. International perspectives on individual differences. Volume 2* (pp. 239-265). Westport: Ablex.

Pajares, F. & Urdan, T. (1996). Exploratory factor analysis of the Mathematics Anxiety Scale.

Measurement and Evaluation in Counseling and Development, 29, 35-47.

Parsons, J.E., Kaczala, C.M. & Meece, J.L. (1982). Socialization of achievement attitudes and beliefs: Classroom influences. *Child Development, 53,* 322-339.

Peixoto, F. & Almeida, L.S. (2010). Self-concept, self-esteem and academic achievement: strategies for maintaining self-esteem in students experiencing academic failure. *European Journal of Psychology of Education, 25,* 157-175.

Pekrun, R. (1983). *Schulische Persönlichkeitsentwicklung. Theorieentwicklungen und empirische Erhebungen von Schülern der 5. bis 10. Klassenstufe.* Frankfurt/Main: Lang.

Pekrun, R. (1985). Classroom climate and test anxiety: Developmental validity of expectancy-value theory of anxiety. In H.M. van der Ploeg, R. Schwarzer & C.D. Spielberger (Eds.), *Advances in test anxiety research. Volume 4* (pp. 147-158). Lisse: Swets and Zeitlinger.

Pekrun, R. (1987). Die Entwicklung leistungsbezogener Identität bei Schülern. In H.-P. Frey & K. Haußer (Hrsg.), *Identität. Entwicklungen psychologischer und soziologischer Forschung* (S. 43-57). Stuttgart: Enke.

Pekrun, R. (1988a). Anxiety and motivation in achievement settings: Towards a system-theoretical approach. *International Journal of Educational Research, 12,* 307-323.

Pekrun, R. (1988b). *Emotion, Motivation und Persönlichkeit.* München: Psychologie Verlags Union.

Pekrun, R. (1991). Schulleistung, Entwicklungsumwelten und Prüfungsangst. In R. Pekrun & H. Fend (Hrsg.), *Schule und Persönlichkeitsentwicklung. Ein Resümee der Längsschnittforschung* (S. 164-180). Stuttgart: Enke.

Petkovic, A. (1980). *Bereichsspezifische Leistungsmotivation und Kausalattribuierung von Erfolg und Mißerfolg bei Schulkindern mit extrem guter und extrem schlechter Rechtschreibleistung.* Technische Universität München, Fakultät für Wirtschafts- und Sozialwissenschaften: Dissertation.

Phan, H.P. (2010). Students' academic performance and various cognitive processes of learning: an integrative framework and empirical analysis. *Educational Psychology, 30,* 297-322.

Phan, H. & Walker, R. (2000). Mathematics self-efficacy in primary schools: Evidence of a hierarchical structure. In R.G. Craven & H.W. Marsh (Eds.), *Self-concept theory, research and practice: Advances for the new millenium* (pp. 343-354). Collected papers of the inaugural Self-Concept Enhancement and Learning Facilitation (SELF) Research Centre international conference, Sydney, Australia, October 5-6, 2000. University of Western Sydney: Self-concept Enhancement and Learning Facilitation (SELF) Centre.

Pintrich, P.R. (2003). Motivation and classroom learning. In W.M. Reynolds & G.E. Miller (Eds.), *Handbook of psychology. Volume 7: Educational psychology* (pp. 103-122). Hoboken: Wiley.

Pintrich, P.R. & De Groot, E.V. (1990). Motivational and self-regulated learning components of classroom academic performance. *Journal of Educational Psychology, 82,* 33-40.

Pintrich, P.R. & Zusho, A. (2002). The development of academic self-regulation: The role of cognitive and motivational factors. In A. Wigfield & J.S. Eccles (Eds.), *Development of achievement motivation* (pp. 249-284). San Diego: Academic Press.

Pinxten, M., De Fraine, B., Van Damme, J. & D'Haenens, E. (2010). Causal ordering of academic self-concept and achievement: Effects of type of achievement measure. *British Journal of Educational Psychology, 80,* 689-709.

Plake, B.S. & Parker, C.S. (1982). The development and validation of a revised version of the Mathematics Anxiety Rating Scale. *Educational and Psychological Measurement, 42,* 551-557.

Pohlmann, B. (2005). *Konsequenzen dimensionaler Vergleiche.* Münster: Waxmann.

Pohlmann, B. & Möller, J. (2006). Vergleichseffekte auf kognitive, affektive und motivationale Variablen. Eine experimentelle Überprüfung. *Zeitschrift für Entwicklungspsychologie und Pädagogische Psychologie, 38,* 79-87.

Pohlmann, B. & Möller, J. (2009). On the benefit of dimensional comparisons. *Journal of Educational Psychology, 101,* 248-258.

Pohlmann, B., Möller, J. & Streblow, L. (2004). Zur Fremdeinschätzung von Schülerselbstkonzepten durch Lehrer und Mitschüler. *Zeitschrift für Pädagogische Psychologie, 18,* 157-169.

Pollak, D. (2009). The self-concept and dyslexia. In J. Soler, F. Fletcher-Campbell & G. Reid (Eds.), *Understanding difficulties in literacy development: Issues and concepts* (pp. 203-215). Los Angeles: Sage Publications.

Poloczek, S., Greb, K. & Lipowsky, F. (2009). Schulisches Selbstkonzept (Zusatzerhebung). In F. Lipowsky, G. Faust & K. Greb (Hrsg.), *Dokumentation der Erhebungsinstrumente des Projekts „Persönlichkeits- und Lernentwicklung von Grundschülern" (PERLE) – Teil 1* (S. 72-75). Frankfurt/Main: Gesellschaft zur Förderung Pädagogischer Forschung/Deutsches Institut für Internationale Pädagogische Forschung.

Poloczek, S., Karst, K., Praetorius, A.-K. & Lipowsky, F. (2011). Generalisten oder Spezialisten? Bereichsspezifität und leistungsbezogene Zusammenhänge des schulischen Selbstkonzepts von Schulanfängern. *Zeitschrift für Pädagogische Psychologie, 25,* 173-183.

Polychroni, F., Koukoura, K. & Anagnostou, I. (2006). Academic self-concept, reading attitudes and approaches to learning of children with dyslexia: do they differ from their peers? *European Journal of Special Needs Education, 21,* 415-430.

Poskiparta, E., Niemi, P., Lepola, J., Ahtola, A. & Laine, P. (2003). Motivational-emotional vulnerability and difficulties in learning to read and spell. *British Journal of Educational Psychology, 73,* 187-206.

Preckel, F. & Brüll, M. (2010). The benefit of being a big fish in a big pond: Contrast and assimilation effects on academic self-concept. *Learning and Individual Differences, 20,* 522-531.

Preckel, F., Zeidner, M., Goetz, T. & Schleyer, E.J. (2008). Female 'big fish' swimming against the tide: The 'big-fish-little-pond effect' and gender-ratio in special gifted classes. *Contemporary Educational Psychology, 33,* 78-96.

Putwain, D.W., Woods, K.A. & Symes, W. (2010). Personal and situational predictors of test anxiety of students in post-compulsory education. *British Journal of Educational Psychology, 80,* 137-160.

Räty, H. & Kasanen, K. (2007). Gendered views of ability in parents' perceptions of their children's academic competencies. *Sex Roles, 56,* 117-124.

Räty, H., Kasanen, K. & Kärkkäinen, R. (2006). School subjects as social categorisations. *Social Psychology of Education, 9,* 5-25.

Räty, H., Vänskä, J., Kasanen, K. & Kärkkäinen, R. (2002). Parents' explanations of their child's performance in mathematics and reading: A replication and extension of Yee and Eccles. *Sex Roles, 46,* 121-128.

Rankin, J.L., Bruning, R.H. & Timme, V.L. (1994). The development of beliefs about spelling and their relationship to spelling performance. *Applied Cognitive Psychology, 8,* 213-232.

Rankin, J.L., Bruning, R.H., Timme, V.L. & Katkanant, C. (1993). Is writing affected by spelling performance and beliefs about spelling? *Applied Cognitive Psychology, 7,* 155-169.

Raviv, A., Bar-Tal, D., Raviv, A. & Bar-Tal, Y. (1980). Causal perceptions of success and failure by advantaged, integrated, and disadvantaged pupils. *British Journal of Educational Psychology, 50,* 137-146.

Rheinberg, F., Vollmeyer, R. & Burns, B.D. (2000). Motivation and self-regulated learning. In J. Heckhausen (Ed.), *Motivational psychology of human development. Developing motivation and motivating development* (pp. 81-108). Amsterdam: Elsevier.

Richards, A., French, C.C., Keogh, E. & Carter, C. (2000). Test-anxiety, inferential reasoning and working memory load. *Anxiety, Stress, and Coping, 13,* 87-109.

Rider, N. & Colmar, S. (2005). *Reading achievement and reading self-concept in Year 3 students.* Paper presented at the AARE Education Research Creative Dissent Constructive Solutions, Parramatta, 27 November - 1 December, 2005.

Riddick, B. (2010). *Living with dyslexia. The social and emotional consequences of specific learning difficulties/disabilities* (2nd ed.). London: Routledge.

Riddick, B., Sterling, C., Farmer, M. & Morgan, S. (1999). Self-esteem and anxiety in the educational histories of adult dyslexic students. *Dyslexia, 5,* 227-248.

Ridsdale, J. (2004). Dyslexia and self-esteem. In M. Turner & J. Rack (Eds.), *The study of dyslexia* (pp. 249-279). New York: Kluwer Academic Publishers.

Rinn, A.N., Plucker, J.A: & Stocking, V.B. (2010). Fostering gifted students' affective development: A look at the impact of academic self-concept. *Teaching Exceptional Children Plus,* 6(4), Article 1, 1-13.

Robertson, J.S. (2000). Is attribution training a worthwhile classroom intervention for K-12 students with learning difficulties? *Educational Psychology Review, 12,* 111-134.

Roesken, B., Hannula, M.S. & Pehkonen, E. (2011). Dimensions of students' views as learners of mathematics. *ZDM Mathematics Education, 43,* 497-506.

Rosen, J.A., Glennie, E.J., Dalton, B.W., Lennon, J.M. & Bozick, R.N. (2010). *Noncognitive skills in the classroom: New perspectives on educational research.* RTI Research Triangle Park: RTI Press publication No. BK-004-1009.

Rosenberg, M. (1979). *Conceiving the self.* New York: Basic Books.

Rosenberg, M., Schooler, C., Schoenbach, C. & Rosenberg, F. (1995). Global self-esteem and specific self-esteem: Different concepts, different outcomes. *American Sociological Review, 60,* 141-156.

Rosenthal, J.H. (1973). Self-esteem in dyslexic children. *Academic Therapy, 9,* 27-39.

Rost, D.H. & Schermer, F.J. (1989). The assessment of coping with test anxiety. In R. Schwarzer, H.M. van der Ploeg & C.D. Spielberger (Eds.), *Advances in test anxiety research. Volume 6* (pp. 179-191). Lisse: Swets and Zeitlinger.

Rost, D.H., Sparfeldt, J.R., Dickhäuser, O. & Schilling, S.R. (2005). Dimensional comparisons in subject-specific academic self-concepts and achievements: A quasi-experimental approach. *Learning and Instruction, 15,* 557-570.

Rost, D.H., Sparfeldt, J.R. & Schilling, S.R. (2007). *DISK-Gitter mit SKSLF-8. Differentielles Selbstkonzept-Gitter mit Skala zur Erfassung des Selbstkonzepts schulischer Leistungen und Fähigkeiten.* Göttingen: Hogrefe.

Rounds, J.B. & Hendel, D.D. (1980). Measurement and dimensionality of mathematics anxiety. *Journal of Counseling Psychology, 27,* 138-149.

Rouxel, G. (2000). Cognitive-affective determinants of performance in mathematics and verbal domains. Gender differences. *Learning and Individual Differences, 12,* 287-310.

Rowe, E.W., Kim, S., Baker, J.A., Kamphaus, R.W. & Horne, A.M. (2010). Student personal perception of classroom climate: Exploratory and confirmatory factor analyses. *Educational and Psychological Measurement, 70,* 858-879.

Rowe, K. (2003). *The importance of teacher quality as a key determinant of students' experiences and outcomes of schooling.* Background paper to keynote address presented at the ACER Research Conference, Melbourne, 19-21 October 2003.

Rubie-Davies, C.M. (2010). Teacher expectations and perceptions of student attributes: Is there a relationship? *British Journal of Educational Psychology, 80,* 121-135.

Rubin, R.A. (1978). Stability of self-esteem ratings and their relations to academic achievement: A longitudinal study. *Psychology in the Schools, 15,* 430-433.

Rustemeyer, R. & Fischer, N. (2005). Sex- and age-related differences in mathematics. *Psychological Reports, 97,* 183-194.

Ryan, R.M. & Grolnick, W.S. (1986). Origins and pawns in the classroom: Self-report and projective assessments of individual differences in children's perceptions. *Journal of Personality and Social Psychology, 50,* 550-558.

Ryckman, D.B. & Peckham, P.D. (1987). Gender differences in attributions for success and failure situations across subject area. *Journal of Educational Research, 81,* 120-125.

Ryckman, D.B., Peckham, P.D., Mizokawa, D.T. & Sprague, D.G. (1990). The Survey of Achievement Responsibility (SOAR): Reliability and validity data on an academic attribution scale. *Journal of Personality Assessment, 54,* 265-275.

Sadker, M., Sadker, D. & Klein, S. (1991). The issue of gender in elementary and secondary education. *Review of Research in Education, 17,* 269-334.

Sarason, I.G. (1986). Test anxiety, worry, and cognitive interference. In R. Schwarzer (Ed.), *Self-related cognitions in anxiety and motivation* (pp. 19–34). Hillsdale: Erlbaum.

Sarason, I.G. & Sarason, B.R. (1987). Cognitive interference as a component of anxiety: Measurement of its state and trait aspects. In R. Schwarzer, H.M. van der Ploeg & C.D. Spielberger (Eds.), *Advances in test anxiety research. Volume 5* (pp. 3-14). Lisse: Swets and Zeitlinger.

Satow, L. & Schwarzer, R. (2000). Selbstwirksamkeitserwartung, Besorgtheit und Schulleistung: Eine Längsschnittuntersuchung in der Sekundarstufe I. *Empirische Pädagogik, 14,* 131-150.

Schilling, S.R., Sparfeldt, J.R. & John, M. (2005). Besser in Mathe – besorgter in Deutsch? Beziehungen zwischen Schulleistungen, schulischen Selbstkonzepten und Prüfungsängsten im Rahmen des I/E-Modells. In S.R. Schilling, J.R. Sparfeldt & C. Pruisken (Hrsg.), *Aktuelle Aspekte pädagogisch-psychologischer Forschung* (S. 159-178). Münster: Waxmann.

Schilling, S.R., Sparfeldt, J.R. & Rost, D.H. (2006). Facetten des schulischen Selbstkonzepts. Welchen Unterschied macht das Geschlecht? *Zeitschrift für Pädagogische Psychologie, 20,* 9-18.

Schneider, W. (1980). *Bedingungsanalysen des Recht-Schreibens.* Stuttgart: Huber.

Schunk, D.H. (1995). Implicit theories and achievement behavior. *Psychological Inquiry, 6,* 311-314.

Schunk, D.H. (2008). Attributions as motivators of self-regulated learning. In D.H. Schunk & B.J. Zimmerman (Eds.), *Motivation and self-regulated learning. Theory, research, and applications* (pp. 245-266). New York: Routledge.

Schunk, D.H. (2012). *Learning theories. An educational perspective* (6th ed.). Boston: Pearson Education.

Schunk, D.H., Pintrich, P.R. & Meece, J.L. (2008). *Motivation in education. Theory, research, and applications* (3rd ed.). Upper Saddle River: Pearson.

Schwarzer, R. (1984). Worry and emotionality as separate components of test anxiety. *International Review of Applied Psychology, 33,* 205-220.

Schwarzer, R. (1996). Thought control of action: Interfering self-doubts. In I.G. Sarason, G. R. Pierce & B.R. Sarason (Eds.), *Cognitive interference: Theory, methods, and findings* (pp. 99-115). Mahwah: Erlbaum.

Schwarzer, R. & Cherkes-Julkowski, M. (1982). Determinants of test anxiety and helplessness. In R. Schwarzer, H.M. van der Ploeg & C.D. Spielberger (Eds.), *Advances in test anxiety research. Volume 1* (pp. 33-43). Lisse: Swets and Zeitlinger.

Schwarzer, R. & Jerusalem, M. (1992). Advances in anxiety theory: A cognitive process approach. In K.A. Hagtvet & T.B. Johnson (Eds.), *Advances in test anxiety research. Volume 7* (pp. 2-17). Lisse: Swets and Zeitlinger.

Schwarzer, R. & Quast, H.-H. (1985). Multidimensionality of the anxiety experience: Evidence for additional components. In H.M. van der Ploeg, R. Schwarzer & C.D. Spielberger (Eds.), *Advances in test anxiety research. Volume 4* (pp. 3-14). Lisse: Swets and Zeitlinger.

Schwarzer, R., Seipp, B. & Schwarzer, C. (1989). Mathematics performance and anxiety: A meta-analysis. In R. Schwarzer, H.M. van der Ploeg & C.D. Spielberger (Eds.), *Advances in test anxiety research. Volume 6* (pp. 105-119). Lisse: Swets and Zeitlinger.

Seaton, M., Marsh, H.W. & Craven, R.G. (2009). Earning its place as a pan-human theory: Universality of the big-fish-little-pond effect across 41 culturally and economically diverse countries. *Journal of Educational Psychology, 101,* 403-419.

Seaton, M., Marsh, H.W. & Craven, R.G. (2010). Big-fish-little-pond effect: Generalizability and moderation – Two sides of the same coin. *American Educational Research Journal, 47,* 390-433.

Sepie, A.C. & Keeling, B. (1978). The relationship between types of anxiety and under-achievement in mathematics. *Journal of Educational Research, 72,* 15-19.

Shavelson, R.J., Hubner, J.J. & Stanton, G.C. (1976). Self-concept: Validation of construct interpretations. *Review of Educational Research, 46,* 407-441.

She, H.-C. (2000). The interplay of a biology teacher's beliefs, teaching practices and gender-based interaction. *Educational Research, 42,* 100-111.

Shell, D.F., Colvin, C. & Bruning, R.H. (1995). Self-efficacy, attribution, and outcome expectancy mechanisms in reading and writing achievement: Grade level and achievement-level differences. *Journal of Educational Psychology, 87,* 386-398.

Shores, M.L. & Shannon, D.M. (2007). The effects of self-regulation, motivation, anxiety, and attribution on mathematics achievement for fifth and sixth grade students. *School Science and Mathematics, 107,* 225-236.

Sideridis, G.D. & Kafetsios, K. (2008). Perceived parental bonding, fear of failure and stress during class presentations. *International Journal of Behavioral Development, 32,* 119-130.

Simpson, S.M., Licht, B.G., Wagner, R.K. & Stader, S.R. (1996). Organization of children's academic ability-related self-perceptions. *Journal of Educational Psychology, 88,* 387-396.

Skaalvik, E.M. (1983). Academic achievement, self-esteem and valuing of the school – Some sex differences. *British Journal of Educational Psychology, 53,* 299-306.

Skaalvik, E.M. (1986a). Age trends in male and female self-esteem in Norwegian samples. *Scandinavian Journal of Educational Research, 30,* 107-119.

Skaalvik, E.M. (1986b). Sex differences in global self-esteem: A research review. *Scandinavian Journal of Educational Research, 30,* 167-179.

Skaalvik, E.M. (1994). Attribution of perceived achievement in school in general and in math and verbal areas: Relations with academic self-concept and self-esteem. *British Journal of Educational Psychology, 64,* 133-143.

Skaalvik, E.M. (1997a). Issues in research on self-concept. In M.L. Maehr & P.R. Pintrich (Eds.), *Motivation and achievement. Volume 10* (pp. 51-97). Greenwich: JAI Press.

Skaalvik, E.M. (1997b). Self-enhancing and self-defeating ego orientation: Relations with task and avoidance orientations, achievement, self-perceptions, and anxiety. *Journal of Educational Psychology, 89,* 71-81.

Skaalvik, E.M. & Hagtvet, K.A. (1990). Academic achievement and self-concept: An analysis of causal predominance in a developmental perspective. *Journal of Personality and Social Psychology, 58,* 292-307.

Skaalvik, E.M. & Rankin, R. J. (1992). Math and verbal achievement and self-concepts: Testing the internal/external frame of reference model. *Journal of Early Adolescence, 12,* 267–279.

Skaalvik, E.M. & Rankin, R.J. (1995). A test of the internal/external frame of reference model at different levels of math and verbal self-perception. *American Educational Research Journal, 32,* 161-184.

Skaalvik, E.M. & Skaalvik, S. (2002). Internal and external frames of reference for academic self-concept. *Educational Psychologist, 37,* 233-244.

Skaalvik, E.M. & Skaalvik, S. (2006). Self-concept and self-efficacy in mathematics: Relation with mathematics motivation and achievement. In S.A. Barab, K.E. Hay & D.T. Hickey (Eds.), *Proceedings of the International Conference of the Learning Sciences ICLS 2006* (pp. 709-715). Bloomington: Indiana University.

Skaalvik, E.M. & Valås, H. (1999). Relations among achievement, self-concept, and motivation in mathematics and language arts: A longitudinal study. *Journal of Experimental Education, 67,* 135-149.

Skaalvik, S. & Skaalvik, E.M. (2004). Gender differences in math and verbal self-concept, performance expectations, and motivation. *Sex Roles, 50,* 241-252.

Skinner, E.A. (1995). *Perceived control, motivation, and coping.* Thousand Oaks: Sage Publications.

Skinner, E.A., Wellborn, J.G. & Connell, J.P. (1990). What it takes to do well in school and whether I've got it: A process model of perceived control and children's engagement and achievement in school. *Journal of Educational Psychology, 82,* 22-32.

Skinner, E.A., Zimmer-Gembeck, M.J. & Connell, J.P. (1998). Individual differences and the development of perceived control. *Monographs of the Society for Research in Child Development, 63*(2/3), 1-231.

Solheim, R. (1989). Socioemotional characteristics. In H.-J. Gjessing & B. Karlsen, *A longi-*

tudinal study of dyslexia. Bergen's multivariate study of children's learning disabilities (pp. 36-58). New York: Springer.

Sparfeldt, J.R., Schilling, S.R., Rost, D.H., Stelzl, I. & Peipert, D. (2005). Leistungsängstlichkeit: Facetten, Fächer, Fachfacetten? Zur Trennbarkeit nach Angstfacette und Inhaltsbereich. *Zeitschrift für Pädagogische Psychologie, 19,* 225-236.

Spielberger, C.D. (1975). Anxiety: State-trait-process. In: C.D. Spielberger & I.G. Sarason (Eds.), *Stress and anxiety. Volume 1* (pp. 115-143). New York: Wiley.

Stapel, D.A. & Suls, J. (2004). Method matters: Effects of explicit versus implicit social comparisons on activation, behavior and self-views. *Journal of Personality and Social Psychology, 87,* 860-875.

Steele, C.M., Spencer, S.J. & Aronson, J. (2002). Contending with group image: The psychology of stereotype and social identity threat. In M.P. Zanna (Ed.), *Advances in experimental social psychology. Volume 34* (pp. 379-440). New York: Academic Press.

Steinmayr, R. & Spinath, B. (2008). Sex differences in school achievement: What are the roles of personality and achievement motivation? *European Journal of Personality, 22,* 185-209.

Stetsenko, A., Little, T.D., Gordeeva, T., Grasshoff, M. & Oettingen, G. (2000). Gender effects in children's beliefs about school performance: A cross-cultural study. *Child Development, 71,* 517-527.

Stevenson, H.W. & Newman, R.S. (1986). Long-term prediction of achievement and attitudes in mathematics and reading. *Child Development, 57,* 646-659.

Stipek, D.J. (1984). Sex differences in children's attributions for success and failure on math and spelling tests. *Sex Roles, 11,* 969-981.

Stipek, D.J. & DeCotis, K.M. (1988). Children's understanding of the implication of causal attributions for emotional experiences. *Child Development, 59,* 1601-1610.

Stipek, D.J. & Gralinski, H. (1991). Gender differences in children's achievement-related beliefs and emotional responses to success and failure in mathematics. *Journal of Educational Psychology, 83,* 361-371.

Stipek, D.J. & Mason, T.C. (1987). Attributions, emotions, and behavior in the elementary school classroom. *Journal of Classroom Instruction, 22*(2), 1-5.

Streblow, L. (2004). *Bezugsrahmen und Selbstkonzeptgenese.* Münster: Waxmann.

Suinn, R.M. & Edwards, R. (1982). The measurement of mathematics anxiety: The Mathematics Rating Scale for Adolescents – MARS-A. *Journal of Clinical Psychology, 38,* 576-580.

Suldo, S.M., Shaffer, E.J. & Shaunessy, E. (2008). An independent investigation of the School Attitude Assessment Survey-Revised. *Journal of Psychoeducational Assessment, 26,* 69-82.

Suppon, V. (2004). Implementing strategies to assist test-anxious students. *Journal of Instructional Psychology, 31,* 292-296.

Terras, M.M., Thompson, L.M. & Minnis, H. (2009). Dyslexia and psycho-social functioning: an exploratory study of the role of self-esteem and understanding. *Dyslexia, 15,* 304-327.

Thijs, J., Verkuyten, M. & Helmond, P. (2010). A further examination of the big-fish-little-pond effect: Perceived position in class, class size, and gender comparisons. *Sociology of Education, 83,* 333-345.

Thomson, M.E. & Hartley, G.M. (1980). Self-concept in dyslexic children. *Academic Thera-*

py, 16, 19-36.

Tiedemann, J. (2000a). Parents' gender stereotypes and teachers' beliefs as predictors of children's concept of their mathematical ability in elementary school. *Journal of Educational Psychology, 92,* 144-151.

Tiedemann, J. (2000b). Gender-related beliefs of teachers in elementary school mathematics. *Educational Studies in Mathematics, 41,* 191-207.

Tiedemann, J. (2002). Teachers' gender stereotypes as determinants of teacher perceptions in elementary school mathematics. *Educational Studies in Mathematics, 50,* 49-62.

Tiedemann, J. & Billmann-Mahecha, E. (2004). Development of self-concept in elementary school classes: A test of theoretical models. In H.W. Marsh, J. Baumert, G.E. Richards & U. Trautwein (Eds.), *Self-concept, motivation, and identity. Where to from here? Proceedings of the Third International Biennial SELF Research Conference.* Berlin: Max Planck Institute for Human Development.

Tiedemann, J. & Billmann-Mahecha, E. (2006). Academic achievement and motivation in difficult classes. A multilevel analysis approach. In A.V. Mitel (Ed.), *Focus on educational psychology* (pp. 327-341). New York: Nova Science Publishers.

Tiedemann, J. & Billmann-Mahecha, E. (2007). Zum Einfluss von Migration und Schulklassenzugehörigkeit auf die Übergangsempfehlung für die Sekundarstufe I. *Zeitschrift für Erziehungswissenschaft, 10,* 108-120.

Tiedemann, J. & Faber, G. (1991). Entwicklung ausagierenden Schülerverhaltens in der Grundschule. In R. Pekrun & H. Fend (Hrsg.), *Schule und Persönlichkeitsentwicklung. Ein Resümee der Längsschnittforschung* (S. 241-253). Stuttgart: Enke.

Tiedemann, J. & Faber, G. (1994). Mädchen und Grundschulmathematik: Ergebnisse einer vierjährigen Längsschnittuntersuchung zu ausgewählten geschlechtsbezogenen Unterschieden in der Leistungsentwicklung. *Zeitschrift für Entwicklungspsychologie und Pädagogische Psychologie, 26,* 101-111.

Tiedemann, J. & Faber, G. (1995). Mädchen im Mathematikunterricht: Selbstkonzept und Kausalattributionen im Grundschulalter. *Zeitschrift für Entwicklungspsychologie und Pädagogische Psychologie, 27,* 61-71.

Tietjens, M., Möller, J. & Pohlmann, B. (2005). Zum Zusammenhang von Leistungen und Selbstkonzepten in verschiedenen Sportarten. *Zeitschrift für Sportpsychologie, 12,* 135-143.

Tobias, S. (1992). The impact of test anxiety on cognition in school learning. In K.A. Hagtvet & T.B. Johnson (Eds.), *Advances in test anxiety research. Volume 7* (pp. 18-31). Lisse: Swets and Zeitlinger.

Trautwein, U. (2003). *Schule und Selbstwert. Entwicklungsverlauf, Bedeutung von Kontextfaktoren und Effekte auf die Verhaltensebene.* Münster: Waxmann.

Trautwein, U., Gerlach, E., & Lüdtke, O. (2008). Athletic classmates, physical self-concept, and free-time physical activity: A longitudinal study of frame of reference effects. *Journal of Educational Psychology, 100,* 988-1001.

Trautwein, U., Lüdtke, O., Köller, O. & Baumert, J. (2006). Self-esteem, academic self-concept, and achievement: How the learning environment moderates the dynamics of self-concept. *Journal of Personality and Social Psychology, 90,* 334-349.

Trautwein, U., Lüdtke, O., Marsh, H.W., Köller, O. & Baumert, J. (2006). Tracking, grading, and student motivation: Using group composition and status to predict self-concept and interest in ninth-grade mathematics. *Journal of Educational Psychology, 98,* 788-806.

Trautwein, U., Lüdtke, O., Marsh, H.W. & Nagy, G. (2009). Within-school social comparison: How students perceive the standing of their class predicts academic self-concept. *Journal of Educational Psychology, 101,* 853-866.

Treutlein, A. & Schöler, H. (2009). Zum Einfluss der schulischen Lernumwelt auf die Schulleistung. In J. Roos & H. Schöler (Hrsg.), *Entwicklung des Schriftspracherwerbs in der Grundschule. Längsschnittanalyse zweier Kohorten über die Grundschulzeit* (S. 109-143). Wiesbaden: Verlag für Sozialwissenschaften.

Trzesniewski, K.H., Donnellan, M.B., Moffitt, T.E., Robins, R.W., Poulton, R. & Caspi, A. (2006). Low self-esteem during adolescence predicts poor health, criminal behavior, and limited economic prospects during adulthood. *Developmental Psychology, 42,* 381-390.

Tsovili, T.D. (2004). The relationship between language teachers' attitudes and the state-trait anxiety of adolescents with dyslexia. *Journal of Research in Reading, 27,* 69-86.

Tuckman, B.W. (1999). *A tripartite model of motivation for achievement: Attitude/drive/strategy.* Paper presented in the symposium: Motivational factors affecting student achievement – current perspectives. Annual Meeting of the American Psychological Association, Boston, August 1999.

Turner, S.L., Steward, J.C. & Lapan, R.T. (2004). Family factors associated with sixth-grade adolescents' math and science career interests. *Career Development Quarterly, 53,* 41-52.

Undheim, A.M., Wichstrøm, L. & Sund, A.M. (2011). Emotional and behavioral problems among school adolescents with and without reading difficulties as measured by the Youth Self-Report: A one-year follow-up study. *Scandinavian Journal of Educational Research, 55,* 291-305.

Usher, E.L. & Pajares, F. (2009). Sources of self-efficacy in mathematics: A validation study. *Contemporary Educational Psychology, 34,* 89-101.

Valentine, J.C. & DuBois, D.L. (2005). Effects of self-beliefs on academic achievement and vice versa. Separating the chicken from the egg. In H.W. Marsh, R.G. Craven & D.M. McInerney (Eds.), *New frontiers for self research* (pp. 53-77). Greenwich: Information Age Publishing.

Valentine, J.C., DuBois, D.L. & Cooper, H. (2004). The relation between self-beliefs and academic achievement: A meta-analytic review. *Educational Psychologist, 39,* 111-133.

Valeski, T.N. & Stipek, D.J. (2001). Young children's feelings about school. *Child Development, 72,* 1198-1213.

Valtin, R. (1972). *Empirische Untersuchungen zur Legasthenie.* Hannover: Schroedel.

Van Aken, M.A.G., Helmke, A. & Schneider, W. (1997). Selbstkonzept und Leistung – Dynamik ihres Zusammenspiels: Ergebnisse aus dem SCHOLASTIK-Projekt. In F.E. Weinert & A. Helmke (Hrsg.), *Entwicklung im Grundschulalter* (S. 341-350). Weinheim: Beltz.

Van Damme, J., Opdenakker, M.-C., De Fraine, B. & Mertens, W. (2004). Academic self-concept and academic achievement: Cause and effect. In H.W. Marsh, J. Baumert, G.E. Richards & U. Trautwein (Eds.), *Self-concept, motivation, and identity. Where to from here?* Proceedings of the Third International Biennial SELF Research Conference. Berlin: Max Planck Institute for Human Development.

Van de gaer, E., Pustjens, H., Van Damme, J. & De Munter, A. (2006). The gender gap in language achievement: The role of school-related attitudes of class groups. *Sex Roles, 55,* 397-408.

Van Kraayenoord, C.E. & Schneider, W.E. (1999). Reading achievement, metacognition, reading self-concept and interest: A study of German students in grades 3 and 4. *European Journal of Psychology of Education, 14,* 305-324.

Van Oudenhoven, J.P., Siero, F., Veen, P. & Siero, S. (1982). Effects of positive feedback on self-evaluations and spelling achievement in a real educational setting. *European Journal of Social Psychology, 12,* 321-325.

Varnhagen, C.K. (2000). Shoot the messenger and disregard the message? Children's attitudes toward spelling. *Reading Psychology, 21,* 115-128.

Viljaranta, J., Nurmi, J.-E., Aunola, K. & Salmelo-Aro, K. (2009). The role of task values in adolescents' educational tracks: A person-oriented approach. *Journal of Research on Adolescence, 19,* 786-798.

Vincent, D. & Claydon, J. (1996). *Diagnostic spelling test. Teacher's guide* (Australian edition). Victoria: Professional Resources Services.

Vispoel, W.P. (2003). Measuring and understanding self-perceptions of musical ability. In H. W. Marsh, R.G. Craven & D.M. McInerney (Eds.), *International advances in self-research* (pp. 151-179). Greenwich: Information Age Publishing.

Vispoel, W.P. & Austin, J.R. (1995). Success and failure in junior high school: A critical incident approach to understanding students' attributional beliefs. *American Educational Research Journal, 32,* 377-412.

Voelkl, K.E. (1996). Measuring students' identification with school. *Educational and Psychological Measurement, 56,* 760-770.

Wagner, C. & Valtin, R. (2004). Determinants of self-esteem in young adolescents. In H.W. Marsh, J. Baumert, G.E. Richards & U. Trautwein (Eds.), *Self-concept, motivation, and identity. Where to from here? Proceedings of the Third International Biennial SELF Research Conference.* Berlin: Max Planck Institute for Human Development.

Wagner, J.W.L. (1977a). *Fragebogen zum Selbstkonzept FSK 4-6.* Weinheim: Beltz.

Wagner, J.W.L. (1977b). *Fragebogen: Einstellung zur Schule FES 4-6.* Weinheim: Beltz.

Wang, M.C., Haertel, G.D. & Walberg, H.J. (1993). Toward a knowledge base for school learning. *Review of Educational Research, 63,* 249-294.

Wasowicz, J., Apel, K., Masterson, J.J. & Whitney, A. (2004). *SPELL-Links to reading and writing.* Evanston: Learning By Design.

Watkins, D. & Gutierrez, M. (1989). Between- and within-construct aspects of academic self-attributions: An investigation of the construct validity of an Australian instrument for Filipino subjects. *Australian Journal of Psychology, 41,* 291-301.

Weiner, B. (2005). Motivation from an attribution perspective and the social psychology of perceived competence. In A.J. Elliott & C.S. Dweck (Eds.), *Handbook of competence and motivation* (pp. 73-84). New York: Guilford.

Weiner, B. (2010). The development of an attribution-based theory of motivation: A history of ideas. *Educational Psychologist, 45,* 28-36.

Weinert, F.E., Schrader, F.-W. & Helmke, A. (1989). Quality of instruction and achievement outcomes. *International Journal of Educational Research, 13,* 895-914.

Whaley-Klahn, M.A., Loney, J., Weissenburger, F.E. & Prinz, R. (1976). Responses of boys and girls to a behaviorally focused school attitude questionnaire. *Journal of School Psychology, 14,* 283-290.

Wheeler, L., & Suls, J. (2005). Social comparison and self-evaluations of competence. In A.J. Elliot & C.S. Dweck (Eds.), *Handbook of competence and motivation* (pp. 566-578). New York: Guilford Press.

Whitley, B.E. & Frieze, I.H. (1985). Children's causal attributions for success and failure in achievement settings: a meta-analysis. *Journal of Educational Psychology, 77*, 608-616.

Wigfield, A. & Eccles, J.S. (1989). Test anxiety in elementary and secondary school students. *Educational Psychologist, 24*, 159-183.

Wigfield, A. & Eccles, J.S. (2000). Expectancy-value theory of achievement motivation. *Contemporary Educational Psychology, 25*, 68-81.

Wigfield, A. & Eccles, J.S. (2002). The development of competence beliefs, expectancies for success, and achievement values from childhood through adolescence. In A. Wigfield & J.S. Eccles (Eds.), *Development of achievement motivation* (pp. 91-120). San Diego: Academic Press.

Wigfield, A., Eccles, J.S., Yoon, K.S., Harold, R.D., Arbreton, A., Freedman-Doan, K. & Blumenfeld, P.C. (1997). Changes in children's competence beliefs and subjective task values across the elementa-ry school years: A three-year study. *Journal of Educational Psychology, 89*, 451-469.

Wigfield, A., Guthrie, J.T., Tonks, S. & Perencevich, K.C. (2004). Children's motivation for reading: Domain specificity and instructional influences. *Journal of Educational Research, 97*, 299-309.

Wigfield, A. & Karpathian, M. (1991). Who am I and what can I do? Children's self-concepts and motivation in achievement situations. *Educational Psychologist, 26*, 233-261.

Wigfield, A. & Meece, J.L. (1988). Math anxiety in elementary and secondary school students. *Journal of Educational Psychology, 80*, 210-216.

Wilgenbusch, T. & Merrell, K.W. (1999). Gender differences in self-concept among children and adolescents: A meta-analysis of multidimensional studies. *School Psychology Quarterly, 14*, 101-120.

Wilkins, J.L.M. (2004). Mathematics and science self-concept: An international investigation. *Journal of Experimental Education, 72*, 331-346.

Wilson, K.M. & Trainin, G. (2007). First-grade students' motivation and achievement for reading, writing, and spelling. *Reading Psychology, 28*, 257-282.

Wine, J.D. (1982). Evaluation anxiety. A cognitive-attentional construct. In H.W. Krohne & L. Laux (Eds.), *Achievement, stress, and anxiety* (pp. 207-219). Washington: Hemisphere.

Winkelmann, H. & Groeneveld, I. (2010). Geschlechterdisparitäten. In O. Köller, M. Knigge & B. Tesch (Hrsg.), *Sprachliche Kompetenzen im Ländervergleich* (S. 177-184). Münster: Waxmann.

Wouters, S., Germeijs, V., Colpin, H. & Verschueren, K. (2011). Academic self-concept in high school: Predictors and effects on adjustment in higher education. *Scandinavian Journal of Psychology, 52*, 586-594.

Xu, M. & Marsh, H. (2009). *The internal/external frame of reference models of academic self-concept among three school subjects for Hong Kong adolescents: The role of native and foreign languages.* Paper presented at the 5th International Biennial SELF Research Conference. Enabling human potential: The centrality of self and identity. Dubai, January 13-15, 2009.

Yee, D., & Eccles, J. (1988). Parent perceptions and attributions for children's math achievement. *Sex Roles, 19*, 317-333.

Yoon, K.S., Eccles, J.S. & Wigfield, A. (1996). *Self-concept of ability, value, and academic achievement: A test of causal relations.* Paper presented at the Annual Meeting of the

American Educational Research Association at New York, April 8-12, 1996.

Zbornik, J.J. & Wallbrown, F.H. (1991). The development and validation of a scale to measure reading anxiety. *Reading Improvement, 28,* 2-13.

Zeidner, M. (1998). *Test anxiety. The state of the art.* New York: Plenum.

Zeidner, M. & Schleyer, E.J. (1999). The big-fish-little-pond effect for academic self-concept, test anxiety, and school grades in gifted children. *Contemporary Educational Psychology, 24,* 305-329.

Zeinz, H. (2006). *Schulische Selbstkonzepte und soziale Vergleiche in der Grundschule: Welche Rolle spielt die Einführung von Schulnoten?* Friedrich-Alexander-Universität Erlangen-Nürnberg, Erziehungswissenschaftliche Fakultät: Dissertation.

Zeleke, S. (2004). Self-concepts of students with learning disabilities and their normally achieving peers: a review. *European Journal of Special Needs Education, 19,* 145-170.

Zimmerman, B.J. (2000). Attaining self-regulation: A social-cognitive perspective. In M. Boekaerts, P.R. Pintrich & M. Zeidner (Eds.), *Handbook of self-regulation* (pp. 13-39). San Diego: Academic Press.

Zimmerman, B.J. & Cleary, T.J. (2009). Motives to self-regulate learning. A social-cognitive account. In K.R. Wentzel & A. Wigfield (Eds.), *Handbook of motivation at school* (pp. 247-264). New York: Routledge.

Zingeler-Gundlach, U., Langheinrich, D. & Kemmler, L. (1973). Fehleranalyse von guten und schwachen Rechtschreibleistungen normalbegabter Grundschüler. In R. Valtin (Hrsg.), *Einführung in die Legasthenieforschung* (S. 33-42). Weinheim: Beltz.

Zuckerman, M. (1976). General and situation-specific traits and states: New approaches to assessment of anxiety and other constructs. In M. Zuckerman & C.D. Spielberger (Eds.), *Emotions and anxiety. New concepts, methods, and applications* (pp. 133-174). Hillsdale: Erlbaum.

Zuckerman, M. (1979). Attribution of success and failure revisited: The motivational bias is alive and well in attribution theory. *Journal of Personality, 47,* 245–287.

APPENDICES

APPENDIX A

Item List: **Spelling-Specific Self-concept**
Final scale version

APPENDIX B

Item List: **Causal Attributions of Dictation Outcome**
Final scale versions

APPENDIX A

Item list: **Spelling-Specific Self-concept** (Final scale version)

Item 02   It is hard to me to understand spelling rules.
Item 04   I don't need to practice for dictations.
Item 05   I am always making the same errors in spelling.
Item 08   It is hard to me to participate in spelling lessons.
Item 09   I had rather that spelling would not be so important in school.
Item 10   I have an easy time at writing dictations.
Item 11   If I misspell a word in dictation, I notice it myself.
Item 12   I am a good speller.
Item 13   With some words, I have to think for a long while before I write them down.
Item 14   If I practice a lot at home, nothing goes wrong any longer in dictations.
Item 15   Most of time I have fun in spelling.
Item 16   In class, I often make quite stupid errors with the easiest words.
Item 17   I try hard in spelling, but still I make more errors than others.
Item 18   During spelling lessons I often think: « That never works out for me. »
Item 19   Prior to dictations, I am certain that I will have most of the words correct.
Item 20   I like doing spelling homework.
Item 21   During dictations, I often misspell words which I usually master.
Item 22   If I could choose, I would omit spelling during homework, and instead I would rather solve some additional math exercises.
Item 23   If the teacher tells me that I have misspelled a word, I would rather not continue spelling and writing at all.
Item 24   When we write dictations I am not worried that it becomes too difficult.
Item 27   I consider spelling boring.
Item 28   I would rather that we would practice spelling much more in class.
Item 30   The other students often mock me for my spelling errors.
Item 31   Some students in my class admire me for my spelling skills. They would like to do their dictations exactly the way I do.

APPENDIX B

Item list: **Causal Attributions of Dictation Outcome** (Final scale versions)

Success Attributions
If I write a particularly good dictation, then it is because

Item 01   … I am really apt at spelling.
Item 02   … I was simply lucky.
Item 03   … I have practiced enough at home.
Item 05   … the dictation was not very difficult.
Item 06   … I am interested in spelling.
Item 08   … the teacher has explained difficult words quite well previously in class.
Item 09   … spelling is fun for me.
Item 10   … the teacher has dictated the words slowly enough.
Item 11   … we have practiced enough previously in class.
Item 12   … the teacher likes me.
Item 13   … nobody has disturbed me during dictation.
Item 14   … I like the teacher.

Failure Attributions
If I write a particularly bad dictation, then it is because

Item 01   … I am not really apt at spelling.
Item 03   … I have not practiced enough at home.
Item 04   … I have not paid enough attention in class.
Item 05   … the dictation was too difficult.
Item 06   … I am not interested in spelling.
Item 08   … the teacher has not explained difficult word well enough previously in class.
Item 09   … spelling is no fun for me.
Item 10   … the teacher has dictated the words too fast.
Item 11   … we have not practiced enough previously in class.
Item 12   … the teacher does not like me.
Item 13   … others have disturbed me during dictation.
Item 14   … I don't like the teacher.

INDEX

A

academic motivation, 47
academic performance, 1, 23, 26, 29, 35, 122, 128, 131, 132, 135, 140, 142
academic self-concepts, 4, 6, 8, 12, 15, 16, 17, 18, 23, 28, 34, 125, 144
academic settings, ix, 8
academic success, 3, 28, 120, 133, 135
academic tasks, 10
adaptation, 134
adjustment, 140, 152
adolescents, ix, xi, 24, 119, 121, 129, 133, 134, 138, 140, 150, 151, 152
adulthood, 131, 137, 150
affective reactions, 58, 60
age, 3, 5, 7, 8, 16, 17, 19, 20, 21, 22, 24, 28, 49, 63, 97, 125, 129, 130, 145
aggression, 125
American Educational Research Association, 153
American Psychological Association, 121, 150
antisocial behavior, 125
anxiety, vii, 11, 13, 26, 27, 28, 29, 30, 31, 32, 34, 37, 41, 44, 45, 46, 49, 60, 79, 80, 81, 83, 84, 85, 88, 89, 90, 92, 104, 113, 119, 121, 122, 123, 124, 125, 126, 129, 130, 131, 132, 133, 134, 136, 139, 140, 141, 142, 144, 145, 146, 147, 148, 149, 150, 152, 153
anxiety reaction, 29
appraisals, ix, 27, 29
aptitude, 24
arithmetic, 52
assessment, 6, 14, 37, 40, 41, 49, 116, 117, 118, 120, 122, 144, 153
assessment procedures, 117
assimilation, 11, 12, 14, 138, 143
athletes, 7
attachment, 34

attitudes, vii, ix, 7, 35, 44, 87, 88, 89, 90, 91, 92, 93, 94, 95, 96, 112, 113, 116, 120, 124, 130, 131, 137, 140, 142, 143, 148, 150, 151
attribution, 22, 23, 24, 25, 26, 28, 40, 41, 45, 48, 98, 99, 102, 103, 107, 108, 110, 115, 116, 130, 131, 133, 135, 137, 138, 144, 145, 146, 151, 153
attribution theory, 153
Australasia, 124
avoidance, 58, 125, 147
avoidance behavior, 125

B

base, 151
basic research, 33
behavioral problems, 119, 150
behaviors, 17, 30, 34, 87, 98, 116
bias, 16, 24, 28, 120, 134, 137, 153
bonding, 135, 146
bottom-up, 7, 34, 77, 84, 139

C

calibration, 134
case study, 135
causal attribution, vii, xi, 22, 23, 24, 25, 26, 32, 33, 34, 35, 37, 38, 40, 42, 48, 51, 97, 98, 99, 101, 104, 108, 109, 112, 113, 115, 116, 117, 118, 123, 125, 128, 140, 141, 148, 152
causal inference, 110
causality, 122, 139
Chicago, 119
chicken, 150
childhood, 135, 141, 152
child-rearing practices, 132
children, ix, xi, 15, 16, 18, 24, 29, 38, 49, 65, 119, 120, 121, 122, 123, 124, 125, 126, 127, 128, 129,

130, 131, 132, 133, 134, 135, 137, 138, 141, 143, 144, 145, 147, 148, 149, 150, 152, 153
city, 49, 133
clarity, 2, 25
class size, 148
classes, 12, 49, 143, 149
classification, 22, 45, 72, 97
classroom, ix, 1, 7, 10, 12, 14, 17, 18, 22, 24, 28, 42, 49, 50, 51, 52, 56, 58, 60, 62, 63, 66, 69, 88, 96, 97, 99, 100, 102, 110, 111, 113, 116, 121, 122, 125, 128, 129, 131, 132, 133, 142, 144, 145, 148
classroom activities, 1, 14, 17
classroom management, 1
classroom settings, 13
climate, 28, 29, 96, 113, 142, 145
close relationships, 32
coding, 53
cognition, 149
cognitive performance, 30
cognitive perspective, 1, 153
cognitive process, 26, 142, 146
cognitive skills, 1, 28, 117
cognitive theory, 120
cognitive trait, 1
communities, 139
comorbidity, 122
complement, 32
complexity, 14, 23, 30, 77
complications, 95
composition, 149
conceptualization, 39, 95, 97, 113
conductors, 49
conference, 122, 142
confrontation, 29
consensus, 23
consent, 49
construct validity, 39, 42, 43, 56, 63, 111, 113, 137, 139, 151
construction, xi, 53, 99, 112
content analysis, 24
coping strategies, 30, 49, 136
correlation, 44, 50, 63, 112, 115
correlations, 30, 40, 41, 45, 53, 59, 66, 73, 88, 91, 102, 103
criminal behavior, 150
cues, 2, 24, 27, 29, 30
cultural differences, 10
curriculum, 30, 126

D

danger, 30
defensiveness, 132

deficit, 30
delinquency, 125
depression, 119, 123, 133, 141
depressive symptoms, 128, 141
devaluation, 51
developmental change, 20, 119
developmental dyslexia, 133
developmental process, 17
dimensionality, 99, 122, 139, 145
disposition, 26, 30
distress, 27, 29
distribution, 56, 106
downward comparison, 9
dyslexia, x, 37, 121, 129, 131, 133, 141, 143, 144, 148, 150

E

education, 122, 123, 139, 146
educational process, 18
educational psychologists, 124
educational psychology, vii, 137, 139, 149
educational research, x, 18, 39, 144
educational settings, xii, 8, 15, 98, 116, 117
educational system, 12
egg, 150
elementary school, ix, 10, 13, 15, 16, 17, 21, 38, 42, 46, 50, 65, 77, 120, 124, 128, 130, 131, 132, 133, 135, 148, 149
elementary students, vii, xi, 72, 79, 85, 110
emotion, 30, 129
emotional experience, 148
emotional problems, ix, 79
emotional responses, 3, 22, 148
emotional state, 7, 53
emotional well-being, x, 84
emotionality, 29, 31, 44, 45, 51, 80, 84, 124, 130, 146
empirical studies, ix, 5, 28, 30, 65
encouragement, 17
enrollment, 140
environment, 12, 13, 18, 102
environmental variables, 29
error estimation, 73, 74, 77, 111, 114
evidence, vii, ix, xi, 5, 6, 8, 11, 12, 14, 15, 16, 17, 18, 19, 24, 26, 28, 29, 30, 31, 34, 35, 37, 56, 71, 87, 110, 122, 132
exercise, 102
expectancy-value theory, 142
exploratory study, 17, 148
external constraints, 98

F

factor analysis, 132, 139, 141
fear, 4, 26, 27, 41, 124, 132, 139, 146
feelings, 7, 23, 26, 28, 29, 30, 35, 42, 45, 53, 55, 63, 77, 80, 81, 84, 85, 88, 98, 105, 117, 121, 150
fish, 12, 14, 113, 122, 132, 136, 137, 138, 141, 143, 146, 148, 153
force, 93
foreign language, xi, 6, 7, 10, 16, 71, 152
formation, viii, ix, xi, 6, 8, 10, 11, 15, 18, 21, 23, 26, 28, 32, 34, 39, 41, 42, 58, 63, 71, 98, 100, 101, 109, 138
fouling, 53
foundations, 120
France, 133
freedom, 80, 89

G

gender differences, 16, 17, 18, 22, 25, 28, 35, 46, 74, 86, 94, 104, 108, 115, 123, 124, 129, 132
gender effects, 86
gender gap, 15, 140, 150
gender stereotyping, 28, 34
gender-dependent achievement, 18
generalizability, 6, 9, 20, 43, 78, 85, 114, 121
gifted, 13, 130, 143, 144, 153
global feeling, 4
grades, xi, 8, 14, 15, 18, 20, 38, 43, 65, 66, 68, 69, 77, 86, 88, 96, 130, 135, 136, 139, 140, 149, 151, 153
grouping, 133
growth, 124
gymnastics, 122

H

Hawaii, 141
health, 150
helplessness, 23, 25, 46, 58, 63, 77, 98, 99, 105, 110, 119, 120, 126, 128, 141, 146
high school, 130, 135, 137, 152
higher education, 152
higher-order thinking, 126
history, x, 28, 151
homework, 2, 17, 56, 120, 156
Hong Kong, 138, 152
human, 124, 134, 135, 138, 144, 146, 152
human development, 144
Hunter, 16, 129
hypothesis, 122, 124

I

ideals, 137
identification, 53, 151
identity, 121, 135, 140, 149, 150, 151, 152
IEA, 129, 133
image, 123, 148
individual development, 41
individual differences, 8, 141, 145
individual personality, 24
individuals, 140
inferences, 125
information processing, ix, 8, 26, 28, 29, 32, 34, 97
inhibition, 132
instructional time, 28
integration, 14, 22, 140
intelligence, 120
interaction effect, 62, 83, 94, 107, 108
interdependence, 9, 140
interface, 39, 71
interference, 145, 146
internalizing, x, 35, 49
interrelations, 4, 32, 61, 104
intervention, 6, 118, 120, 144
intrinsic motivation, 129
intrinsic value, 20
inversion, 75
issues, xii, 127, 132

J

junior high school, 151
justification, 137

K

kindergarten, 131, 135
knowledge acquisition, 33

L

languages, 10, 125, 138
latent mathematics, 5
lead, ix, 8, 11, 16, 17, 18, 22, 23, 29, 30, 53, 55, 56, 65, 87, 95, 98
learned helplessness, 47, 122, 125, 128
learners, xi, 7, 16
learning, ix, x, xi, 1, 2, 4, 6, 7, 11, 13, 16, 17, 18, 21, 22, 24, 25, 28, 30, 32, 33, 34, 35, 37, 38, 42, 46, 55, 56, 58, 60, 63, 66, 71, 74, 77, 79, 87, 91, 92, 93, 94, 97, 98, 99, 100, 102, 103, 105, 106, 107,

108, 109, 110, 111, 115, 116, 117, 120, 121, 123, 124, 125, 126, 128, 129, 131, 132, 133, 134, 135, 138, 139, 140, 142, 143, 144, 146, 148, 149, 153
learning behavior, x, 21, 22, 25, 34, 35, 98, 115
learning difficulties, 58, 144
learning disabilities, x, 120, 121, 126, 134, 135, 140, 148, 153
learning environment, 11, 124, 133, 149
learning outcomes, 2, 18, 19, 25, 32, 98
learning process, ix, 18, 117
learning skills, 30, 124
light, 110
literacy, ix, x, xi, 37, 39, 65, 88, 123, 129, 132, 143
locus, 99, 110, 112
longitudinal study, vii, xi, 9, 38, 120, 123, 131, 132, 133, 139, 141, 145, 147, 148, 149
long-term memory, 3

M

magnitude, ix, 9, 11, 13, 14, 16, 17, 18, 19, 20, 32, 37, 40, 53, 58, 66, 76, 80, 88, 95, 103
majority, 23, 49
management, 110, 123
masking, 20
materials, 115
mathematical achievement, 136
mathematics, xi, 5, 6, 7, 9, 10, 11, 13, 14, 15, 16, 17, 20, 31, 40, 42, 43, 50, 56, 59, 65, 72, 88, 103, 104, 115, 119, 123, 124, 129, 130, 131, 135, 136, 137, 140, 141, 143, 144, 145, 146, 147, 148, 149, 150
mathematics education, 136
math-gender stereotypes, 16
matter, x, 6, 35, 36, 38, 72, 95, 110, 120
measurement, vii, 13, 19, 20, 40, 41, 47, 48, 50, 51, 52, 53, 55, 56, 57, 58, 59, 60, 62, 63, 66, 67, 68, 73, 74, 75, 80, 83, 88, 89, 90, 92, 93, 95, 99, 100, 101, 102, 103, 104, 105, 106, 107, 108, 111, 112, 115, 116, 117, 122, 124, 130, 134, 137, 138, 139, 148
median, 106
memory, 30, 137
memory performance, 30
meta-analysis, 19, 126, 134, 135, 136, 141, 146, 152
metacognition, 150
methodological procedures, 6
methodology, 116
models, 1, 16, 19, 21, 22, 36, 53, 60, 66, 67, 111, 119, 126, 132, 139, 140, 149, 152
moderates, 149
modules, 118

motivation, ix, 6, 7, 20, 53, 79, 120, 121, 124, 126, 129, 130, 131, 133, 136, 138, 139, 140, 141, 142, 144, 145, 146, 147, 148, 149, 150, 151, 152, 153
motivational beliefs, ix
multidimensional, vii, xi, 6, 7, 19, 26, 27, 31, 32, 38, 40, 41, 42, 60, 71, 88, 97, 123, 130, 133, 134, 135, 137, 138, 139, 152
multiple regression, 45, 53, 60, 74, 104
multiple regression analyses, 53, 60, 74, 104
multivariate, 46
multivariate analysis, 46
multivariate statistics, 121

N

natural science, 50
negative attitudes, 52, 92, 95
negative consequences, 27, 29, 30, 88
negative effects, 9, 138
negative outcomes, 97
negative relation, 8, 9, 10, 14, 28, 34
nervousness, 29
Netherlands, 139
New Zealand, 123
null, 21

O

optimism, 131
outcome standards, 8
overlap, 18, 22, 32, 59, 61, 75, 80, 89, 113

P

parallel, 50
parenting, 29
parents, 11, 17, 29, 34, 49, 120, 143
path analysis, 130, 140
pathways, 29
peer group, 14
peer influence, 17
perceived control, 147
perceived self-efficacy, 120
personal control, 3, 99
personality, ix, xi, 1, 28, 31, 32, 35, 121, 126, 134, 139, 148
personality constructs, 32
personality development, ix, 35, 126
personality traits, 1
person-oriented approach, 151
pessimism, 139
physical activity, 149

physical education, 123
physics, 11
physiological arousal, 26, 29, 30, 125
pilot study, 56, 115
pleasure, 138
poor performance, 25, 43, 50
poor readers, 122
positive attitudes, 35
positive correlation, 87, 110
positive feedback, 151
positive relationship, 8
post-compulsory education, 143
predictive validity, 137
predictor variables, 59
primary school, 131, 134, 142
prior knowledge, 2
probability, 39, 71
problem solving, 72
processing stages, 27
programming, 122
project, 42, 46
protection, 27, 125
psychological processes, 30
psychology, 120, 126, 128, 142, 144, 148
psychometric properties, 7, 47, 48, 63, 73, 99, 111
psychosocial development, 26, 34
punishment, 29

Q

questionnaire, xi, 7, 39, 40, 42, 47, 50, 52, 53, 111, 151

R

reactions, 27, 28, 29, 30, 31, 39, 80
reading, ix, x, xi, 7, 12, 16, 21, 38, 65, 119, 120, 121, 122, 123, 125, 132, 135, 139, 141, 143, 144, 146, 148, 150, 151, 152, 153
reading difficulties, 7, 150
reading skills, 119
realism, 131
reasoning, 144
recommendations, 138
redundancy, 106
reform, 124
regression, 9, 19, 20, 38, 44, 45, 59, 75, 93
regression analysis, 9
regression weights, 44, 45
relevance, xii, 101, 102, 116, 117
reliability, 40, 50, 136
relief, 25, 131

remedial spelling training, 117, 118, 127, 128
replication, 47, 48, 124, 143
repression, 30
reputation, 124
requirements, ix, 10, 22, 23, 33, 55, 58, 117
resilience, 34, 123, 139, 140
resources, 30, 133
response, 38, 115
response format, 115
risk, 20, 25, 29, 30, 31, 34, 37, 49, 63, 77, 79, 85, 98
risks, 26
rules, 115, 156

S

schemata, 3, 128
school, vii, xi, xii, 1, 3, 6, 7, 8, 10, 11, 12, 14, 15, 16, 17, 18, 20, 21, 24, 32, 34, 39, 44, 49, 52, 87, 88, 89, 90, 91, 92, 93, 94, 95, 96, 112, 113, 116, 119, 121, 123, 124, 128, 129, 131, 132, 133, 134, 135, 136, 137, 138, 139, 140, 141, 147, 148, 149, 150, 151, 152, 153, 156
school achievement, 135, 141, 148
school climate, 52, 88, 128
school failure, 136
school learning, xi, 1, 129, 149, 151
school performance, 128, 132, 148
school success, 141
schooling, viii, 35, 52, 87, 88, 95, 145
science, 6, 10, 13, 15, 20, 120, 121, 123, 128, 130, 133, 135, 141, 150, 152
scope, 5, 9, 13, 36, 43
second language, 123
secondary education, 13, 141, 145
secondary school achievement, 141
secondary school students, 13, 152
secondary schools, 133
secondary students, 5, 17, 20, 140
selective attention, 28
selectivity, 38
self-awareness, 28
self-confidence, 58, 80, 130, 141
self-consistency, 110
self-doubt, 30, 146
self-efficacy, 3, 7, 12, 39, 71, 77, 98, 115, 117, 121, 123, 128, 130, 133, 134, 139, 142, 147, 150
self-enhancement, 18, 21, 65, 66
self-esteem, vii, x, xi, xii, 4, 6, 20, 24, 26, 28, 32, 34, 35, 37, 43, 44, 48, 49, 53, 56, 60, 63, 73, 74, 75, 76, 77, 79, 80, 81, 82, 83, 84, 85, 88, 89, 90, 91, 92, 93, 94, 95, 96, 104, 105, 111, 112, 119, 125, 133, 134, 136, 137, 138, 142, 144, 145, 147, 148, 150, 151

self-evaluations, 16, 34, 63, 79, 80, 133, 139, 141, 151
self-monitoring, 1
self-perceptions, vii, x, xi, 5, 7, 8, 10, 12, 15, 16, 28, 37, 38, 42, 43, 48, 51, 55, 56, 62, 65, 66, 68, 71, 74, 79, 84, 87, 97, 110, 112, 117, 118, 123, 130, 135, 139, 147, 151
self-regulation, 34, 133, 142, 146, 153
self-view, 148
self-worth, 18, 26, 27, 28, 34, 35, 37, 53, 63, 77, 79, 81, 85, 88, 110, 121, 124, 125, 129, 130
sex, 130, 135, 137, 147
sex differences, 147
simulation, 54
skill acquisition, 2
social anxiety, 28
social class, 124
social comparison, 3, 7, 8, 11, 14, 18, 23, 28, 38, 42, 69, 132, 136, 139, 148, 150
social identity, 148
social psychology, 129, 137, 148, 151
socialization, 16, 18
software, 53
solution, 40, 43, 57, 100
special education, 126
spelling, vii, viii, ix, x, xi, xii, 37, 38, 40, 41, 42, 43, 44, 45, 46, 47, 48, 49, 50, 51, 55, 56, 57, 58, 59, 60, 62, 63, 65, 66, 67, 68, 69, 71, 72, 73, 74, 75, 76, 77, 79, 80, 81, 83, 84, 85, 86, 88, 91, 92, 93, 94, 95, 96, 98, 99, 102, 103, 104, 105, 106, 107, 108, 109, 110, 111, 112, 113, 114, 115, 116, 117, 118, 126, 128, 144, 148, 151, 152, 156, 157
SPSS software, 53
stability, 22, 56, 68, 85, 99, 110, 112, 115, 122, 138
stable self-beliefs, ix
standard deviation, 52
state, vii, 27, 29, 30, 37, 40, 79, 110, 121, 145, 150, 153
states, 30, 80, 153
statistics, 52, 53, 56, 128
stereotypes, 16, 17, 18, 21, 25, 35, 120, 121, 124, 135, 149
strategy use, 140
stress, 29, 30, 43, 46, 63, 86, 126, 133, 146, 152
stressors, 121
structural characteristics, 35
structural equation modeling, 9, 53, 60, 61, 66, 68, 69, 73, 74, 76, 81, 82, 89, 90, 91, 92, 93, 120, 125, 134, 137
structure, 5, 6, 7, 47, 48, 53, 56, 63, 71, 73, 97, 98, 121, 122, 129, 134, 139, 142
student achievement, 134, 150
student motivation, 139, 149

style, 29, 128, 141
subgroups, 106, 112
subtraction, 7
suppression, 75
sympathy, 102
symptoms, 29, 58, 84
synthesis, 139

T

tactics, 123
target, x, 14, 125
task difficulty, 23, 45, 98, 102
taxonomy, 24
teacher instruction, 99
teacher support, 24, 88, 96, 97, 116, 124
teachers, 11, 14, 17, 28, 34, 45, 49, 50, 59, 119, 121, 149, 150
techniques, 131, 137
test anxiety, vii, xi, xii, 4, 11, 13, 26, 27, 28, 29, 30, 31, 32, 33, 34, 35, 37, 38, 41, 42, 44, 45, 46, 47, 48, 49, 51, 56, 60, 74, 79, 80, 81, 82, 83, 84, 85, 87, 88, 89, 90, 91, 92, 93, 95, 96, 103, 111, 112, 117, 118, 120, 122, 124, 125, 126, 128, 129, 130, 131, 132, 134, 135, 142, 143, 144, 145, 146, 149, 153
test items, 66
test scores, 50, 139
testing, 9, 43, 49, 80, 89, 125
theoretical approaches, 32
theoretical assumptions, 6, 47, 63, 77, 80, 83, 94, 95, 107, 111, 112
thoughts, 29
top-down, 7, 77
tracks, 13, 16, 18, 36, 37, 151
training, 144
traits, 153
treatment, xii, 17, 131, 135

U

upward comparisons, 15, 122

V

valence, 2, 27
validation, xi, 6, 31, 32, 35, 38, 42, 44, 45, 46, 47, 50, 51, 56, 60, 73, 99, 123, 131, 138, 139, 141, 143, 150, 153
variable factor, 112
variables, vii, x, xi, xii, 1, 6, 8, 9, 12, 18, 19, 20, 21, 25, 26, 28, 29, 31, 32, 34, 40, 41, 42, 43, 44, 45,

46, 47, 48, 49, 50, 53, 56, 57, 58, 60, 61, 62, 66, 67, 73, 74, 75, 76, 80, 81, 83, 89, 90, 91, 92, 94, 95, 99, 100, 103, 105, 106, 108, 111, 112, 113, 115, 116, 133
varimax rotation, 53, 57
verbal component, vii, 5
vulnerability, 143

W

Washington, 121, 126, 152

weakness, 68, 84
well-being, 100
working memory, 30, 119, 130, 132, 136, 144
worry, 29, 30, 31, 44, 45, 51, 80, 84, 140, 145

Y

Yale University, 130
yield, xi, 30, 53, 58, 66, 92, 95, 97
young adults, 133